AMHARIC
DICTIONARY & PHRASEBOOK

AMHARIC
DICTIONARY & PHRASEBOOK

Compiled by
Binyam Sisay Mendisu &
Abdu Ahmed Ali

Hippocrene Books
New York

For information, address:
HIPPOCRENE BOOKS, INC.
171 Madison Avenue
New York, NY 10016
www.hippocrenebooks.com

Library of Congress Cataloging-in-Publication Data

Names: Binyam Sisay Mendisu, compiler. | Abdu Ahmed Ali, compiler.
Title: Amharic-English/English-Amharic dictionary & phrasebook / compiled by Binyam Sisay Mendisu and Abdu Ahmed Ali.
Description: New York : Hippocrene Books, 2018.
Identifiers: LCCN 2018035764| ISBN 9780781813822 (pbk.) | ISBN 0781813824 (pbk.)
Subjects: LCSH: Amharic language--Dictionaries--English. | English language--Dictionaries--Amharic. | Amharic language--Conversation and phrase books--English.
Classification: LCC PJ9237.E7 M39 2018 | DDC 492.87321--dc23
LC record available at https://lccn.loc.gov/2018035764

Printed in the United States of America.

CONTENT

INTRODUCTION TO THE AMHARIC LANGUAGE

Amharic is an Afro-Asiatic language that belongs to the Semitic language family. It is spoken in Ethiopia by more than 30 million people both as a first and second language. It is the working language of the Federal Democratic Republic of Ethiopia and it serves as a main lingua franca among the different ethnic groups of the country. Its written records date back to the thirteenth century and it uses the Ethiopic script. Amharic has different regional dialects, but this book mainly focuses on the variety spoken around the capital city as it is gradually emerging as a standard variety.

PHONOLOGY

Consonants		Amharic Examples	English Equivalents
p [p]	*as in*	ፖምፓ [pompa]	pope
b [b]	*as in*	በግ [beg]	burn
t [t]	*as in*	ተስፋ [tesfa]	ten
d [d]	*as in*	ዶሮ [doro]	double
k [k]	*as in*	ከበሮ [kebero]	kite
g [g]	*as in*	ገንዘብ [genzeb]	gain
j [ɟ/ǧ]	*as in*	ጆሮ [joro]	job
sh [ʃ]	*as in*	ሽንት [shint]	shoe
h [h]	*as in*	ሀገር [hager]	hotel
kh [ħ]	*as in*	መኸር [mekher]	
l [l]	*as in*	ሌላ [lela]	light
m [m]	*as in*	ሞት [mot]	mango
n [n]	*as in*	ነጭ [nech]	not
f [f]	*as in*	ፊት [fit]	fun
s [s]	*as in*	ሰርግ [serg]	senior
v [v]	*as in*	ቪላ [villa]	vain
w[w]	*as in*	ወንበር [wenber]	wine
y [y/j]	*as in*	የብስ [yebs]	you
z [z]	*as in*	ዘፈን [zefen]	zero
zh [ž]	*as in*	ረዥም [rezhim]	collage

r [r]	*as in*	ሩቅ [ruq]	cry
q [q]	*as in*	ቀይ [qeyy]	
ch [č]	*as in*	ችሎታ [chilota]	chain
ch [č']	*as in*	ጨው [chew]	
ng [ñ/ɲ]	*as in*	ሰኞ [segno]	cologne
t [t']	*as in*	ጥቁር [tiqur]	
ts [s']	*as in*	ፀሎት [tselot]	
p [p']	*as in*	ኢትዮጲያ [ityop'iya]	
a [ɔ]	*as in*	አይን [ayn]	

Note: European-language speakers usually face difficulties in pronouncing plosive consonants such as p', s', t', č', and q; they tend to replace them with fricative counterparts such as p, s, t, č, and k, respectively. For example, "ityopiya" for "ityop'iya" ኢትዮጲያ (*Ethiopia*), "sehay" for "s'ehay" ፀሀይ (*sun*), "tifir" for "t'ifir" ጥፍር (*nail*), "čewata" for "č'ewata" ጨዋታ (*play*), and "keyy" for "qeyy" ቀይ (*red*).

Vowels		Amharic Examples	English Equivalents
e [ə]	*as in*	በግ [beg]	turn
i [i]	*as in*	ፊት [fit]	sick
ea[e]	*as in*	ኤሊ [eli]	many

ɨ [i]	*as in*	እህት [ihit]	
a [a]	*as in*	አንድ [and]	annual
o [o]	*as in*	ሞት [mot]	photo
u [u]	*as in*	ዱባ [dubba]	put

Notes:

The semi-vowel w is used in combination with other vowels for making a complex consonant sound preceding the combined vowels:

[u] before [a] = [w] in "quanqua" written "qwanqwa" ቋንቋ (*language*)

[o] before [a] = [w] in "semtoal" written "semtwal" ሰምቷል (*he has heard*)

Because of the absence of the open vowels on early typewriters, [ə] and [ɨ] are written as [e] and [i] respectively.

Consonant gemination is represented by doubling.

GRAMMAR

Verbs

Syntactically, Amharic verbs may be:

Transitive:

Monotransitive:
በሩን ዝጋ berun ziga (*close the door*)
መብራቱን አጥፋ mebratun atfa (*turn off the light*)

Ditransitive:
ዳቦ ግዛልኝ dabbo gizallign (*buy me a bread*)
ስልክ ደውልልኝ silk dewwilillign (*give me a call*)

Intransitive:
Example: ሩጥ rut (*run*)
ተኛ tegna (*sleep*)

The verb to be:

ነው / ናት / ናቸው
new / nat / nachew

is used as a linking verb:
ሰነፍ ነው/ናት/ናቸው
Senef new/nat/nachew.
He/She/They is/are lazy.

or as locative:
ኩባያው እዚህ ነው
Kubayyaw izzih new.
The cup is here.

Sentence Construction

Sentence construction in Amharic takes these syntactic structures:

SVi (Subject) Verb intransitive:

ሮጠ
Rote.
He ran (from 'rot-')

SOV (Subject) Object + Verb transitive, i.e., Direct object:

ጫማ ገዛ
Chamma gezza.
He bought a shoe. (from 'gezz-')

SOOV (Subject) + Indirect object + Direct object + Verb):

ለወንድሙ ጫማ ገዛለት
Lewendimmu chamma gezzallet.
He bought his brother a shoe. (from 'gezz-')

SCV (Subject) + Complement + Verb:

ልጁ አስተዋይ ነው
Liju asteway new.
The boy is clever. (from 'n-')

ፊቱ ነጭ ሆነ
Fitu nech hone.
His face became white. (from 'hon-')

Verb Conjugation

Verb conjugation takes into account adverbs of time to determine the suitable suffix that conveys the tense form. For example, using ቆ-ረ-ጠ qorret- (*to cut*), we can observe the tense forms from the past (1-3) through the present (4) to the future (5):

1. Past tense 3:
ባለፈው ሳምንት ቆርጬ ነበር
Ballefew sammint qoriche nebber.
I had cut last week. (Say three or more days ago)

2. Past tense 2:
ትናንት ቆርጫለሁ
Tinant qorichallehu.
I cut yesterday. (Say one or two days ago)

3. Past tense 1:
አሁን ቆረጥኩ
Ahun qorretku.
I cut a moment ago.

4. Present tense 0 (habitual):
እቆርጠዋለሁ
Iqortewallehu.
I usually cut it.

5. Future tense:
ነገ/ወደፊት እቆርጠዋለሁ
Nege/Wedefit iqortewallehu.
I will cut it tomorrow. (any time in the future)

Note: The past auxiliary ነበር "nebber" combines with the main verb to indicate a distant past action (1). Present tense (habitual) and Future tense have similar conjugations (4), (5).

Using the verb በል- bell- (*to eat*):

1. በልተሀ ነበር belteh nebber
   You had eaten (long ago/the other day/three days ago)

2. በልተሃል beltehall
   You ate (yesterday, two days ago, this morning)

3. በላሀ bellah
   You had/have eaten (a minute ago)

4. ትበላለሀ tibelalleh
   You eat (usually)

5. ትበላለሀ tibelalleh
   You will eat (some day).

Note again (4) and (5) spelled the same way but (5) should be contextualized or (otherwise carry a future time indicator) to differentiate it from the habitual present tense.

Nouns and Adjectives

Amharic distinguishes between countable and uncountable nouns. Singular countable nouns and uncountable nouns are unmarked while plurality is indicated by the suffix -(w)och. Modifier adjectives usually indicate plurality by repeating their middle root consonant. For example:

ትልቅ tilliq *big* (sg.)
ትላልቅ tilalliq *big* (pl.)

ትንሽ tinnish *small* (sg.)
ትናንሽ tinannish *small* (pl.)

ቀይ qeyy *red* (sg.)
ቀያይ qeyayy *red* (pl.)

ጥቁር tiqur *black* (sg.)
ጥቋቁር tiquaqqur black (pl.)

Nominal suffixes

-Ø (sg.)

ሰው sew *man*

አንድ ትልቅ ሰው እዚህ ሊበላ መጥቷል
and tilliq sew izzih libela mettoal.
one big man here has come to eat.
A big man has come to eat here.

-och (pl.)

ሰዎች sewoch *men*

ትላልቅ ሰዎች እዚህ ሊበሉ መጥተዋል
tilalliq sewoch izzih libelu mettewal.
big (pl.) *men here has come to eat.*
Big men came to eat here.

-ø (sg.)

ፍየል fiyyel *goat*

አንድ ፍየል ዛሬ ተገዝቷል
and fiyyel zare tegeztoal.
one goat today has been bought.
One goat has been bought today.

በግ beg *sheep*

አንድ በግ ዛሬ ተሸጧል
and beg zare teshetoal.
one sheep today has been sold
One sheep has been sold today.

-och (pl.)

ፍየሎች fiyyeloch *goats*

ሶስት ፍየሎች ዛሬ ተገዝተዋል
sost fiyyeloch zare tegeztewal.
three goats today have been bought.
Three goats have been bought today.

በጎች begoch *sheep*

ሶስት በጎች ዛሬ ተሸጠዋል
sost begoch zare teshetewal.
three sheep today have been sold
Three sheep have been sold today.

-Ø (No sg. / pl. for generic and abstract nouns)

ቆሻሻ qoshasha *dirt*

ቆሻሻ ታይቷል
qoshasha taytoal.
Dirt has been noticed.

ሰብዓዊነት sebawinnet *humanity*

ሰብዓዊነት ታይቷል
sebawinnet taytoal.
Humanity has been displayed.

ዕምነት imnet *faith*

ዕምነትህ አድኖሃል
imnetih adinohal.
Faith yours has saved you.
Your faith has saved you.

-Ø (No sg./pl. for liquid)

ውሃ wiha *water*

ውሃ ፈሷል
wiha fessoal.
Water has been spilled.

ደም dem *blood*

ደም ፈሷል
dem fessoal.
Blood has been shed.

In Amharic, the noun functioning as a topic in a sentence dictates agreement with the verbal inflection or bound subject in singular/plural or neutral number, and numeral modifier. But the head noun itself is dictated by the form of the adjectival modifier before it dictates the overall verbal inflection. Note, for example the sentences below:

አንድ/ሁለት በግ አለኝ/አሉኝ
and/hulet beg allegn/*allugn.
one/two sheep have.
I have one/two sheep.

ሁለት በጎች አሉኝ/አለኝ
hulet begoch allugn/*allegn.
two sheep (pl.) *have.*
I have two sheep.

ትልቅ/ትላልቅ ቤት አለኝ/አሉኝ
tilliq/*tilalliq bet allegn/*allugn.
*big/*big* (pl.) *house have.*
I have a big house.

ትላልቅ ቤቶቸ/ቤት አሉኝ/አለኝ
tilalliq betoch/*bet allugn/*allegn.
big (pl.) *houses/*house have.*
I have big houses.

TRANSLITERATION KEY

ha ሀ/ሃ/ሐ	hu ሁ	hi ሂ		he ሄ	h/hi ህ	ho ሆ	hua ኋ
le ለ	lu ሉ	li ሊ	la ላ	le ሌ	l/li ል	lo ሎ	lua ሏ
me መ	mu ሙ	mi ሚ	ma ማ	me ሜ	m/mi ም	mo ሞ	mua ሟ
se ሰ/ሠ	su ሱ/ሡ	si ሲ/ሢ	sa ሳ/ሣ	se ሴ/ሤ	s/si ስ/ሥ	so ሶ/ሦ	sua ሷ/ሧ
she ሸ	shu ሹ	shi ሺ	sha ሻ	she ሼ	sh/shi ሽ	sho ሾ	shua ሿ
re ረ	ru ሩ	ri ሪ	ra ራ	re ሬ	r/ri ር	ro ሮ	rua ሯ
qe ቀ	qu ቁ	qi ቂ	qa ቃ	qe ቄ	q/qi ቅ	qo ቆ	qua ቋ
be በ	bu ቡ	bi ቢ	ba ባ	be ቤ	b/bi ብ	bo ቦ	bua ቧ
te ተ	tu ቱ	ti ቲ	ta ታ	te ቴ	t/ti ት	to ቶ	tua ቷ

che ቸ	chu ቹ	chi ቺ	cha ቻ	che ቼ	ch/chi ች	cho ቾ	chua ቿ
ne ነ	nu ኑ	ni ኒ	na ና	ne ኔ	n/ni ን	no ኖ	nua ኗ
gne ኘ	gnu ኙ	gni ኚ	gna ኛ	gne ኜ	gn/gni ኝ	gno ኞ	gnua ኟ
a አ/ዐ/ኣ	u ኡ/ዑ	i ኢ/ዒ		ea ኤ/ዔ	e እ/ዕ	o ኦ/ዖ	
ke ከ	ku ኩ	ki ኪ	ka ካ	ke ኬ	k/ki ክ	ko ኮ	kua ኳ
khe ኸ	khu ኹ	khi ኺ	kha ኻ	khe ኼ	kh/khi ኽ	kho ኾ	
we ወ	wu ዉ	wi ዊ	wa ዋ	we ዌ	w/wi ው	wo ዎ	
ze ዘ	zu ዙ	zi ዚ	za ዛ	ze ዜ	z/zi ዝ	zo ዞ	zua ዟ
zhe ዠ	zhu ዡ	zhi ዢ	zha ዣ	zhe ዤ	zh/zhi ዥ	zho ዦ	zhua ዧ
te ጠ	tu ጡ	ti ጢ	ta ጣ	te ጤ	t/ti ጥ	to ጦ	tua ጧ

che ጨ	chu ጩ	chi ጪ	cha ጫ	che ጬ	ch/chi ጭ	cho ጮ	chua ጯ
de ደ	du ዱ	di ዲ	da ዳ	de ዴ	d/di ድ	do ዶ	dua ዷ
je ጀ	ju ጁ	ji ጂ	ja ጃ	je ጄ	j/ji ጅ	jo ጆ	jua ጇ
ge ገ	gu ጉ	gi ጊ	ga ጋ	ge ጌ	g/gi ግ	go ጎ	gua ጓ
ye የ	yu ዩ	yi ዪ	ya ያ	ye ዬ	y/yi ይ	yo ዮ	
tse ጸ/ፀ	tsu ጹ/ፁ	tsi ጺ/ፂ	tsa ጻ/ፃ	tse ጼ/ፄ	ts/tsi ጽ/ፅ	tso ጾ/ፆ	tsua ጿ
pe ጰ	pu ጱ	pi ጲ	pa ጳ	pe ጴ	p/pi ጵ	po ጶ	pua ጷ
pe ፐ	pu ፑ	pi ፒ	pa ፓ	pe ፔ	p/pi ፕ	po ፖ	pua ፗ
fe ፈ	fu ፉ	fi ፊ	fa ፋ	fe ፌ	f/fi ፍ	fo ፎ	fua ፏ
ve ቨ	vu ቩ	vi ቪ	va ቫ	ve ቬ	vi ቭ	vo ቮ	vua ቯ

AMHARIC-ENGLISH DICTIONARY

ሀ ha / ሁ hu / ሂ hi / ሄ he / ህ hi / ሆ ho / ኋ hua

ሀሙስ **ha-mus** Thursday
ሀምሌ **ham-le** July
ሀምሳ **ham-sa** fifty
ሀሳብ **has-sab** thought
ሀረግ **ha-reg** phrase
ሀቀኛ **haq-qegn-gna** honest
ሀብሀብ **hab-hab** melon
ሀኪም **ha-kim** doctor, physician
ሀውልት **ha-wult** monument, statue
ሀያ **ha-ya** twenty
ሀይል **ha-yil** energy
ሀይል **ha-yil** might
ሀይማኖት **hay-ma-not** religion
ሀይቅ **ha-yiq** lake
ሀዲድ **ha-did** rail

ሁለተኛ **hu-let-tegn-gna** second (*adj. / ord. num.*)
ሁለት ጊዜ **hu-let gi-ze** twice
ሁሉም **hul-lum** all
ሁልጊዜ **hul-gi-ze** always, ever
ሁኔታ **hu-ne-ta** event

ሂሳብ **hi-sab** bill; math

ሄሎ **he-lo** hello
ሄደ **he-de** go
ሄደ **he-de** leave

ህመም **hi-mem** pain; illness
ህመም ማስታገሻ **hi-mem mas-ta-ge-sha** painkiller
ህመምተኛ **hi-mem-tegn-gna** sick
ህብረት **hib-ret** union
ህንጻ **hin-tsa** building
ህክምና **hik-ki-min-na** medicine

ህዝብ **hizb** crowd; population
ህያው **hiy-yaw** alive
ህይወት **hiy-wet** life
ህዳር **hi-dar** November
ህገ መንግስት **hig-ge men-gist** constitution
ህገ ወጥ **hig-ge wet** illegal
ህጋዊ **hig-ga-wi** legal
ህግ **higg** law
ህግ መተላለፍ **higg te-lal-le-fe** trespassing
ህግ አውጪ ክፍል **higg aw-chi ki-fil** legislature
ህግ ፊት አቀረበ **higg fit a-qer-re-be** prosecute
ህጻን **hi-tsan** baby

ሆስቴል **hos-tel** hostel
ሆስፒታል **hos-pi-tal** hospital
ሆቴል **ho-tel** hotel
ሆነ **ho-ne** become
ሆድ **hod** stomach
ሆድ ድርቀት ያመመው **hod dir-qet yam-me-mew**
constipated

ኋላ **hua-la** rear

ለ le / ሊ li / ላ la / ሌ le / ል li / ሎ lo

ለማኝ **lem-magn** beggar
ለማዳ **lem-mad-da** domestic
ለማዳ እንሰሳ **lem-mad-da in-se-sa** pet
ለምን **le-min** why
ለስላሳ **les-las-sa** soft
ለቆ ወጣ **leq-qo wet-ta** evacuate
ለበሰ **leb-be-se** wear, dress (*v.*)
ለብቻ **le-bi-cha** alone
ለብቻ መሆን **le-bich-cha me-hon** privacy
ለአካለ መጠን ያልደረሰ **le-ka-le me-ten yal-der-re-se** minor (*n.*)
ለወጠ **lew-we-te** alter, change (*v.*)
ለውዝ **lewz** almonds, peanuts, nuts
ለውጥ **lewt** change (*n.*)
ለየ **ley-ye** identify, recognize
ለፋፊ **lef-fa-fi** announcer

ሊሆን የሚችል **li-hon yem-mi-chil** probably
ሊትር **li-tir** liter
ሊግ **lig** league
ሊጥ **lit** dough

ላስቲክ **las-tik** plastic
ላብ **lab** sweat
ላከ **la-ke** send
ላውንደሪ **la-wun-de-ri** laundry
ላውንጅ **la-wunj** lounge
ላይ **lay** on; up (*adv.*)
ላጤ **lat-te** single (*n.*)
ላጨ **lach-che** shave
ላፕቶፕ **lap-top** laptop

ሌሊት **le-lit** night

ሌላ **le-la** other
ሌባ **le-ba** intruder, thief
ሌንስ **lens** lens

ልል **lil** loose
ልምድ **limd** experience
ልስልስ **lis-lis** smooth (*adj.*)
ልብ **libb** heart
ልብ ድካም **libb di-kam** heart attack
ልብስ **libs** cloth
ልብስ ሰፋ **libs sef-fa** sew
ልኬት **lik-ket** measure
ልክ **lik** exact, fitting
ልውውጥ **li-wiw-wit** exchange
ልዩ **liy-yu** special; different
ልደት **li-det** birthday
ልጃገረድ **li-ja-ge-red** girl
ልጅ **lij** child
ልጅ ያዥ **lij yazh** babysitter

ሎሚ **lo-mi** lemon

መ me / ሙ mu / ሚ mi / ማ ma / ሜ me / ም mi / ሞ mo

መሐላ **me-hal-la** swear
መሃል **me-hal** middle
መሐል ከተማ **me-hal ke-te-ma** downtown
መሐንዲስ **me-han-dis** engineer
መለሰ **mel-le-se** repay, refund (*v.*)
መለኪያ **me-lek-ki-ya** pint
መለኪያ ክፍል **me-lek-ki-ya ki-fil** fitting room
መለዋወጫ **me-le-wa-we-cha** spare part
መለያ **mel-le-ya** identification
መለጊያ **me-leg-gi-ya** bat (*sports equipment*)
መልስ **mel-liss** reply
መልሶ ክፍያ **mel-li-so ki-fiy-ya** repayment
መልዕክተኛ **mel-ek-tegn-gna** messenger
መልዕክት **mel-ekt** message
መልካም **mel-kam** nice
መልክ **mel-kam** look
መመሪያ **mem-me-ri-ya** directions
መመገቢያ ክፍል **mem-me-ge-bi-ya ki-fil** dining room
መምሪያ **mem-ri-ya** guidebook, manual (*n.*)
መሰለ **mes-se-le** appear, seem
መሰረተ ልማት **me-se-re-te li-mat** infrastructure
መሠረት **me-se-ret** base
መሰናክል **me-se-na-kil** barrier
መሳሪያ **mes-sa-ri-ya** equipment, tool
መሳቢያ **me-sa-bi-ya** drawer
መሳፈሪያ **mes-sa-fe-ri-ya** fare
መስማት የተሳነው **mes-mat yet-te-sa-new** deaf
መስተንግዶ **mes-ten-gi-do** accommodation; hospitality
መስታዎት **mes-ta-wot** mirror
መስከረም **mes-ke-rem** September
መስክ **mesk** field
መስኮት **mes-kot** window

መስጊድ **mes-gid** mosque
መረመረ **me-rem-me-re** inspect, check (*v.*)
መረጃ **mer-re-ja** information
መረጠ **mer-re-te** prefer, select (*v.*)
መሪ **me-ri** wheel; leader, guide (*n.*)
መራራ **me-ra-ra** sour
መራር **mer-rar** bitter
መሬት **me-ret** earth, land
መሬት መንቀጥቀጥ **me-ret men-qet-qet** earthquake
መርከብ **mer-keb** ship
መርዝ **merz** poison
መርፌ **mer-fe** needle, syringe
መርፌ ወጋ **mer-fe weg-ga** inject
መሿለኪያ **mesh-shau-le-ki-ya** subway
መቀመጫ **meq-qe-me-cha** seat
መቀስ **me-qes** scissors
መቀየሪያ ክፍል **me-qey-ye-ri-ya ki-fil** changing room
መቅለሚያ **meq-le-mi-ya** dye
መቅሰፍት **meq-seft** disaster
መቆያ **me-qoy-ya** snack (*n.*)
መቆፈሪያ **me-qof-fe-ri-ya** pick
መብራት **meb-rat** lamp
መብት **me-bit** right (*n.*)
መተላለፊያ **me-te-la-le-fi-ya** aisle, lobby
መታ **met-ta** kick
መታወቂያ ወረቀት **met-ta-we-qi-ya we-re-qet** ID card
መታጠቢያ ቤት **me-ta-te-bi-ya bet** bathroom
መታጠፊያ **met-ta-te-fi-ya** turn
መቶ **me-to** hundred
መቶኛ **me-togn-gna** percent
መቼ **me-che** when
መነሻ **men-ne-sha** departure
መነኩሲት **me-nek-ku-sit** nun
መነጽር **me-ne-tsir** eyeglasses
መንሸራተቻ **men-she-ra-te-cha** skis (*n.*)
መንበር **men-ber** altar

መንታ **men-ta** twin
መንደር **men-der** village
መንጃ ፈቃድ **men-ja fe-qad** driver's license
መንገድ **men-ged** pavement, road, route
መንገድ መምሪያ **men-ged mem-ri-ya** road map
መንግስት **men-gist** government
መንጠሪያ **men-te-ri-ya** spring (*metal coil*)
መኖሪያ **me-no-ri-ya** home
መኝታ ቤት **megn-gni-ta bet** bedroom
መዓዛ **me-a-za** odor
መኪና **me-ki-na** car
መኪና ማቆሚያ **me-ki-na ma-qo-mi-ya** parking
መካነ መቃብር **me-ka-ne me-qa-bir** cemetery
መካከለኛ **me-kak-ke-legn-gna** mild; medium (*adj.*)
መኮንን **me-kon-nin** officer
መኸር **me-kher** autumn
መኻን **me-khan** sterile
መወጣጫ **mew-we-ta-cha** step (*n.*)
መውጫ **mew-cha** exit
መዋቢያ **mew-wa-bi-ya** cosmetics
መዘነ **mez-ze-ne** weigh
መዘግየት **me-zeg-yet** delay
መዝናኛ **mez-nagn-gna** entertainment
መዝገበ ቃላት **mez-ge-be qa-lat** dictionary
መዝገብ **mez-geb** record
መደበኛ **me-de-begn-gna** formal; regular
መደብር **me-deb-bir** store, department store
መደወያ ካርድ **me-dew-we-ya kard** phone card
መዳረሻ **med-da-re-sha** destination
መድሐኒት **med-ha-nit** drug, medication
መድሐኒት መደብር **med-ha-nit me-deb-bir** drugstore, pharmacy
መድረሻ **med-re-sha** arrival
መድረክ **med-rek** platform, stand
መጀመሪያ **me-jem-me-ri-ya** start
መገለል **meg-ge-lel** withdrawal

መገናኛ **meg-ga-na-gna** junction
መገኛ ቦታ **meg-gegn-gna bo-ta** location
መጋዝ **me-gaz** saw (*n. / tool*)
መግለጫ **meg-le-cha** announcement
መግቢያ **meg-bi-ya** entrance, access (*n.*)
መግቢያ ክፍያ **meg-bi-ya ki-fiy-ya** cover charge
መግቢያ ቪዛ **meg-bi-ya vi-za** entry visa
መጓጓዣ **meg-gua-gua-zha** transport, transportation
መጠለያ **met-te-le-ya** shelter
መጠለያ ስፍራ **met-te-le-ya sif-ra** sanctuary
መጠበቅ **me-teb-beq** wait
መጠን **me-ten** amount, size; limit (*n.*)
መጠን ያለፈ **me-ten yal-le-fe** overdose
መጠጊያ **met-te-gi-ya** refuge
መጠጥ **me-tet** beverage, drink (*n.*)
መጣ **met-ta** come
መጥበሻ **met-be-sha** pan
መጥፎ **me-ti-fo** bad
መጸዳጃ **mets-tse-ga-ja** toilet
መጻህፍት መደብር **me-tsa-hift me-deb-bir** bookstore
መጽሐፍ **me-tsi-haf** book
መጽሐፍ ቅዱስ **me-tsi-haf qi-dus** bible
መፍትሔ **mef-ti-he** remedy (*n.*)

ሙሉ **mu-lu** full
ሙሉ ልብስ **mu-lu libs** suit
ሙስሊም **mus-lim** Muslim
ሙቀት **mu-qet** heat; temperature
ሙቅ **muq** hot
ሙት **mut** dead
ሙከራ **muk-ke-ra** test
ሙከራ **mik-ke-ra** trial
ሙዚቀኛ **mu-zi-qegn-gna** musician
ሙዚቃ **mu-zi-qa** music
ሙዚየም **mu-zi-yem** museum
ሙዝ **muz** banana

ሙያዊ **mu-ya-wi** professional
ሙግት **mug-git** argument
ሙጫ **much-cha** glue

ሚልዮን **mil-yon** million
ሚስት **mist** wife
ሚያዝያ **mi-ya-zi-ya** April

ማህተም **mah-tem** stamp
ማሰሮ **ma-se-ro** pot
ማሳ **ma-sa** farm
ማሳጅ **ma-saj** massage
ማስታወሻ **mas-ta-we-sha** note
ማስታወቂያ **mas-ta-we-qi-ya** advertisement
ማስጠንቀቂያ **mas-ten-qe-qi-ya** warning
ማረ **ma-re** forgive, pardon (*v.*)
ማር **mar** honey
ማርሽ **marsh** gear
ማሻገሪያ **mash-sha-ge-ri-ya** ferry
ማሽን **ma-shin** machine
ማቀዝቀዣ **ma-qez-qe-zha** refrigerator
ማቅለሽለሽ **maq-lesh-lesh** motion sickness, nausea
ማቆሚያ **ma-qo-mi-ya** stop
ማበጠሪያ **ma-bet-te-ri-ya** comb
ማተሚያ **mat-te-mi-ya** printer
ማን **man** who
ማንኛውም **ma-ni-gna-wim** any
ማንኛውም ሰው **ma-ni-gna-wim sew** anyone
ማንኛውም ነገር **ma-ni-gna-wim ne-ger** anything
ማንኛውም አካል **ma-ni-gna-wim a-kal** anybody
ማንኪያ **man-ki-ya** spoon
ማንጫ **man-cha** detergent
ማዕቀብ **ma-i-qeb** sanction
ማዕበል **ma-i-bel** storm
ማዕከል **ma-i-kel** center
ማዕዘን **ma-i-zen** corner

ማክሰኞ **mak-segn-gno** Tuesday
ማውጫ **maw-cha** directory
ማዞሪያ **ma-zo-ri-ya** dialing code
ማይል **ma-yil** mile
ማይክሮዌቭ **may-ki-ro-wev** microwave
ማይግሬን **may-gi-ren** migraine
ማደንዘዣ **ma-den-ze-zha** anesthetic
ማድቤት **mad-bet** kitchen
ማገዶ **ma-ge-do** firewood
ማጠቢያ ማሽን **ma-te-bi-ya ma-shin** washing machine
ማጣጣሚያ **mat-ta-ta-mi-ya** dessert
ማጤስ **ma-tes** smoking
ማጭበርበር **mach-ber-ber** fraud

ሜትር **me-tir** meter
ሜንታ **men-ta** mint
ሜካኒክ **me-ka-nik** mechanic
ሜዳ **me-da** plain

ምህረት **mi-hi-ret** pardon (*n.*)
ምሉዕ **mi-lu-i** perfect
ምላጭ **mi-lach** razor
ምልክት **mi-lik-kit** signal
ምልክት **mi-lik-kit** symptom
ምሳ **mi-sa** lunch
ምሳሌ **mis-sa-le** example
ምስል **mi-sil** picture
ምስራቅ **mis-raq** east
ምስጢር **mis-tir** secret
ምርመራ **mir-me-ra** diagnosis
ምርመራ **mir-me-ra** inquiry
ምርኩዝ **mir-kuz** crutches
ምርጫ **mir-cha** election, selection
ምሽት **mish-shit** evening
ምቹ **mich-chu** comfortable, convenient
ምቾት **mi-chot** comfort

ምን **min** what
ምንም **mi-nim** nothing
ምንዛሬ **mi-niz-za-re** currency
ምንጣፍ **min-taf** carpet
ምንጭ **minch** source; fountain; spring (*water*)
ምዕራብ **mi-i-rab** west
ምዕራፍ **mi-i-raf** chapter
ምክንያቱም **mi-ki-ni-ya-tum** because of
ምክንያት **mi-kin-yat** ground (*n.*); reason
ምዝገባ **miz-ge-ba** registration
ምድር **mi-dir** ground (*adj.*)
ምድር ቤት **mi-dir bet** basement
ምድጃ **mi-dij-ja** oven, stove
ምግብ **mi-gib** dish, food, meal
ምግብ ቤት **mi-gib bet** restaurant
ምግብ አብሳይ **mi-gib ab-say** cook (*n.*)
ምጣኔ ሐብት **mit-ta-ne hebt** economy

ሞላ **mol-la** fill
ሞቃት **moq-qat** warm
ሞተ **mo-te** die
ሞተር **mo-ter** engine, motor
ሞተር መመንጨቂያ ሽቦ **mo-ter me-men-che-qi-ya shi-bo** jumper cables
ሞተርሳይክል **mo-ter-say-kil** motorcycle
ሞቴል **mo-tel** motel
ሞከረ **mok-ke-re** try

ሰ se / ሱ su / ሲ si / ሳ sa / ሴ se / ሶ so

ሰላም **se-lam** peace
ሰላምታ **se-lam-ta** greeting
ሰላሳ **se-la-sa** thirty
ሰላጣ **se-la-ta** lettuce, salad
ሰማ **sem-ma** hear
ሰማንያ **se-man-ya** eighty
ሰማያዊ **se-ma-ya-wi** blue
ሰማይ **se-may** sky
ሰሜን **se-men** north
ሰሜን ምስራቅ **se-men mis-raq** northeast
ሰሜን ምዕራብ **se-men mi-i-rab** northwest
ሰረቀ **ser-re-qe** steal
ሰረዘ **ser-re-ze** cancel
ሰራ **ser-ra** knit; make (*v.*); work (*v.*)
ሰራተኞች **ser-ra-tegn-gnoch** staff
ሰራዊት **se-ra-wit** army
ሰርግ **serg** wedding
ሰርጥ **sert** alley
ሰርቨር **ser-ver** server
ሰበሰበ **se-bes-se-be** collect
ሰበረ **seb-be-re** break
ሰባ **se-ba** seventy
ሰባራ **se-ba-ra** broken
ሰባት **se-bat** seven
ሰብዓዊ መብት **seb-a-wi mebt** human rights
ሰነድ **se-ned** document
ሰኔ **se-ne** June
ሰንሰለት **sen-se-let** chain
ሰኞ **segn-gno** Monday
ሰዓት **se-at** clock; hour; o'clock
ሰዓት እላፊ **se-at il-la-fi** curfew
ሰከንድ **se-kend** second (*n. / in time*)
ሰካራም **sek-ka-ram** drunk
ሰዋሰው **se-wa-sew** grammar

ሰው **sew** folk, human, people; man
ሰጠ **set-te** give
ሰፈር **se-fer** neighborhood
ሰፋ **sef-fa** stitch

ሱሪ **sur-ri** pants
ሱቅ **suq** shop
ሱፍ **suf** wool
ሱፐርማርኬት **sup-per-mar-ket** supermarket

ሲሚንቶ **sim-min-to** cement
ሲባጎ **si-ba-go** cord
ሲኒማ **si-ni-ma** cinema
ሲኒማ ቤት **si-ni-ma bet** movie theater
ሲናጎግ **si-na-gog** synagogue
ሲዲ **si-di** CD
ሲጋራ **si-ga-ra** cigarette
ሲቪል **si-vil** civilian

ሳህን **sa-hin** plate
ሳል **sal** cough
ሳልቫትዮ **sal-va-ti-yo** gas tank
ሳሎን **sa-lon** salon
ሳመ **sa-me** kiss
ሳሙና **sa-mu-na** soap
ሳምንት **sam-mint** week
ሳር **sar** grass
ሳር ቅጠል **sar qi-tel** vegetarian
ሳቀ **sa-qe** laugh
ሳተላይት **sa-te-layt** satellite
ሳንቲም **san-tim** cent
ሳንዱች **san-duch** sandwich
ሳይንስ **sa-yins** science
ሳጥን **sa-tin** locker; box (*n.*)
ሴሚናር **se-mi-nar** seminar
ሴት **set** woman
ሴት ልጅ **set lij** daughter
ሴት አያት **set a-yat** grandmother

ስህተት **sih-tet** incorrect, wrong
ስለ **si-le** about
ስለታም **si-le-tamm** sharp
ስልሳ **sil-sa** sixty
ስልክ **silk** phone, telephone
ስልክ ቁጥር **silk qu-tir** phone number
ስሜት **sim-met** feel
ስም **sim** name
ስምምነት **si-mi-mi-net** agreement
ስምንት **sim-mint** eight
ስራ **si-ra** business, job, work, occupation
ስርቆት (የሱቅ ውስጥ) **sir-qot (ye-suq wist)** shoplifting
ስርዓት **sir-at** system
ሲቃይ **si-qay** torture
ስብሰባ **sib-se-ba** meeting
ስነ ኮረንቲ **si-ne kor-ren-ti** electricity
ስኒ **si-ni** cup
ስንዴ **sin-de** wheat
ስካነር **is-ka-ner** scanner
ስኳር **sik-kuar** diabetes
ስኳር **sik-kuar** sugar
ስደተኛ **sid-de-tegn-gna** immigrant, refugee
ስደት **sid-det** immigration
ስድስት **sid-dist** six
ስጋ **si-ga** meat
ስጋ ሻጭ **si-ga shach** butcher
ስጋት **si-gat** threat (*n.*); worry (*n.*)
ስጋጃ **si-gaj-ja** rug
ስጎ **si-go** sauce
ስጦታ **si-to-ta** gift
ስፌት **si-fet** seam
ስፍራ **sif-ra** area, scene

ሶስት **sost** three
ሶስት ማዕዘን **sost ma-i-zen** triangle
ሶኬት **sok-ket** plug

ረ re / ሩ ru / ሪ ri / ራ ra / ር ri / ሮ ro

ረሳ **res-sa** forget
ረቡዕ **re-bu-i** Wednesday
ረብሻ **reb-sha** riot
ረዥም **rezh-zhim** long; tall
ረዳ **red-da** aid (*v.*)
ረዳት **red-dat** aide (*n.*)
ረድፍ **redf** queue
ረገጠ **reg-ge-te** step (*v.*)

ሩቅ **ruq** far
ሩብ **rub** quarter
ሩዝ **ruz** rice

ሪሳይክል **ri-say-kil** recycle
ሪባን **ri-ban** ribbon
ሪችት **ri-chit** fireworks
ሪዝ **riz** moustache
ሪፐብሊክ **ri-peb-lik** republic

ራስ **ras** head
ራሽን **ra-shin** ration
ራቁት **ra-qut** naked
ራት **rat** dinner
ራት በላ **rat bel-la** dine
ራዲዮ **ra-di-yo** radio
ራጅ **raj** x-ray
ራግቢ **rag-bi** rugby

ርምጃ **ir-mij-ja** walk (*n.*)
ርቱዕ **ri-tu-i** fluent
ርካሽ **rik-kash** cheap
ርክክብ **ri-kik-kib** delivery
ርዳታ **ir-da-ta** help

ሮጠ **ro-te** run

ሸ she / ሹ shu / ሻ sha / ሼ she / ሽ shi / ሾ sho

ሸለቆ **she-le-qo** basin
ሸመተ **shem-me-te** buy, purchase
ሸሚዝ **she-miz** shirt
ሸረሪት **she-re-rit** spider
ሸቀጥ **she-qet** goods
ሸካራ **she-ka-ra** rough
ሸክላ **shek-la** brick
ሸክላ ስራ **shek-la si-ra** pottery
ሸጠ **she-te** sell
ሸጦ ጨረሰ **she-to cher-re-se** sold out

ሹካ **shuk-ka** fork

ሻምፓኝ **sham-pagn** champagne
ሻምፖ **sham-po** shampoo
ሻረ **sha-re** undo
ሻርክ **shark** shark
ሻንጣ **shan-ta** suitcase
ሻይ **shay** tea
ሻይ ቤት **shay bet** cafe

ሼፍ **shef** chef

ሺ **shi** thousand
ሽልማት **shil-li-mat** prize
ሽምብራ **shim-bi-ra** chickpeas
ሽርሽር **shir-shir** hike
ሽርሽር **shir-shir** picnic
ሽቦ **shi-bo** cable
ሽቦ **shi-bo** wire
ሽታ **shit-ta** smell
ሽንኩርት **shin-kurt** onion
ሽፋን **shi-fan** cover

ሾርባ **shor-ba** soup

ቀ qe / ቁ qu / ቃ qa / ቄ qe / ቅ qi / ቆ qo / ቋ qua

ቀለም **qe-lem** color
ቀለበሰ **qe-leb-be-se** reverse
ቀለበት **qe-le-bet** ring (*jewelry*)
ቀለጠ **qel-le-te** melt
ቀላል **qel-lal** light, portable, minor (*adj.*)
ቀላቀለ **qel-lal** mix
ቀሚስ **qe-mis** dress (*n.*)
ቀበረ **qeb-be-re** bury
ቀበቶ **qe-bet-to** seat belt
ቀትር **qe-tir** noon
ቀነ ገደብ **qe-ne ge-deb** deadline
ቀናኢ **qe-na-i** zealous
ቀን **qen** day, daytime
ቀዝቃዛ **qez-qaz-za** cold (*adj.*)
ቀይ **qeyy** red
ቀዳ **qed-da** pour
ቀዳሚ **qe-da-mi** first
ቀዳዳ **qe-da-da** puncture
ቀዶ ጠጋኝ **qed-do teg-gagn** surgeon
ቀዶ ጥገና **qed-do tig-ge-na** surgery
ቀጠለ **qet-te-le** carry-on, resume
ቀጠሮ **qe-te-ro** appointment
ቀጣ **qet-ta** punish
ቀጣሪ **qe-ta-ri** employer
ቀጥሎ **qet-ti-lo** next
ቀጥታ **qet-ti-ta** live (*adj.*); straight
ቀጭን **qech-chin** thin

ቁልፍ **qulf** button; ignition; key
ቁምሳጥን **qum-sa-tin** cabinet
ቁስለት **qus-let** infection
ቁስል **qu-sil** sore (*n.*)
ቁራጭ **qur-rach** piece

ቁርስ **qurs** breakfast
ቁርጭምጭሚት **qur-chim-chi-mit** ankle
ቁንጫ **qu-nich-cha** flea
ቁጡ **qut-tu** sensitive
ቁጥር **qu-tir** number

ቃል **qal** word
ቃል ገባ **qal geb-ba** promise (*v.*)
ቃልኪዳን **qal-ki-dan** promise (*n.*)
ቃሬዛ **qa-re-za** litter
ቃና **qa-na** flavor

ቄስ **qes** priest

ቅመም **qi-mem** seasoning
ቅመም የበዛበት **qi-mem ye-bez-zab-bet** spicy
ቅማል **qi-mal** lice
ቅርብ **qirb** near
ቅርጫት **qir-chat** basket
ቅርጫት ኳስ **qir-chat kuas** basketball
ቅርጻ ቅርጽ **qir-tsa qirts** sculpture
ቅርጽ **qirts** engraving
ቅበላ **qi-be-la** admission
ቅባት **qi-bat** cream
ቅቤ **qi-be** butter
ቅናሽ **qin-nash** discount, sale
ቅይጥ ጾታ **qiy-yit tso-ta** heterosexual
ቅዱስ **qid-dus** holy, sacred
ቅዳሜ **qi-da-me** Saturday
ቅዳሜና እሁድ **qi-da-men-na e-hud** weekend
ቅጂ **qij-ji** copy
ቅጣት **qi-tat** penalty
ቅጽበት **qits-bet** instant, moment

ቆለፈ **qol-le-fe** lock
ቆረጠ **qor-re-te** cut
ቆሻሻ **qo-sha-sha** dirty, trash

ቆንስላ **qon-si-la** consulate
ቆንጆ **qon-jo** beautiful
ቆይታ **qoy-yi-ta** stay
ቆዳ **qo-da** leather; skin
ቆጠበ **qot-te-be** save

ቋሊማ **qua-li-ma** sausage
ቋሚ **qua-mi** permanent
ቋት **quat** reservoir
ቋንቋ **quan-qua** language
ቋጠሮ **qua-te-ro** knot

በ **be** through
በኋላ **be-hua-la** after, later
በለስ **be-les** fig
በላ **bel-la** eat
በሰበሰ **be-seb-be-se** rot
በረሐ **be-re-ha** desert
በረረ **ber-re-re** fly (*v.*)
በረራ **be-re-ra** flight
በረዶ **be-re-do** ice; snow (*n.*)
በረዶ ዘነበ **be-re-do zen-ne-be** snow (*v.*)
በር **ber** door
በርሜል **ber-mel** barrel
በርበሬ **ber-be-re** pepper
በሽታ **besh-shi-ta** disease
በቀር **be-qer** except
በቂ **be-qi** enough
በቆሎ **beq-qol-lo** corn
በቡጢ መታ **be-but-ti met-ta** box (*v.*)
በተጨማሪም **be-te-chem-ma-rim** also
በነፍሳት መነደፍ **be-nef-sat men-ne-def** insect bite
በአቅራቢያ **be-aq-rab-bi-ya** nearby
በዓል **be-al** festival, holiday
በከለ **bek-ke-le** infect
በድብቅ የሚሰራ **be-dib-biq yem-mis-ser-ra** underground
በገንዘብ ደለለ **be-gen-zeb del-le-le** bribe (*v.*)
በጊዜ **be-gi-ze** early
በጋ **be-ga** summer
በጋራ **be-ga-ra** together
በግ **beg** sheep
በጠቅላላ **be-teq-lal-la** entire
በጣም **be-tam** very
በፊት **be-fit** before

በፍጹም **be-fits-tsum** never (*adv.*)

ቡሎን **bu-lon** screw
ቡና **bun-na** coffee
ቡና ቤት **bun-na bet** bar (*n. / place for drinking*)
ቡናማ **bun-nam-ma** brown
ቡድን **bu-din** group
ቡጢ **but-ti** fist; punch

ቢላዋ **bil-la-wa** knife
ቢራ **bi-ra** beer
ቢሮ **bi-ro** office
ቢሮክራሲ **bi-ro-ki-ra-si** bureaucracy
ቢጫ **bi-cha** yellow

ባህላዊ ኪነት **ba-hi-la-wi ki-net** folk art
ባህል **ba-hil** culture
ባህር **ba-hir** sea
ባህር ሐይል **ba-hir ha-yil** navy (*n. / military*)
ባለ ስልጣን **ba-le sil-tan** official
ባለመኝታ መኪና **ba-le-megn-gni-ta me-ki-na** sleeping car
ባለሱቅ **ba-le-suq** shopkeeper
ባለስልጣን **ba-le-sil-tan** authority
ባለቤት **ba-le-bet** owner
ባለትዳር **ba-le-ti-dar** married
ባለዚፕ ብርድ ልብስ **ba-le-zipp bird libs** sleeping bag
ባለዛጎል ዓሳ **ba-le-za-gol a-sa** shellfish
ባለጌ **ba-le-ge** impolite, rude
ባለጎማ ጫማ **ba-le-gom-ma cham-ma** skate (*n.*)
ባላንድ አቅጣጫ **ba-land aq-tach-cha** one-way
ባል **bal** husband
ባልኮኒ **bal-ko-ni** balcony
ባረከ **bar-re-ke** bless
ባርኔጣ **bar-net-ta** hat
ባሻገር **bash-shag-ger** across
ባቄላ **ba-qe-la** bean

ባቡር **ba-bur** train
ባቡር ጣቢያ **ba-bur ta-bi-ya** train station
ባብዛኛው **bab-za-gnaw** often (*adv.*)
ባት **bat** thigh
ባትሪ (የእጅ) **bat-ri (ye-ijj)** battery
ባትሪ **bat-ri** flashlight
ባንክ **bank** bank
ባንዲራ **ban-di-ra** flag
ባዕድ አገር **ba-id a-ger** foreign
ባከፓክ **bak-pak** backpack
ባዶ **ba-do** empty, vacant

ቤተ መቅደስ **be-te meq-des** temple
ቤተ መጻህፍት **be-te me-tsa-hift** library
ቤተሰብ **be-te-seb** family
ቤተክርስትያን **be-te-ki-ris-ti-yan** church
ቤት **bet** house
ቤንዚን **ben-zin** petrol, gasoline

ብልህ **bi-lih** wise
ብልሹ **bi-lish-shu** corrupt
ብልጭታ **bil-lich-ta** flash
ብስክሌት **bis-ki-let** bicycle
ብረት **bi-ret** metal, iron
ብር **birr** silver
ብርሐን **bir-han** lighting
ብርቱካን **bir-tu-kan** orange
ብርድልብስ **bir-di-libs** blanket
ብርጭቆ **bir-chiq-qo** glass
ብቻ **bich-cha** only
ብዕር **bi-ir** ink; pen
ብክለት **bik-let** pollution
ብዙ **bi-zu** many, much
ብዛት **bi-zat** quantity
ብድር **bid-dir** credit
ብድር **bid-dir** loan (*n.*)
ብጥብጥ **bi-tib-bit** violence

ቦምብ **bomb** bomb
ቦርሳ **bor-sa** bag, purse
ቦቲ **bot-ti** boot
ቦታ **bo-ta** place
ቦነስ **bo-nes** bonus

ቧምቧ መክፈቻ **buam-bua mek-fe-cha** faucet

ተ te / ቲ ti / ታ ta / ቴ te / ት ti / ቶ to

ተላላፊ **te-la-la-fi** contagious
ተመለሰ **te-mel-le-se** return
ተመለከተ **te-me-lek-ke-te** watch (*v.*)
ተመላሽ ገንዘብ **te-mel-lash gen-zeb** refund (*n.*)
ተመሳሳይ **te-me-sa-say** same
ተመሳሳይ ጾታ **te-me-sa-say tso-ta** homosexual
ተማረ **te-ma-re** learn
ተማሪ **te-ma-ri** student
ተምር **te-mir** date
ተሟገተ **te-muag-ge-te** argue
ተስማሚ **tes-ma-mi** fit
ተስማማ **tes-mam-ma** agree
ተረተረ **te-ret-te-re** rip
ተረጎመ **te-reg-go-me** interpret, translate
ተራመደ **te-ram-me-de** walk (*v.*)
ተራራ **te-ra-ra** mountain
ተርጓሚ **ter-gua-mi** interpreter, translator
ተሸከመ **te-shek-ke-me** carry
ተሽከርካሪ **tesh-ker-ka-ri** vehicle
ተቀላቀለ **te-qe-laq-qe-le** join
ተቀመጠ **te-qem-me-te** sit
ተቀማጭ **te-qem-mach** deposit; reserve
ተቀማጭ ሒሳብ **te-qe-mach hi-sab** account
ተቀበለ **te-qeb-be-le** accept, receive; admit
ተቀያሪ **te-qey-ya-ri** substitute
ተቀጣሪ **te-qet-ta-ri** employee
ተቃራኒ **te-qa-ra-ni** opposite
ተቃወመ **te-qaw-we-me** against
ተቃውሞ **te-qaw-mo** protest
ተቅማጥ **teq-mat** diarrhea
ተቋም **te-quam** institution
ተባባሪ **te-bab-be-re** associate (*n.*)
ተባይ **te-bay** pest

ተነፈሰ **te-nef-fe-se** breathe (*v.*)
ተናደደ **te-nad-de-de** angry
ተናገረ **te-nag-ge-re** speak
ተንሸራተተ **ten-she-rat-te-te** ski (*v.*)
ተንቀሳቀሰ **ten-qe-saq-qe-se** move (*v.*)
ተንቀሳቃሽ ምስል **ten-qe-sa-qash mi-sil** video
ተንቀሳቃሽ ስልክ **ten-qe-sa-qash silk** mobile phone
ተንኮል **ten-kol** trick (*n.*)
ተኛ **tegn-gna** asleep; sleep
ተከላከለ **te-ke-lak-ke-le** protect
ተከራይ **te-ke-ray** tenant
ተከተለ **te-ket-te-le** follow
ተከታዮች **te-ket-ta-yoch** suite
ተከፍሏል **te-kef-lual** paid
ተኩስ **te-kus** shot
ተካ **tek-ka** replace
ተክል **te-kil** plant
ተኮሰ **tek-ko-se** shoot (*v.*)
ተወላጅ **te-wel-laj** native
ተወጋጅ **te-weg-gaj** disposable
ተዋናይ **te-wa-nay** actor
ተዘጋበት **te-zeg-gab-bet** lock out
ተየበ **tey-ye-be** type (*v.*)
ተደወለ **te-dew-we-le** toll (*v.*)
ተገነዘበ **te-ge-nez-ze-be** understand
ተግባር **te-gi-bar** activity
ተግባቦት **teg-ba-bot** communication
ተጎዳኘ **te-go-dagn-gne** associate (*v.*)
ተጓዘ **te-gua-ze** travel
ተጓዥ **te-guazh** passenger
ተጠማ **te-tem-ma** thirsty
ተጠርጣሪ **te-ter-ta-ri** suspect (*n.*)
ተጠቀመ **te-teq-qe-me** use (*v.*)
ተጠነቀቀ **te-te-neq-qe-qe** beware
ተጨማሪ **te-chem-ma-ri** extra
ተጨባጭ **te-cheb-bach** concrete

ተጫወተ **te-chaw-we-te** play (*v.*)
ተጫጫነ **te-cha-cha-ne** dizzy
ተጽዕኖ **te-tsi-i-no** influence
ተፈጥሮ **te-fet-ro** nature
ተፈጥሯዊ **te-fet-rua-wi** organic

ቲማቲም **ti-ma-tim** tomato
ቲኬት **tik-ket** ticket

ታህሳስ **ta-hi-sas** December
ታላቅ **tal-laq** great
ታማሚ **ta-ma-mi** patient (*n.*)
ታምፑን **tam-pun** tampon
ታች **tach** down
ታክሲ **tak-si** cab, taxi
ታዲያስ **ta-di-yas** hey (*interj.*)
ታዳጊ **tad-da-gi** young
ታዳጊ ልጅ **tad-da-gi lij** kid
ታጋች **tag-gach** hostage

ቴሌቪዥን **te-le-vi-zhin** television
ቴምብር **tem-bir** postage
ቴፕ **tepp** tape

ትሁት **ti-hut** polite
ትህትና **ti-hi-tin-na** courtesy
ትል **til** worm
ትልቅ **til-liq** large, big
ትምህርት **ti-mi-hirt** education
ትምህርት ቤት **ti-mi-hirt bet** school
ትሪ **ti-ri** tray
ትራስ **ti-ras** pillow
ትራፊክ **ti-ra-fik** traffic
ትርታ **tir-ri-ta** pulse
ትርኢት **tir-it** show (*n.*)
ትርጉም **tir-gum** interpretation
ትርፍ **tirf** profit

ትርፍ **tirf** spare (*adj.*)
ትርፍ አንጀት **tirf an-jet** appendicitis
ትናንት **ti-nant** yesterday
ትንሽ **tin-nish** small
ትንሽ ሆቴል **tin-nish ho-tel** inn
ትዕምርት **ti-im-mirt** symbol
ትእዛዝ **ti-i-zaz** order
ትዕይንት **ti-iy-yint** scenery
ትእግስት **ti-i-gist** patience
ትከሻ **ti-kesh-sha** shoulder
ትኩሳት **tik-ku-sat** fever
ትኩስ **tik-kus** fresh
ትክክለኛ **ti-kik-ki-legn-gna** accurate, correct, right (*adj.*)
ትውኪያ **tiw-ki-ya** vomit
ትያትር **ti-ya-tir** theater

ቶሎ **to-lo** soon (*adv.*)

ቸ che / ቻ cha / ቼ che / ች chi

ቸኮሌት **chek-ko-let** chocolate

ቻለ **cha-le** able, can (*modal verb*)
ቻርኔላ **char-ne-la** zipper
ቻናል **cha-nal** channel

ቼክ **chek** check (*n.*)

ችላ አለ **chil-la a-le** ignore
ችግር **chig-gir** problem
ችግር **chig-gir** trouble

ነ ne / ኒ ni / ና na / ን ni / ኖ no

ነሐሴ ne-ha-se August
ነርስ ners nurse
ነርቭ nerv nerve
ነቃ neq-qa wake
ነበልባል ne-bel-bal flame, flare
ነካ nek-ka touch
ነዋሪ ne-wa-ri occupant
ነው new be (*v. / am, is, are, was, were, been*)
ነዳ ned-da drive
ነዳጅ ne-daj fuel
ነዳጅ (መርገጫ) ne-daj (me-ri-ge-cha) accelerator (gas pedal)
ነገ ne-ge tomorrow
ነገረ neg-ge-re tell
ነገር ne-ger thing
ነገድ ne-ged tribe
ነጋዴ neg-ga-de merchant
ነጎድጓድ ne-god-guad thunder
ነጠላ ne-te-la single (*adj.*)
ነጠላ ጫማ ne-te-la cham-ma sandals
ነጥብ ne-tib point, score (*n. / sports*)
ነጭ nech white
ነጭ ጋዝ nech gaz gasoline
ነጻ ne-tsa free
ነፋስ nefs wind
ነፍሰጡር nef-se-tur pregnant
ነፍሱን ስቶ nef-sun si-to unconscious
ነፍሳት nef-sat insect
ነፍሳት ማባረሪያ nef-sat mab-ba-re-ri-ya insect repellant
ነፍስ ዘራ nefs zer-ra revive

ኒውክሌር niw-ki-ler nuclear

ናሙና **na-mu-na** sample
ናፍታ **naf-ta** diesel
ናፕሳክ **nap-sak** knapsack
ናፕኪን **nap-kin** napkin

ንቅለ ተከላ **niq-le te-ke-la** transplant
ንብ **nib** bee
ንብረት **nib-ret** property
ንክሻ **ni-kish-sha** bite
ንጉሳዊ ቤተሰብ **ni-gu-sa-wi be-te-seb** royalty
ንጋት **ni-gat** dawn
ንግስት **ni-gist** queen
ንግድ **nigd** trade
ንጹህ **ni-tsuh** clean, pure, innocent

ኖረ **no-re** live (*v.*)
ኖራ **no-ra** lime

አ a / ዓ a / ኤ e / እ i / ኦ o

አሁን a-hun now
አለ a-le say
አለመግባባት a-le-meg-ba-bat misunderstanding; dispute (*v.*)
አለማዊ al-ma-wi secular
አለም አቀፍ a-lem aq-qef international
አለርጂ a-ler-ji allergy
አለቀሰ a-leq-qe-se cry
አለቃ a-le-qa chief (*adj.*)
አለፋ a-lef-fa exhaust
አላማ a-la-ma purpose
አልባሌ a-lib-ba-le casual
አልባሳት al-ba-sat clothing
አልተስማማም al-tes-mam-mam disagree
አልኮል al-kol alcohol
አልጋ al-ga bed
አልጋ ለቆ ወጣ al-ga leq-qo wet-ta check out
አልጋ ያዘ al-ga ya-ze check in
አመሰግናለሁ a-me-seg-gi-nal-le-hu thank you
አመታዊ a-me-ta-wi annual
አመታዊ ክብረ በዓል a-me-ta-wi ki-bi-re be-al anniversary
አመነ am-me-ne believe, trust
አመድ a-med ash
አመጣ a-met-ta bring
አመጽ a-mets rebellion
አማራጭ am-ma-rach option
አማች a-mach mother-in-law
አማከረ am-mak-ke-re consult
አማጺ am-ma-tsi rebel
አሜሪካ a-me-ri-ka United States
አምስት am-mist five
አምቡላንስ am-bu-lans ambulance

አምባሳደር **am-ba-sad-der** ambassador
አምና **am-na** last year
አሰመጠ **a-sem-me-te** drown
አሰሳ **a-se-sa** navigation
አሰረ **as-se-re** tie (*v.*)
አሰበ **as-se-be** think
አሰጋ **a-seg-ga** threaten
አሳ **a-sa** fish
አሳ ማስገሪያ ዘንግ **a-sa mas-ge-ri-ya zeng** fishing rod
አሳ ማስገር **a-sa mas-ger** fishing
አሳ ማስገር ይፈቀዳል **a-sa mas-ger yif-feq-qe-dal** fishing permitted
አሳ አስጋሪ **a-sa as-ga-ri** fisherman
አሳማ **a-sa-ma** pig
አሳማሚ **a-sam-ma-mi** painful
አሳሰበ **a-sas-se-be** recommend; alarm, worry (*v.*)
አሳንሰር **a-san-ser** elevator, escalator
አሳዛኝ **a-saz-zagn** sad
አሳየ **a-say-ye** exhibit, show (*v.*)
አስመጣ **as-met-ta** import
አስማት **as-mat** spell
አስም **asm** asthma
አስራ ሁለት **as-ra hu-let** twelve
አስራ ሰባት **as-ra se-bat** seventeen
አስራ ስምንት **as-ra sim-mint** eighteen
አስራ ስድስት **as-ra sid-dist** sixteen
አስራ አምስት **as-ra am-mist** fifteen
አስራ አራት **as-ra a-rat** fourteen
አስራ አንድ **as-ra and** eleven
አስራ ዘጠኝ **as-ra ze-tegn** nineteen
አስር **as-sir** ten
አስርተ ዓመት **as-sir-te a-met** decade
አስቀረ **as-qer-re** exclude
አስቀየመ **as-qey-ye-me** offend
አስቂኝ **as-si-qign** funny
አስቆጠረ **as-qot-te-re** score (*v.*)

አስቆጣ **as-qot-ta** irritate
አስቤዛ **as-be-za** supplies
አስተላለፈ **as-te-lal-le-fe** postpone; transfer
አስተማማኝ **as-te-ma-magn** reliable
አስተማሪ **as-te-ma-ri** teacher
አስተሳሰብ **as-te-sa-seb** idea
አስተዋይ **as-te-way** reasonable
አስተዳደር **as-te-da-der** administration
አስታወሰ **as-taw-we-se** remember
አስታወቀ **as-taw-we-qe** pronounce
አስቸጋሪ **as-cheg-ga-ri** difficult
አስወገደ **as-weg-ge-de** avoid
አስወገደ **as-weg-ge-de** remove
አስደሳች **as-des-sach** pleasant
አስገነዘበ **as-ge-nez-ze-be** remind
አስገድዶ መድፈር **as-ged-di-do med-fer** rape (*n.*)
አስገድዶ ደፈረ **as-ged-di-do def-fe-re** rape (*v.*)
አስጠነቀቀ **as-te-neq-qe-qe** warn
አስጠኚ **as-tegn-gni** tutor
አስጣለ **as-ta-le** rescue
አስፈሪ **as-fer-ri** scary
አስፕሪን **as-pi-rin** aspirin
አረንጓዴ **a-ren-gua-de** green
አረጋገጠ **ar-re-gag-ge-te** confirm
አረፍተ ነገር **a-ref-te ne-ger** sentence
አሩስቶ **ar-rus-to** roasted
አራት **a-rat** four
አራት ማዕዘን **a-rat ma-i-zen** rectangle
አርባ **ar-ba** forty
አርብ **arb** Friday
አርትራይቲስ **ar-ti-ray-tis** arthritis
አርክቴክቸር **ar-ki-tek-chur** architecture
አሸባሪ **ash-sheb-ba-ri** terrorist
አሸነፈ **ash-shen-ne-fe** win
አሸዋ **a-she-wa** sand
አቀዘቀዘ **a-qe-zeq-qe-ze** freeze

አቃቤ ህግ **aq-qa-be hig** attorney, lawyer
አቅጣጫ **aq-tach-cha** direction
አቆመ **a-qo-me** halt; park (*v.*)
አበሰለ **a-bes-se-le** cook (*v.*)
አበቃ **a-beq-qa** qualify
አበበ **ab-be-be** flourish
አበባ **a-be-ba** flower
አበደረ **a-bed-de-re** loan (*v.*)
አባል **a-bal** member
አባት **ab-bat** father
አቤቱታ አቀረበ **a-be-tu-ta a-qer-re-be** complain
አብራራ **ab-rar-ra** explain
አብዛኛውን **ab-zagn-gna-wun** most (*adv.*)
አብዮት **a-bi-yot** revolution
አተር **a-ter** pea
አታለለ **at-tal-le-le** trick (*v.*)
አትክልት **a-ti-kilt** vegetable
አትክልት ስፍራ **a-ti-kilt sif-ra** garden (*n.*)
አቶ **a-to** Mr. (*title*)
አነሳ **a-nes-sa** lift
አነስተኛ **a-nes-tegn-gna** minimum
አነቀ **an-ne-qe** choke
አነቃ **a-neq-qa** awake
አነቃነቀ **an-ne-qan-ne-qe** rock (*v.*)
አነበበ **a-neb-be-be** read
አነጋገር (ቅላጼ) **an-ne-ga-ger (qi-la-tse)** accent
አንሶላ **an-so-la** sheet
አንተ **an-te** you
አንቲባዮቲክስ **an-ti-ba-yo-tiks** antibiotics
አንቲሴፕቲክ **an-ti-sep-tik** antiseptic
አንቲፍሪዝ **an-ti-fi-riz** antifreeze
አንኳኳ **an-kuak-kua** knock
አንዴ **an-de** once
አንድ **and** one
አንድ አይነት **and ay-net** uniform
አንገት **an-get** neck

አንጻራዊ **an-tsa-ra-wi** relative
አኘከ **agn-gne-ke** chew
አከመ **ak-ke-me** treat
አከራየ **ak-ke-ray-ye** rent (*v.*)
አከርካሪ **a-ker-ka-ri** spine
አከበረ **a-keb-be-re** respect (*v.*)
አኩሪ አተር **a-ku-ri a-ter** soy
አካል **a-kal** body; organ
አካል ጉዳተኛ **a-kal gu-da-tegn-gna** handicapped, disabled
አካል ጉዳት **a-kal gu-dat** disability
አካውንታንት **ak-ka-wun-tant** accountant
አካዳሚ **ak-ka-da-mi** academy
አክሰል **ak-sil** axle
አክብሮት **ak-bi-rot** respect (*n.*)
አወቀ **aw-we-qe** know
አወከ **aw-we-ke** disturb
አወዳደረ **aw-we-dad-de-re** compare
አወጀ **aw-we-je** declare
አዋለ **a-wa-le** spend
አዋቂ **a-wa-qi** adult
አውራ ጎዳና **aw-ra go-da-na** highway
አውራ ጣት **aw-ra tat** thumb
አውራጃ **aw-raja-ja** district
አውሮፓ **aw-rop-pa** Europe
አውሮፓዊ **aw-rop-pa-wi** European
አውሮፕላን **aw-rop-pi-lan** airplane, plane
አውቶማቲክ **aw-to-ma-tik** automatic
አውቶማቲክ ስርጭት **aw-to-ma-tik si-rich-chit** automatic transmission
አውቶሞቢል **aw-to-mo-bil** automobile
አውቶቡስ **aw-to-bus** bus
አውድቅ ያለበት **aw-diq yal-leb-bet** epileptic
አዎ **a-wo** yes
አዘዘ **az-ze-ze** dictate
አየ **ay-ye** see

አየር **ay-yer** air
አየር መንገድ **ay-yer men-ged** airline
አየር ማረፊያ **ay-yer ma-re-fi-ya** airport
አየር ንብረት **ay-yer nib-ret** climate
አይሁድ **ay-hud** Jew
አይብ **a-yib** cheese
አይነ ስውር **ay-ne si-wur** blind
አይነርግብ **ay-ner-gib** veil
አይነት **ay-net** type (*n.*)
አይን **ayn** eye
አይጥ **a-yit** mouse
አይጥ **a-yit** rat
አደረሰ **a-der-re-se** deliver
አደረቀ **a-der-re-qe** drain
አደረገ **a-der-re-ge** do, act
አደባባይ **ad-de-ba-bay** square (*town square*)
አደነ **ad-de-ne** hunt
አደንዛዥ **a-den-zazh** sedative
አደገኛ **a-de-gegn-gna** serious
አደጋ **a-de-ga** accident; danger, hazard, risk
አዲስ **ad-dis** new
አዳመጠ **ad-dam-me-te** listen
አዳራሽ **ad-da-rash** hall
አዳር **a-dar** layover; overnight (*adv.*)
አዳነ **a-da-ne** cure
አዳኝ **ad-dagn** hunter
አድራሻ **ad-rash-sha** address (*n.*)
አገለለ **a-gel-le-le** withdraw
አገለገለ **a-ge-leg-ge-le** serve
አገልጋይ **a-gel-gay** servant
አገልግሎት **a-gel-gi-lot** service
አገራዊ ኮድ **a-ge-ra-wi kod** country code
አገር **a-ger** country, nation
አገር ማየት **a-ger ma-yet** sightseeing
አገባ **a-geb-ba** marry
አገተ **ag-ge-te** kidnap

አገኘ **a-gegn-gne** find, retrieve; get; meet
አገዘ **ag-ge-ze** assist
አገዛዝ **ag-ge-zaz** regime
አጋራ **ag-gar-ra** share
አጋር **ag-gar** partner
አጋዥ **ag-gazh** assistant
አግባብ **ag-bab** proper
አጎት **ag-got** uncle
አጎረሰ **a-gor-re-se** tip (*v.*)
አጎበር **a-go-ber** mosquito net
አጠመደ **a-tem-me-de** catch, trap (*v.*)
አጠቃ **a-teq-qa** attack (*v.*)
አጠቃላይ **at-te-qa-lay** general; total
አጠበ **at-te-be** bathe, wash
አጣ **at-ta** lose
አጥር **a-tir** fence
አጥንት **a-tint** bone
አጨበጨበ **a-che-bech-che-be** clap
አጭር **ach-chir** short
አፈቀረ **a-feq-qe-re** love (*v.*)
አፍ **af** mouth
አፍንጫ **a-fin-cha** nose
አፏጨ **a-fua-che** whistle (*v.*)
አፓርታማ **a-par-ta-ma** apartment
ኢሜል **i-mel** e-mail
ኢንሱሊን **in-su-lin** insulin
ኢንተርኔት **in-ter-net** Internet
ኢንፍሉዌንዛ **in-fi-lu-wen-za** influenza
ኢንቬሎፕ **in-ve-lop** envelope

ዓለም **a-lem** world
ዓመት **a-met** year

ኤምባሲ **em-ba-si** embassy
ኤሲ **e-si** air conditioning
ኤቲኤም **e-ti-aem** ATM

ኤች አይ ቪ **ech-ay-vi** HIV
ኤክስፐረስ ባቡር **e-kis-pi-res ba-bur** express train
ኤድስ **eds** AIDS
ኤጀንሲ **e-jen-si** agency
ኤግዚቢት **eg-zi-bit** exhibit (*n.*)

እህት **i-hit** sister
እምነት **im-net** trust (*n.*)
እሱ **is-su** he
እሱ (ለነገር) **is-su (le-ne-ger)** it
እሳት **i-sat** fire
እስረኛ **is-regn-gna** prisoner
እስራት **is-si-rat** arrest (*n.*)
እስር ቤት **i-sir bet** jail
እስቴድየም **is-te-di-yem** stadium
እስከዚያ **is-kez-zi-ya** until
እስክስታ **is-kis-ta** dance
እስፖርት **is-port** sport
እስፖርቶች **is-por-toch** sports
እሷ **is-sua** she
እረፍት **i-reft** rest
እርሳስ **ir-sas** pencil
እርሾ **ir-sho** yeast
እርዳታ **ir-da-ta** aid (*n.*)
እርጎ **ir-go** yogurt
እሺ **ish-shi** OK, okay
እቃ **i-qa** item; kit
እቃ ማጠቢያ **i-qa ma-te-bi-ya** sink (*n.*)
እቅድ **iq-qid** plan, project
እቅፍ አደረገ **iq-qif a-der-re-ge** hug
እባብ **i-bab** snake
እባክዎ **i-ba-ki-wo** please
እብድ **ibd** mad
እብጠት **ib-tet** swelling
እነሱ **in-nes-su** they
እና **in-na** and

እናት **in-nat** mother
እኔ **i-ne** I
እንስሳ **in-si-sa** animal
እንስት **i-nist** female
እንሽላሊት **in-shi-la-lit** lizard
እንቁላል **in-qu-lal** egg
እንቆቅልሽ **in-qo-qil-lish** mystery, puzzle
እንኳን ደህና መጣህ **in-kuan deh-na met-tah** welcome
እንደገና **in-de-ge-na** again
እንዴት **in-det** how
እንጉዳይ **in-gu-day** mushroom
እንግሊዝኛ ቋንቋ **in-gi-li-zign-gna quan-qua** English language
እንግዳ **in-gi-da** guest; unfamiliar
እንጨት **in-chet** wood
እኛ **ign-gna** we
እከክ **i-kek** itch
እኩለ ሌሊት **ik-ku-le le-lit** midnight
እኩለ ቀን **ik-ku-le qen** midday
እኩል **ik-kul** equal, even
እውነተኛ **iw-ne-tegn-gna** true
እውነት **iw-net** truth
እውናዊ **i-wu-na-wi** actual
እዚህ **iz-zih** here
እዚያ **iz-zi-ya** there
እያንዳንዱ **iy-yan-dan-du** every
እይታ **iy-yi-ta** view
እዳ **i-da** debt
እድለኛ **id-di-legn-gna** lucky
እድል **id-dil** fortune
እድሜ **id-me** age
እድፍ **i-dif** dirt
እጅ **ijj** hand
እጅ ሰጠ **ijj set-te** surrender (*v.*)
እጅ በእጅ ከፈለ **ijj bejj kef-fe-le** cash (*v.*)
እግረኛ **ig-regn-gna** pedestrian

እግር **i-gir** foot; leg
እግር ኳስ **i-gir kuas** football, soccer
እጥፍ **i-tif** double
እጽ **its** herb

ኦክስጅን **ok-si-jin** oxygen
ኦክቶፐስ **ok-to-pes** octopus
ኦፔራ **op-pe-ra** opera
ኦፕሬተር **op-pi-re-ter** operator

ከ ke / ኩ ku / ኪ ki / ካ ka / ኬ ke / ክ ki / ኮ ko / ኳ kua

ከ **ke** if
ከ ... አጠገብ **ke ... a-te-geb** next to
ከኋላ **ke-hua-la** behind
ከለከለ **ke-lek-ke-le** prohibit
ከላይ **ke-lay** above, over (*prep.*)
ከመካከል **ke-me-kak-kel** among
ከሰሰ **ke-se-se** accuse
ከሰዓት በኋላ **ke-se-at be-hua-la** afternoon
ከስምምነት ደረሰ **ke-si-mim-min-net** compromise
ከሰር **ke-sir** under
ከረሜላ **ke-re-mel-la** candy
ከረባት **ke-re-bat** tie (*n.*)
ከርሞ **ker-mo** next year
ከቀረጥ ነጻ **ke-qe-ret ne-tsa** duty-free
ከባድ **keb-bad** heavy; sore (*adj.*)
ከብት **kebt** cattle
ከተማ **ke-te-ma** city, town
ከተበ **ket-te-be** vaccinate
ከታች **ke-tach** below
ከንፈር **ken-fer** lip
ከፈለ **kef-fe-le** pay; separate (*v.*)
ከፈተ **kef-fe-te** unlock
ከፍተኛ **kef-fi-tegn-gna** senior
ከፍታ **kef-fi-ta** altitude

ኩላሊት **ku-la-lit** kidney
ኩባንያ **kub-ba-niy-ya** company

ኪሎ ሜትር **ki-lo me-tir** kilometer
ኪሎ ግራም **ki-lo gi-ram** kilogram
ኪስ **kis** pocket
ኪራይ **ki-ray** rent (*n.*)
ኪነ ጥበብ **ki-ne ti-beb** art

ኪኒን **ki-nin** pill

ካላንደር **ka-lan-der** calendar
ካልሲ **kal-si** sock
ካሜራ **ka-me-ra** camera
ካምፕ **kamp** camp
ካምፕግራውንድ **kamp-gi-ra-wund** campground
ካሳ **ka-sa** compensation
ካሬ **ka-re** square (*form*)
ካርታ **kar-ta** map
ካርድ **kard** card
ካሮት **ka-rot** carrot
ካቴድራል **ka-ted-ral** cathedral
ካካዎ **ka-ka-wo** cocoa
ካደ **ka-de** deny
ካፊያ **kaf-fi-ya** shower

ኬሚካል **ke-mi-kal** chemical
ኬክ **kek** cake
ኬክ ቤት **kek bet** pastry

ክለብ **ki-leb** club
ክሊኒክ **ki-li-nik** clinic
ክልል **kil-lil** region
ክስ **kiss** prosecution
ክረምት **ki-remt** winter
ክብ **kibb** circle
ክትባት **kit-ti-bat** vaccination
ክንድ **kind** arm
ክንፍ **kinf** wing
ክዳን **ki-dan** lid
ክፍለ ዘመን **kif-le ze-men** century
ክፍለ ጊዜ **kif-le gi-ze** period
ክፍል **ki-fil** class; room; section
ክፍልፋይ **ki-fil-fay** ratio
ክፍት **kift** open
ክፍት የስራ ቦታ **kift ye-si-ra bo-ta** vacancy

ክፍያ **ki-fiy-ya** payment, fee

ኮሚሽን **ko-mi-shin** commission
ኮሜዲ **ko-me-di** comedy
ኮምፒዩተር **kom-pi-yu-ter** computer
ኮረብታ **ko-reb-ta** hill
ኮረንቲ **kor-ren-ti** electric
ኮረንቲ አስተላላፊ **kor-ren-ti as-te-la-la-fi** conductor
ኮርማ **kor-ma** bull
ኮርቻ **ko-rich-cha** saddle
ኮሸር **ko-sher** kosher
ኮት **kot** coat
ኮንዶም **kon-dom** condom
ኮክ **kok** peach
ኮኮብ ቆጣሪ **kok-kob qo-ta-ri** fortuneteller
ኮኮነት **ko-ko-net** coconut

ኳስ **kuas** ball

ወ we / ዋ wa / ው wi

ወህኒ **weh-ni** prison
ወለወለ **we-lew-we-le** dust (*v.*)
ወሊድ መከላከል **we-lid mek-ke-la-kel** contraception
ወላጅ **we-laj** parent
ወሰነ **wes-se-ne** decide; limit (*v.*)
ወሰደ **wes-se-de** take
ወረቀት **we-re-qet** paper
ወረወረ **we-rew-we-re** throw
ወሬ **we-re** talk
ወር **wer** month
ወርቅ **werq** gold
ወቀሳ **we-qe-sa** accusation
ወቀጠ **weq-qe-te** pound (*v.*)
ወቅታዊ **weq-ta-wi** seasonal
ወቅት **weqt** season
ወተት **we-tet** milk
ወታደር **wet-tad-der** soldier
ወንበር **wen-ber** chair
ወንዝ **wenz** river
ወንድ ልጅ **wend lij** boy; son
ወንድ አያት **wend a-yat** grandfather
ወንድም **wen-dimm** brother
ወንጀል **wen-jel** crime
ወኪል **we-kil** agent
ወይም **we-yim** or
ወይነጠጅ **wey-ne-tejj** purple
ወይን **weyn** grape
ወይንጠጅ **weyn-tejj** wine
ወይዘሪት **wey-ze-rit** Ms. (*title*)
ወይዘሮ **wey-ze-ro** lady; Mrs. (*title*)
ወደብ **we-deb** harbor
ወደደ **wed-de-de** like (*v.*)
ወዲያ **we-di-ya** away

ወጣ **wet-ta** climb; out (*adv.*)
ወጣት **wet-tat** youth
ወጥ **wett** original
ወጥመድ **wet-med** trap (*n.*)
ወጪ **we-chi** expense
ወፍራም **wef-ram** fat

ዋስትና **was-tin-na** insurance
ዋሻ **wash-sha** tunnel, cave
ዋቢ **wa-bi** reference
ዋና **wan-na** main (*adj.*)
ዋኖስ **wa-nos** pigeon
ዋኘ **wagn-gne** swim
ዋጋ **wa-ga** charge (*n.*)
ዋጋ **wa-ga** cost, price, rate
ዋጠ **wa-te** swallow (*v.*)

ውሃ **wi-ha** water
ውሃ ለቀቀ **wi-ha leq-qe-qe** flush
ውሃ ቋጠረ **wi-ha quat-te-re** blister
ውል **wil** contract
ውሎ አድሮ **wi-lo ad-ro** eventually
ውሳኔ **wis-sa-ne** decision
ውስብስብ **wi-sib-sib** complicated
ውስጥ **wist** inside
ውሸት **wi-shet** lie
ውሻ **wish-sha** dog
ውቅያኖስ **wiq-ya-nos** ocean
ውድ **wid** expensive
ውድ ያልሆነ **wid yal-ho-ne** inexpensive
ውድቀት **wid-qet** fall (*n. / descent*)
ውጊያ **wig-gi-ya** battle (*n.*)
ውጤት **wit-tet** product
ውጭ **wich** outside

ዘ ze / ዙ zu / ዛ za / ዜ ze / ዝ zi / ዧ zha

ዘለፋ **ze-le-fa** insult
ዘልማዳዊ **zel-ma-da-wi** traditional
ዘልማድ **zel-mad** tradition
ዘመን መለወጫ **ze-men me-lew-we-cha** New Year
ዘመን ተሻጋሪ **ze-men te-sha-ga-ri** classic
ዘረፈ **zer-re-fe** rob
ዘራፊ **ze-ra-fi** robber
ዘር **zer** seed
ዘብ **zeb** guard (*n.*)
ዘነበ **zen-ne-be** rain (*v.*)
ዘንቢል **zen-bil** shopping basket
ዘይት **ze-yit** oil
ዘገባ **ze-ge-ba** report
ዘጋ **zeg-ga** close, shut (*v.*)
ዘጋቢ **zeg-ga-bi** reporter
ዘግይቶ **zeg-yi-to** late
ዘጠና **ze-te-na** ninety
ዘጠኝ **ze-tegn** nine
ዘፈነ **zef-fe-ne** sing
ዘፈን **ze-fen** song

ዙሪያ **zu-ri-ya** around
ዙሮ መሄድ **zu-ro me-hed** detour

ዛሬ **za-re** today
ዛሬ ምሽት **za-re mish-shit** tonight

ዜሮ **ze-ro** zero
ዜና **ze-na** news
ዜጋ **ze-ga** citizen

ዝላይ **zil-lay** jump
ዝምተኛ **zim-mi-tegn-gna** quiet
ዝርዝር **zir-zir** list

ዝርግ **zirg** flat
ዝቅተኛ **ziq-qi-tegn-gna** low
ዝናብ **zi-nab** rain (*n.*)
ዝንብ **zinb** fly (*n. / insect*)
ዝንጀሮ **zin-jo-ro** monkey
ዝግ **zig** closed
ዝግታ **zig-gi-ta** slow
ዝግጁ **zi-gij-ju** ready

ዣንጥላ **zhan-ti-la** umbrella

የ ye / ዩ yu / ያ ya / ዪ yi

የህዝብ **ye-hizb** public
የህዝብ ላውንደሪ **ye-hizb la-wun-de-ri** laundromat
የህዝብ መጓጓዣ **ye-hizb meg-gua-gua-zha** public transportation
የህዝብ መጸዳጃ **ye-hizb mets-tse-da-ja** public toilet
የህዝብ ስልክ **ye-hizb silk** public telephone
የሕግ መወሰኛ ምክር ቤት **ye-higg me-wes-se-gna mi-kir bet** senate
የሕግ መወሰኛ ምክር ቤት አባል **ye-higg me-wes-se-gna mi-kir bet a-bal** senator
የህጻናት ማበሻ **ye-hi-tsa-nat mab-be-sha** baby wipes
የሕጻናት እንክብካቤ **ye-hi-tsa-nat en-ki-bik-ka-be** childcare
የሆነ ሰው **ye-ho-ne sew** someone
የሆነ ነገር **ye-ho-ne ne-ger** something
የለም **yel-lem** no
የሌሊት ወፍ **ye-le-lit wef** bat (*animal*)
የልብ **ye-libb** intimate
የልደት ቀን **ye-li-det qen** date of birth
የልደት ካርድ **ye-li-det kard** birth certificate
የመረጃ ዴስክ **ye-mer-re-ja desk** information desk
የመርከብ መድረክ **ye-mer-keb med-rek** deck
የመርከብ ማራገፊያ **ye-mer-keb mar-ra-ge-fi-ya** dock
የመርከብ ሸራ **ye-mer-keb she-ra** sail
የሙብት ተሟጋች **ye-me-bit te-mua-gach** activist
የመታጠቢያ ልብስ **ye-met-ta-te-bi-ya libs** bathing suit
የመንገድ ስልክ **ye-men-ged silk** phone booth
የመንገዶች መገናኛ **ye-men-ge-doch meg-ge-na-gna** intersection
የመኪና መጨናነቅ **ye-me-ki-na mech-che-na-neq** jam
የመድሐኒት ማዘዣ **ye-med-ha-nit ma-ze-zha** prescription
የመጀመሪያ ህክምና ርዳታ ቁሳቁስ **ye-me-jem-me-ri-ya hik-ki-min-na ir-da-ta qu-sa-qus** first-aid kit

የመጨረሻ **ye-me-cher-re-sha** last
የመጨረሻ (ከፍተኛ) **ye-me-cher-re-sha (kef-fi-te-gna)** maximum
የመጨረሻ ዝቅተኛ **ye-me-cher-re-sha zi-qi-tegn-gna** bottom
የመጸዳጃ ክፍል **ye-mets-tse-da-ja ki-fil** lavatory
የመጸዳጃ ወረቀት **ye-mets-tse-da-ja we-re-qet** toilet paper
የሙዚቃ መሳሪያ **ye-mu-zi-qa mes-sa-ri-ya** musical instrument
የሙዚቃ ትርኢት **ye-mu-zi-qa tir-et** concert
የሙዚቃ ጓድ **ye-mu-zi-qa guad** orchestra
የሚቻል **yem-mich-chal** possibly
የሚያንጎላጅ **yem-mi-yan-go-laj** drowsy
የሚገኝ **yem-mig-gegn** available
የማዕረግ **ye-ma-i-reg** first-class
የማያጨስ **yem-ma-ya-ches** non-smoking
የማይመች **yem-ma-yim-mech** uncomfortable
የማይበቃ **yem-may-be-qa** insufficient
የማይገኝ **yem-ma-yig-gegn** rare
የምርጫ ድምጽ **ye-mir-cha dimts** vote
የምሽት ሕይወት **ye-mish-shit hiy-wot** nightlife
የምንዛሬ ዋጋ **ye-mi-niz-za-re wa-ga** exchange rate
የምግብ መመረዝ **ye-mi-gib mem-me-rez** food poisoning
የምግብ መደብር **ye-mi-gib me-deb-bir** grocery store
የምግብ ዝርዝር **ye-mi-gib zir-zir** menu
የምግብ ፍላጎት **ye-mi-gib fil-la-got** appetite
የሰፈራ ቦታ **ye-se-fe-ra bo-ta** settlement
የሳል ሽሮፕ **ye-sal shi-ropp** cough syrup
የሴት ጓደኛ **ye-set guad-de-gna** girlfriend
የስልክ ጥሪ **ye-silk tir-ri** call (*n.*)
የስራ ቀን **ye-si-ra qen** weekday
የስነ ልቦና ባለሙያ **ye-si-ne lib-bo-na ba-le-mu-ya** psychologist
የስኳር ታማሚ **ye-sik-kuar ta-ma-mi** diabetic
የቀዘቀዘ **ye-qe-zeq-qe-ze** frozen

የራስ መስተንግዶ ye-ras mes-ten-gi-do self-service
የራስ ቅል ye-ras qil skull
የራቁት መዝናኛ የባህር ዳርቻ ye-ra-qut mez-nagn-gna ye-ba-hir da-rich-cha nudist beach
የሽያጭ ደረሰኝ ye-shiy-yach der-re-segn sales receipt
የሽያጭ ግብር ye-shiy-yach gi-bir sales tax
የቀብር ስነስርዓት ye-qe-bir si-ne-sir-at funeral
የቃል ye-qal oral
የቅርብ ye-qirb close (*adj.*)
የበረራ ቁጥር ye-be-re-ra qu-tir flight number
የበሬ ስጋ ye-be-re si-ga beef
የበጎ ፈቃድ አገልግሎት ሰጠ ye-beg-go fe-qad a-gel-gi-lot set-te volunteer (*v.*)
የቡሎን መፍቻ ye-bu-lon mef-cha screwdriver
የባህር ምግብ ye-ba-hir mi-gib seafood
የባህር ዳርቻ ye-ba-hir da-rich-cha beach
የባህር ጉዞ ህመም ye-ba-hir gu-zo hi-mem seasick
የባቡር ሐዲድ ye-ba-bur ha-did railroad
የባቡር ጣቢያ ye-ba-bur ta-bi-ya metro station
የባንክ አካውንት ye-bank ak-ka-wint bank account
የቤተሰብ መጠሪያ ye-be-te-seb met-te-ri-ya surname
የቤት ሰራተኛ ye-bet ser-ra-tegn-gna maid
የቤት እቃ ye-bet i-qa furniture
የቤት ውስጥ ye-bet wist indoor
የብቻ ክፍል ye-bich-cha ki-fil private room
የብድር ካርድ ye-bird kard credit card
የተለመደ yet-te-lem-me-de normal, ordinary, usual
የተለየ yet-te-ley-ye separate (*adj.*)
የተመዘገበ ቃል yet-te-me-zeg-ge-be qal entry
የተሰረቀ yet-te-ser-re-qe stolen
የተራበ yet-te-ra-be hungry
የተሸጠ yet-te-she-te sold
የተበላሸ yet-te-be-lash-she rotten
የተበከለ yet-te-bek-ke-le infected
የተትረፈረፈ yet-tet-re-fer-re-fe excess
የተኛ ጎማ ye-tegn-gna gom-ma flat tire

የተክል ቦታ **ye-te-kil bo-ta** orchard
የተወሰነ **yet-te-wes-se-ne** some
የተገደበ **yet-te-ged-de-be** restricted (*adj.*)
የተጋደመ መወጣጫ **yet-te-gad-de-me mew-we-ta-cha** ramp
የተጨናነቀ **yet-te-che-nan-ne-qe** busy
የተፈቀደ **ye-te-fe-qe-de** allowed
የት **yet** where
የትም ቦታ **ye-tim bo-ta** anywhere
የትም ቦታ **ye-tim bo-ta** nowhere
የኔ **ye-ne** mine
የንጽህና ወረቀት **ye-ni-tsi-hin-na we-re-qet** sanitary napkin
የንፋስ ማጽጃ **ye-ni-fas mats-ja** dry cleaner
የኛ **yegn-gna** our
የአልቤርጎ ዋጋ **ye-al-ber-go wa-ga** room rate
የአልኮል መጠጥ **ye-al-kol me-tet** liquor
የአሳ ማስገር ፈቃድ **ya-sa mas-ger fe-qad** fishing license
የአሳማ ስጋ **ye-a-sa-ma si-ga** pork
የአእምሮ **ye-a-i-mi-ro** mental
የአካል ጉዳተኛ ወንበር **ye-a-kal gu-da-tegn-gna wen-ber** wheelchair
የአውቶቡስ ፌርማታ **ye-aw-to-bus fer-ma-ta** bus terminal
የአየር ማረፊያ ቀረጥ **ye-ay-yer ma-re-fi-ya qe-ret** airport tax
የአየር ጠባይ **ye-ay-yer te-bay** weather
የአይን ብርሐን **ye-ayn bir-han** sight
የአገልግሎት ጊዜ **ye-a-gel-gi-lot gi-ze** expiration date
የኤሌክትሪክ አውቶቡስ **ye-ae-lek-ti-rik aw-to-bus** trolley
የእሳት አደጋ ደወል **ye-i-sat a-de-ga de-wel** fire alarm
የእረፍት ጊዜ **ye-i-reft gi-ze** vacation
የእቃ መግቢያ **ye-qa meg-bi-ya** baggage check
የእንስሳት ማኖሪያ **ye-in-si-sat ma-no-ri-ya** zoo
የእንቅልፍ ክኒን **ye-in-qilf ki-nin** sleeping pills
የእጅ አንጓ **ye-ijj an-gua** wrist
የእግር መንገድ **ye-i-gir men-ged** footpath
የእግር መንገድ **ye-i-gir men-ged** path

የከተማ ዳርቻ **ye-ke-te-ma da-rich-cha** suburb
የከንፈር ወዳጅ **ye-ken-fer we-daj** boyfriend
የካቲት **ye-ka-tit** February
የክፍል መስተንግዶ **ye-ki-fil mes-ten-gi-do** room service
የወሊድ መከላከያ **ye-we-lid mek-ke-la-ke-ya** contraceptive
የወር አበባ **ye-wer a-be-ba** menstruation
የወባ ትንኝ **ye-we-ba ti-nign** mosquito
የወተት ውጤቶች **ye-we-tet wit-te-toch** dairy
የወንበር ቁጥር **ye-wen-ber qu-tir** seat number
የወንድም (የእህት) ወንድ ልጅ **ye-wen-dim (ye-i-hit) wend lij** nephew
የወንድም (የእህት) ሴት ልጅ **ye-wen-dim (ye-i-hit) set lij** neice
የወይራ ፍሬ **ye-wey-ra fi-re** olive
የወደፊት **ye-we-de-fit** future
የውሃ ጉድጓድ **ye-wi-ha gud-guad** well (*n. / for water*)
የውስጥ ልብስ **ye-wist libs** underwear
የውሸት **ye-wi-shet** false
የውጭ **ye-wich** outdoor (*adj.*)
የውጭ ምንዛሬ **ye-wich mi-niz-za-re** currency exchange
የውጭ ቋንቋዎች **ye-wich quan-qua-woch** foreign languages
የውጭ ንግድ **ye-wich nigd** export
የውጭ አገር ገንዘብ **ye-wich a-ger gen-zeb** foreign currency
የዘመን መለወጫ ዕለት (እንቁጣጣሽ) **ye-ze-men me-lew-we-cha i-let (in-qu-ta-tash)** New Year's Day
የዘመን መለወጫ ዋዜማ **ye-ze-men me-lew-we-cha wa-ze-ma** New Year's Eve
የይለፍ ቃል **ye-yi-lef qal** password
የደም አይነት **ye-dem ay-net** blood type
የደረጃ እድገት **ye-de-re-ja id-get** promotion
የደርሶ መልስ ቲኬት **ye-der-so mels tik-ket** round-trip ticket
የዱሮ **ye-du-ro** old
የጅ ሰዓት **yejj se-at** watch (*n. / timepiece*)

የጆሮ ህመም **ye-jo-ro hi-mem** earache
የገላ መታጠቢያ **ye-ge-la me-ta-te-bi-ya** bath
የገበያ ማዕከል **ye-ge-be-ya ma-e-kel** shopping center
የገንዘብ ቦርሳ **ye-gen-zeb bor-sa** wallet
የጉምሩክ አዋጅ **ye-gum-ruk a-waj** customs declaration
የጉባኤ አዳራሽ **ye-gu-ba-ae ad-da-rash** conference room
የግል **ye-gill** personal, private
የግል ንብረት **ye-gill nib-ret** private property
የግዴታ **ye-gid-de-ta** mandatory
የግድ **ye-gidd** ought
የግድግዳ ስዕል **ye-gid-gid-da si-el** mural
የጎሳ **ye-go-sa** ethnic
የጎዳና ገበያ **ye-go-da-na ge-be-ya** flea market
የጠላት **ye-te-lat** hostile
የጠፋ **ye-tef-fa** lost
የጠፋ **ye-tef-fa** off (*adv./adj.*)
የጤና ዋስትና **ye-te-na was-tin-na** health insurance
የጥርስ ሐኪም **ye-tirs ha-kim** dentist
የጥርስ ህመም **ye-tirs hi-mem** toothache
የጥርስ ሳሙና **ye-tirs sa-mu-na** toothpaste
የጥርስ ብሩሽ **ye-tirs bi-rush** toothbrush
የጥንት **ye-tint** antique
የጥገና መደብር **ye-tig-ge-na me-deb-bir** repair shop
የጦር ሰራዊት **ye-tor se-ra-wit** military
የጭነት መኪና **ye-chi-net me-ki-na** truck
የጭንቅላት ግጭት **ye-chin-qil-lat gich-chit** concussion
የጸሎት ቤት **ye-tse-lot bet** chapel
የፊት ለፊት ዴስክ **ye-fit le-fit desk** front desk
የፍቅር **ye-fi-qir** romantic
የፍጥነት ገደብ **ye-fit-net ge-deb** speed limit

ዩኒቨርሲቲ **yu-ni-ver-si-ti** university

ያ **ya** that
ያለ **ya-le** without
ያልተለመደ **yal-te-lem-me-de** unusual

ያልተደሰተ **yal-te-des-se-te** unhappy
ያልተገራ **yal-te-ger-ra** wild
ያልታሰበ አስደሳች ነገር **yal-tas-se-be ne-ger** surprise
ያልጋ ልብስ **yal-ga libs** bedding
ያነሰ **yan-ne-se** less
ያኔ **yan-ne** then (*adv.*)
ያንገት ሐብል **yan-get ha-bil** necklace
ያንገት ልብስ **yan-get libs** scarf
ያዘ **ya-ze** arrest, keep (*v.*)
ያደጋ ደወል **ya-de-ga de-wel** siren
ያገለገሉ እቃዎች መደብር **ya-ge-leg-ge-lu i-qa-woch me-deb-bir** secondhand store
ያገር ውስጥ **ya-ger wust** local

ይህ **yih** this
ይቅርታ **yi-qir-ta** apology; sorry
ይቅርታ ለመነ **yi-qir-ta le-me-ne** apologize
ይበልጥ **yi-belt** more (*adv.*)
ይግባኝ **yig-ba-gn** appeal

ዴ de / ዱ du / ዲ di / ዳ da / ዶ de / ድ di / ዶ do

ደህና **deh-na** safe
ደህንነት **deh-nin-net** safety, security
ደመረ **dem-me-re** add
ደመወዝ **de-me-wez** salary
ደማ **dem-ma** bleed
ደም **dem** blood
ደም ማነስ ያለበት **dem ma-nes yal-le-bet** anemic
ደም ስር **dem sir** vein
ደሴት **des-set** island
ደስተኛ **des-si-tegn-gna** happy
ደረሰ **de-re-se** arrive
ደረሰኝ **der-re-segn** receipt
ደረቀ **der-re-qe** dry (*v.*)
ደረቅ **de-req** dry (*adj.*)
ደረጃ **de-re-ja** level, standard
ደራሲ **de-ra-si** author
ደርሶ መልስ ጉዞ **der-so mels gu-zo** round-trip
ደርዘን **der-zen** dozen
ደቂቃ **de-qi-qa** minute
ደበቀ **deb-be-qe** conceal
ደቡብ **de-bub** south
ደብዳቤ **deb-dab-be** letter (*written note*)
ደንበኛ **den-begn-gna** customer, client
ደንብ **denb** rule
ደከመ **dek-ke-me** tire (*v.*)
ደወለ **dew-we-le** call, ring, dial (*v.*)
ደወል **de-wel** bell
ደጅ **dejj** outdoors (*n.*)
ደገመ **deg-ge-me** repeat
ደግ **degg** kind

ዱር **dur** jungle
ዱቄት **du-qet** flour

ዱካ **duk-ka** trail

ዲሞክራሲ **di-mok-ra-si** democracy
ዲሽ **dish** cable TV
ዲዮድራንት **di-yo-di-rant** deodorant
ዲፕሎማት **dip-pi-lo-mat** diplomat
ዲቪዲ **di-vi-di** DVD

ዳርቻ **da-rich-cha** shore
ዳቦ **dab-bo** bread, loaf
ዳቦ ቤት **da-bo bet** bakery
ዳኘ **dagn-gne** referee (*v.*)
ዳኛ **dagn-gna** judge, referee (*n.*)
ዳይፐር **day-per** diaper

ዴስክ **desk** desk
ዴፖ **dep-po** depot

ድህነት **di-hin-net** poverty
ድልድይ **dil-diy** bridge
ድመት **dim-met** cat
ድምጽ **dimts** ring, sound, voice (*n.*)
ድራማ **di-ra-ma** drama
ድራየር **di-ra-yer** dryer
ድርጊት **dir-git** act (*n.*)
ድንበር **din-ber** border
ድንች **din-nich** potato
ድንኳን **din-kuan** tent
ድንገተኛ **din-ge-tagn-gna** emergency
ድንገተኛ ክፍል **din-ge-tegn-gna ki-fil** emergency room
ድንጋይ **din-gay** rock, stone (*n.*)

ዶላር **do-lar** dollar
ዶሮ **do-ro** chicken
ዶሮ ርባታ **do-ro ir-ba-ta** poultry

ጀ je / ጁ ju / ጂ ji / ጃ ja / ጄ je / ጅ ji / ጆ jo

ጀልባ **jel-ba** boat
ጀርባ **jer-ba** back
ጀበና **je-be-na** kettle

ጁስ **jus** juice

ጂም **jim** gym
ጂንስ **jins** jeans

ጃኬት **ja-ket** jacket

ጄሪካን **je-ri-kan** jar

ጅማሮ **jim-ma-ro** beginning

ጆሮ **jo-ro** ear
ጆግ **jog** jug

ገ ge / ጉ gu / ጊ gi / ጋ ga / ጌ ge / ግ gi / ጎ go / ጓ gua

ገለልተኛ **ge-lel-tegn-gna** neutral
ገለልታ **ge-lel-ta** quarantine
ገለጸ **gel-le-tse** express
ገላጭ ወረቀት **ge-lach we-re-qet** tag
ገመተ **gem-me-te** estimate
ገመድ **ge-med** rope
ገመድ አልባ ኢንተርኔት **ge-med al-ba in-ter-net** wireless Internet
ገበረ **geb-be-re** tax (*v.*)
ገበያ **ge-be-ya** marketplace
ገቢ **ge-bi** income
ገባ **geb-ba** enter
ገንዘብ **gen-zeb** money
ገንዳ **gen-da** pool
ገዛ **gez-za** own (*v.*)
ገደለ **ged-de-le** kill
ገደል **ge-del** cliff
ገደብ **ge-deb** reservation
ገጽ **gets** page
ገፋ **gef-fa** push

ጉልህ **gu-lih** loud
ጉልበት **gul-bet** knee; power
ጉምሩክ **gum-ruk** customs
ጉርሻ **gur-sha** tip (*n.*)
ጉርድ ቀሚስ **gurd qe-mis** skirt
ጉሮሮ **gu-ro-ro** throat
ጉበት **gub-bet** liver
ጉባኤ **gu-ba-ae** conference
ጉብኝት **gu-bign-gnit** visit (*n.*)
ጉንፋን **gun-fan** flu; cold (*n. / illness*)
ጉዞ **gu-zo** itinerary, trip
ጉዳት **gu-dat** damage, harm, injury; toll

ጉዳይ **gud-day** case, issue
ጉድጓድ **gud-guad** hole

ጊዜ **gi-ze** time
ጊዜያዊ **gi-ze-ya-wi** temporary

ጋለበ **gal-le-be** mount, ride
ጋስቴር **gas-ter** aluminum foil
ጋሪ **gar-ri** cart
ጋሻ **ga-sha** acre (0.4 hectares)
ጋበዘ **gab-be-ze** invite
ጋብቻ **ga-bi-cha** marriage
ጋዜጠኛ **ga-ze-tegn-gna** journalist
ጋዜጣ **ga-ze-ta** newspaper

ጌታዬ **ge-ta-ye** sir
ጌጣጌጥ **ge-ta-get** jewelry

ግለሰብ **gil-le-seb** individual, person
ግማሽ **gim-mash** half
ግስ **giss** verb
ግራ **gi-ra** left
ግራም **gi-ram** gram
ግብር **gi-bir** tax (*n.*)
ግብርና **gib-ri-na** agriculture
ግብዣ **gib-zha** party
ግን **gin** but
ግንባር **gin-bar** forehead
ግንባር **gin-bar** front
ግንኙነት **gi-nign-gnun-net** relationship
ግንድ **gind** trunk
ግዛት **gi-zat** territory, state
ግድያ **gi-diy-ya** murder
ግድግዳ **gid-gid-da** wall
ግጥሚያ **git-mi-ya** game
ግጥም **gi-tim** poem

ጎማ **gom-ma** rubber; tire (*n.*)
ጎረቤት **go-re-bet** neighbor
ጎርፍ **gorf** flood
ጎበኘ **go-begn-gne** visit (*v.*)
ጎብኚ **gob-gni** tourist
ጎብኚ **gob-gni** visitor
ጎተተ **got-te-te** pull
ጎን **gonn** profile
ጎን **gonn** side
ጎዳ **god-da** hurt
ጎዳና **go-da-na** street
ጎዳና (አደባባይ) **go-da-na (ad-de-ba-bay)** avenue
ጎዳና ተዳዳሪ **go-da-na te-da-da-ri** homeless
ጎድን **go-din** rib

ጓዝ **guaz** baggage, luggage
ጓደኛ **guad-degn-gna** companion, friend

ጠ te / ጡ tu / ጣ ta / ጤ te / ጥ ti / ጦ to / ጧ tua

ጠለቀ **tel-le-qe** dive
ጠላት **te-lat** enemy
ጠረገ **ter-re-ge** wipe
ጠረጠረ **te-ret-te-re** suspect (*v.*)
ጠረጴዛ **te-req-pe-za** table
ጠረፍ **te-ref** coast
ጠራ **ter-ra** summon
ጠርሙስ **ter-mus** bottle
ጠቀለለ **te-qel-le-le** wrap (*v.*)
ጠቀሜታ **te-qe-me-ta** use (*n.*)
ጠቅላይ ግዛት **teq-lay gi-zat** province
ጠበሰ **teb-be-se** fry
ጠበቀ **teb-be-qe** guard (*v.*)
ጠበቃ **te-be-qa** lawyer
ጠባሳ **te-ba-sa** scar
ጠባብ **teb-bab** narrow
ጠባብ መንገድ **teb-bab men-ged** lane
ጠቦት **teb-bot** lamb
ጠንካራ **ten-kar-ra** hard
ጠየቀ **tey-ye-qe** ask, question, request (*v.*); demand (*n.*)
ጠገነ **teg-ge-ne** fix, repair
ጠጣ **tet-ta** drink (*v.*)

ጡንቻ **tun-cha** muscle

ጣሪያ **ta-ri-ya** roof
ጣቢያ **ta-bi-ya** station
ጣት **tat** finger
ጣዕም **ta-im** taste
ጣፋጭ **ta-fach** sweet
ጣፋጭ (ከምግብ በኋላ) **ta-fach (ke-mi-gib be-hua-la)** pudding

ጤና **te-na** health

ጥልቅ **tilq** deep
ጥሩ **ti-ru** good; well (*interj.*)
ጥራት **ti-rat** quality
ጥራጥሬ **ti-ra-ti-re** cereal
ጥሬ **ti-re** raw
ጥሬ ገንዘብ **ti-re gen-zeb** cash (*n.*)
ጥር **tir** January
ጥርስ **tirs** tooth
ጥቁር **ti-qur** black
ጥቂት **ti-qit** little
ጥቃት **ti-qat** assault, attack (*n.*)
ጥቃት ሰነዘረ **ti-qat se-ne-ze-re** assault (*v.*)
ጥቅል **ti-qill** package, parcel
ጥቅምት **ti-qimt** October
ጥበብ **ti-beb** wisdom
ጥብስ **tibs** steak
ጥናት **ti-nat** study
ጥንድ **tind** pair
ጥኡም **ti-um** delicious
ጥያቄ **tiy-ya-qe** query, question, request (*n.*)
ጥይት **tiy-yit** bullet
ጥድፊያ **tid-fi-ya** hurry
ጥጥ **tit** cotton
ጥፋተኛ **ti-fa-tegn-gna** guilty

ጦር መሳሪያ **tor mes-sa-ri-ya** gun
ጦርነት **to-rin-net** war

ጧት **tuat** morning

ጨ che / ጩ chu / ጫ cha / ጭ chi / ጮ cho

ጨለማ **chel-le-ma** dark
ጨረቃ **che-re-qa** moon
ጨርቅ **cherq** fabric
ጨቅላ **cheq-la** infant
ጨዋታ **che-wa-ta** fun
ጨው **chew** salt

ጩኸት **chu-khe** shout

ጫማ **cham-ma** shoe
ጫነ **cha-ne** load (*v.*)
ጫና **cha-na** load (*n.*)
ጫካ **chak-ka** forest, woods
ጫጉላ **cha-gu-la** honeymoon
ጫጫታ **cha-cha-ta** noise
ጫፍ **chaf** peak, top

ጭስ **chis** smoke
ጭቃ **chi-qa** mud
ጭነት **chi-net** pack
ጭውውት **chi-wiw-wit** play (*n.*)
ጭጋግ **chi-gag** fog

ጮኸ **cho-khe** yell

ጸ tse / ጺ tsi / ጻ tsa / ጾ tso

ጸሐይ **tse-hay** sun
ጸሐይ መከላከያ **tse-hay mek-ke-la-ke-ya** sunblock
ጸሐይ ያቃጠለው **tse-hay yaq-qat-te-lew** sunburn
ጸሐፊ **tse-ha-fi** secretary
ጸለየ **tsel-le-ye** pray
ጸደይ **tse-dey** spring (*season*)
ጸጉረ ልውጥ **tse-gu-re liw-wut** stranger
ጸጉር **tse-gur** hair
ጸጉር አስተካካይ **tse-dur as-te-ka-kay** barber

ጺም መላጫ ሳሙና **tsim me-la-cha sa-mu-na** shaving cream

ጻፈ **tsa-fe** write

ጾታ **tso-ta** sex

ፈ fe / ፉ fu / ፊ fi / ፋ fa / ፍ fi / ፎ fo

ፈለገ **fel-le-ge** need, require, seek, want (*v.*)
ፈሊጥ **fe-lit** idiom
ፈሳሽ **fe-sash** fluid, liquid
ፈረስ **fe-res** horse
ፈራ **fer-ra** afraid
ፈቀደ **fe-qe-de** allow, permit
ፈቃደኛ **fe-qa-degn-gna** volunteer (*n.*)
ፈቃድ **fe-qad** license, permit, permission
ፈተሸ **fet-te-she** search (*v.*)
ፈተነ **fet-te-ne** examine
ፈገግ አለ **fe-gegg a-le** smile (*v.*)
ፈገግታ **fe-geg-ta** smile (*n.*)
ፈጣን **fet-tan** fast, quick, rapid (*adj.*)

ፉጨት **fu-chet** whistle (*n.*)

ፊልም **film** film, movie; screen
ፊርማ **fir-ma** signature
ፊት **fit** face

ፋሻ **fash-sha** bandage
ፋክስ **faks** fax (*n.*)
ፋክስ አደረገ **faks a-der-re-ge** fax (*v.*)

ፍላሽ ፎቶግራፊ **fi-lash fo-to-gi-ra-fi** flash photography
ፍራሽ **fi-rash** mattress
ፍራንክ **fi-rank** coin
ፍሬ **fi-re** berry, fruit
ፍሬን **fi-ren** brake (*n.*)
ፍርሃት **fir-hat** scare
ፍርስራሽ **fi-ris-rash** ruins
ፍርድ ቤት **fird bet** court
ፍርግርግ **fi-rig-rig** cage
ፍቅር **fi-qir** love, romance (*n.*)

ፍተሻ **fit-te-sha** search (*n.*)
ፍተሻ ኬላ **fit-te-sha kel-la** checkpoint
ፍትሐዊ **fit-ha-wi** just
ፍትህ **fi-tih** justice
ፍንጭ **finch** sign
ፍየል **fiy-yel** goat
ፍጥነት **fit-net** speed
ፍጥነት መለኪያ **fit-net me-lek-ki-ya** speedometer
ፍጻሜ **fits-tsa-me** end

ፎቅ **foq** floor; stairs
ፎቶግራፍ **fo-to-gi-raf** photograph
ፎጣ **fo-ta** bath towel, towel

ፐ pe / ፒ pi / ፓ pa / ፔ pe / ፕ pi / ፖ po

ፒራሚድ **pi-ra-mid** pyramid
ፒያኖ **pi-ya-no** piano
ፒጃማ **pi-ja-ma** pajamas
ፒፓ **pip-pa** pipe

ፓስታ **pas-ta** pasta
ፓስፖርት **pas-port** passport
ፓርላማ **par-la-ma** parliament
ፓርክ **park** park (*n.*)
ፓውንድ **pa-wind** pound (*n. / monetary*)
ፓይ **pay** pie

ፔዳል **pe-dal** pedal

ፕሬዝዳንት **pi-rez-dant** president
ፕሮግራም **pi-rog-ram** program, schedule
ፕሮፌሰር **pi-ro-fe-ser** professor

ፖለቲካ **po-le-ti-ka** politics
ፖሊስ **po-lis** police
ፖሊስ ጣቢያ **po-lis ta-bi-ya** police station
ፖም **pom** apple
ፖምፓ **pom-pa** pump
ፖስታ **pos-ta** mail (*n.*)
ፖስታ ላከ **pos-ta la-ke** mail (*v.*)
ፖስታ ሳጥን **pos-ta sa-tin** postbox
ፖስታ ሳጥን ቁጥር **pos-ta sa-tin qu-tir** postal code
ፖስታ ቤት **pos-ta bet** post office
ፖስትካርድ **pos-ti-kard** postcard

ቪ vi / ቫ va

ቪዛ **vi-za** visa

ቫኒላ **va-ni-la** vanilla
ቫይረስ **vay-res** virus

ENGLISH-AMHARIC DICTIONARY

A

able ቻለ cha-le
about ስለ si-le
above ከላይ ke-lay
academy አካዳሚ ak-ka-da-mi
accelerator (gas pedal) ነዳጅ (መርገጫ) ne-daj (me-ri-ge-cha)
accent አነጋገር (ቅላጼ) an-ne-ga-ger (qi-la-tse)
accept ተቀበለ te-qe-be-le
access (*n.*) መግቢያ meg-bi-ya
accident አደጋ a-de-ga
accommodation መስተንግዶ mes-ten-gi-do
account ተቀማጭ ሒሳብ te-qe-mach hi-sab
accountant አካውንታንት ak-ka-win-tant
accurate ትክክለኛ ti-kik-ki-legn-gna
accusation ወቀሳ we-qe-sa
accuse ከሰሰ ke-se-se
acre (0.4 hectares) ጋሻ gash-sha
across ባሻገር ba-sha-ger
act (*v.*) አደረገ a-der-re-ge / (*n.*) ድርጊት dir-git
activist የመብት ተሟጋች ye-me-bit te-mua-gach
activity ተግባር te-gi-bar
actor ተዋናይ te-wa-nay
actual እውናዊ i-wi-na-wi
add ደመረ dem-me-re
address (*n.*) አድራሻ ad-rash-sha
administration አስተዳደር as-te-da-der
admission ቅበላ qib-be-la
admit ተቀበለ te-qeb-be-le
adult አዋቂ a-wa-qi
advertisement ማስታወቂያ mas-ta-we-qi-ya
afraid ፈራ fer-ra
after በኋላ be-hua-la
afternoon ከሰዓት በኋላ ke-se-at be-hua-la

again እንደገና in-de-ge-na
against ተቃወመ te-qa-we-me
age እድሜ id-me
agency ኤጀንሲ e-jen-si
agent ወኪል we-kil
agree ተስማማ tes-mam-ma
agreement ስምምነት si-mi-mi-net
agriculture ግብርና gib-ri-na
aid (*n.*) እርዳታ ir-da-ta / (*v.*) ረዳ red-da
aide (*n.*) ረዳት red-dat
AIDS ኤድስ eds
air አየር ay-yer
air conditioning ኤሲ e-si
airline አየር መንገድ ay-yer men-ged
airplane አውሮፕላን aw-rop-pi-lan
airport አየር ማረፊያ ay-yer ma-re-fi-ya
airport tax የአየር ማረፊያ ቀረጥ ye-ay-yer ma-re-fi-ya qe-ret
aisle መተላለፊያ met-te-la-le-fi-ya
alarm አሳሰበ a-sas-se-be
alcohol አልኮል al-kol
alive ሕያው hiy-yaw
all ሁሉም hul-lum
allergy አለርጂ a-ler-ji
alley ሰርጥ sert
allow ፈቀደ fe-qe-de
allowed የተፈቀደ ye-te-fe-qe-de
almond ለውዝ lewz
alone ለብቻ le-bi-cha
also በተጨማሪም be-te-che-ma-ri
altar መንበር men-ber
alter ለወጠ lew-we-te
altitude ከፍታ kef-fi-ta
aluminum foil ጋስቴር gas-ter
always ሁልጊዜ hul-gi-ze
ambassador አምባሳደር am-ba-sad-der

ambulance አምቡላንስ am-bu-lans
amenities መመቻቻ mem-me-cha-cha
among ከመካከል ke-me-kak-kel
amount መጠን me-ten
and እና in-na
anemic ደም ማነስ ያለበት dem ma-nes yal-leb-bet
anesthetic ማደንዘዣ ma-den-ze-zha
angry ተናዳጅ te-na-daj
animal እንስሳ in-si-sa
ankle ቁርጭምጭሚት qur-chim-chi-mit
anniversary አመታዊ ክብረ በዓል a-me-ta-wi ki-bi-re be-al
announcement መግለጫ meg-le-cha
announcer ለፋፊ lef-fa-fi
annual አመታዊ a-me-ta-wi
antibiotics አንቲባዮቲክስ an-ti-ba-yo-tiks
antifreeze አንቲፍሪዝ an-ti-fi-riz
antique የጥንት ye-tint
antiseptic አንቲሴፕቲክ an-ti-sep-tik
any ማንኛውም ma-ni-gna-wim
anybody ማንኛውም አካል ma-ni-gna-wim a-kal
anyone ማንኛውም ሰው ma-ni-gna-wim sew
anything ማንኛውም ነገር ma-ni-gna-wim ne-ger
anywhere የትም ቦታ ye-tim bo-ta
apartment አፓርታማ a-par-ta-ma
apologize ይቅርታ ለመነ yi-qir-ta le-me-ne
apology ይቅርታ yi-qir-ta
appeal ይግባኝ yig-ba-gn
appear መሰለ mes-se-le
appendicitis ትርፍ አንጀት tirf an-jet
appetite የምግብ ፍላጎት ye-mi-gib fil-la-got
apple ፖም pom
appointment ቀጠሮ qe-te-ro
apricot አፕሪኮት ap-ri-kot
April ሚያዝያ mi-ya-zi-ya
architecture አርክቴክቸር ark-tek-cher
area ስፍራ sif-ra
argue ተሟገተ te-muag-ge-te

argument ሙግት mug-git
arm ክንድ kind
army ሰራዊት se-ra-wit
around ዙሪያ zu-ri-ya
arrival መድረሻ med-re-sha
arrest (*v.*) ያዘ ya-ze / (*n.*) እስራት es-si-rat
arrive ደረሰ der-re-se
art ኪነ ጥበብ ki-ne ti-beb
arthritis አርትራይቲስ ar-ti-ray-tis
ash አመድ a-med
ask ጠየቀ tey-ye-qe
asleep ተኛ tegn-gna
aspirin አስፒሪን as-pi-rin
assault (*n.*) ጥቃት ti-qat / (*v.*) ጥቃት ሰነዘረ ti-qat se-nez-ze-re
assist (*n.*) እገዛ ig-ge-za; (*v.*) አገዘ ag-ge-ze
assistant አጋዥ ag-gazh
associate (*n.*) ተባባሪ te-ba-ba-ri / (*v.*) ተጎዳኘ te-go-dagn-gne
asthma አስም asm
ATM ኤቲኤም e-ti-aem
attack (*v.*) አጠቃ a-teq-qa / (*n.*) ጥቃት ti-qat
attorney አቃቤ ህግ aq-qa-be hig
August ነሐሴ ne-ha-se
author ደራሲ de-ra-si
authority ባለስልጣን ba-le-sil-tan
automatic አውቶማቲክ aw-to-ma-tik
automatic transmission አውቶማቲክ ስርጭት aw-to-ma-tik si-rich-chit
automobile አውቶሞቢል aw-to-mo-bil
autumn መኸር me-kher
available የሚገኝ yem-mig-gegn
avenue ጎዳና (አደባባይ) go-da-na (ad-de-ba-bay)
avoid አስወገደ as-we-ge-de
awake አነቃ a-neq-qa
away ወዲያ we-di-ya
axle አክሰል ak-sil

B

baby ህጻን hi-tsan
baby wipes የህጻናት ማበሻ ye-hi-tsa-nat mab-be-sha
babysitter ልጅ ያዥ lij yazh
back ጀርባ jer-ba
backpack ባክፓክ bak-pak
bad መጥፎ met-fo
bag ቦርሳ bor-sa
baggage ጓዝ guaz
baggage check የእቃ መግቢያ ye-qa meg-bi-ya
bakery ዳቦ ቤት dab-bo bet
balcony ባልኮኒ bal-ko-ni
ball ኳስ kuas
banana ሙዝ muz
bandage ፋሻ fash-sha
bank ባንክ bank
bank account የባንክ አካውንት ye-bank ak-ka-wunt
bar (*n. / place for drinking*) ቡና ቤት bun-na bet
barber ጸጉር አስተካካይ tse-dur as-te-ka-kay
barrel በርሜል ber-mel
barrier መሰናክል me-se-na-kil
base መሠረት me-se-ret
basement ምድር ቤት mi-dir bet
basin ሸለቆ she-le-qo
basket ቅርጫት qir-chat
basketball ቅርጫት ኳስ qir-chat kuas
bat (*animal*) የሌሊት ወፍ ye-le-lit wef; (*sports equipment*) መለጊያ me-leg-gi-ya
bath የገላ መታጠቢያ ye-ge-la me-ta-te-bi-ya
bath towel ፎጣ fo-ta
bathe አጠበ at-te-be
bathing suit የመታጠቢያ ልብስ ye-met-ta-te-bi-ya libs
bathroom መታጠቢያ ቤት me-ta-te-bi-ya bet
battery ባትሪ ba-ti-ri

battle (*n.*) ውጊያ wig-gi-ya
be (*v.* / **am, is, are, was, were, been**) ነው new
beach የባህር ዳርቻ ye-ba-hir da-rich-cha
bean ባቄላ ba-qe-la
beautiful ቆንጆ qon-jo
because of ምክንያቱም mi-kin-ya-tum
become ሆነ ho-ne
bed አልጋ al-ga
bedding ያልጋ ልብስ yal-ga libs
bedroom መኝታ ቤት megn-gni-ta bet
bee ንብ nib
beef የበሬ ስጋ ye-be-re si-ga
beer ቢራ bi-ra
before በፊት be-fit
beggar ለማኝ lem-magn
beginning ጅማሮ jim-ma-ro
behind ከኋላ ke-hua-la
believe አመነ am-me-ne
bell ደወል de-wel
below ከታች ke-tach
berry ፍሬ fi-re
beverage መጠጥ me-tet
beware ተጠነቀቀ te-te-neq-qe-qe
bible መጽሐፍ ቅዱስ me-tsi-haf qid-dus
bicycle ብስክሌት bis-ki-let
big ትልቅ til-liq
bill ሒሳብ hi-sab
birth certificate የልደት ካርድ ye-li-det kard
birthday ልደት li-det
bite ንክሻ ni-kish-sha
bitter መራር mer-rar
black ጥቁር ti-qur
blanket ብርድልብስ bir-di-libs
bleed ደማ dem-ma
bless ባረከ bar-re-ke
blind አይነ ስውር ay-ne siw-wir

blister እባጭ wu-ha quat-te-re
blood ደም dem
blood type የደም አይነት ye-dem ay-net
blue ሰማያዊ se-ma-ya-wi
boat ጀልባ jel-ba
body አካል a-kal
bomb ቦምብ bomb
bone አጥንት a-tint
bonus ቦነስ bo-nes
book መጽሐፍ me-tsi-haf
bookstore መጻሀፍት መደብር me-tsa-hift me-de-bir
boot ቦቲ bot-ti
border ድንበር din-ber
bottle ጠርሙስ ter-mus
bottom የመጨረሻ ዝቅተኛ ye-me-cher-re-sha zi-qi-tegn-gna
box (*n.*) ሳጥን sa-tin / (*v.*) በቡጢ መታ be-but-ti met-ta
boy ወንድ ልጅ wend lij
boyfriend የከንፈር ወዳጅ ye-ken-fer we-daj
brake (*n.*) ፍሬን fi-ren
bread ዳቦ dab-bo
break ሰበረ seb-be-re
breakfast ቁርስ qurs
breathe (*v.*) ተነፈሰ te-nef-fe-se
bribe (*v.*) በገንዘብ ደለለ be-gen-zeb del-le-le
brick ሸክላ shek-la
bridge ድልድይ dil-diy
bring አመጣ a-met-ta
broken ሰባራ se-ba-ra
brother ወንድም wen-dimm
brown ቡናማ bun-nam-ma
building ህንጻ hin-tsa
bull ኮርማ kor-ma
bullet ጥይት tiy-yit
bureaucracy ቢሮክራሲ bi-rok-ra-si
bury ቀበረ qeb-be-re

bus አውቶቡስ aw-to-bus
bus terminal የአውቶቡስ ፌርማታ ye-aw-to-bus fer-ma-ta
business ስራ si-ra
busy የተጨናነቀ yet-te-che-nan-ne-qe
but ግን gin
butcher ሥጋ ሻጭ si-ga shach
butter ቅቤ qi-be
button ቁልፍ qulf
buy ሸመተ shem-me-te

C

cab ታክሲ tak-si
cabinet ቁምሳጥን qum-sa-tin
cable ሽቦ shi-bo
cable TV ዲሽ dish
cafe ሻይ ቤት shay bet
cage ፍርግርግ fi-rig-rig
cake ኬክ kek
calendar የቀን መቁጠሪያ ye-qen me-qu-te-ri-ya
call (*v.*) ደወለ dew-we-le / (*n.*) የስልክ ጥሪ ye-silk tir-ri
camera ካሜራ ka-me-ra
camp ካምፕ kamp
campground ካምፕግራውንድ kamp-gi-ra-wund
can (*modal verb*) ቻለ cha-le
cancel ሰረዘ ser-re-ze
candy ከረሜላ ke-re-mel-la
car መኪና me-ki-na
card ካርድ kard
carpet ምንጣፍ min-taf
carrot ካሮት ka-rot
carry ተሸከመ te-shek-ke-me
carry-on ቀጠለ qet-te-le
cart ጋሪ gar-ri

case ጉዳይ gud-day
cash (*v.*) እጅ በእጅ ከፈለ ijj bejj kef-fe-le / (*n.*) ጥሬ ገንዘብ ti-re gen-zeb
casual አልባሌ a-lib-ba-le
cat ድመት dim-met
catch (*v.*) አጠመደ a-tem-me-de
cathedral ካቴድራል ka-ted-ral
cattle ከብት kebt
cave ዋሻ wash-sha
CD ሲዲ si-di
cement ሲሚንቶ sim-min-to
cemetery መካነ መቃብር me-ka-ne me-qa-bir
cent ሳንቲም san-tim
center ማዕከል ma-i-kel
century ክፍለ ዘመን kif-le ze-men
cereal ጥራጥሬ ti-ra-ti-re
chain ሰንሰለት sen-se-let
chair ወንበር wen-ber
champagne ሻምፓኝ sham-pagn
change (*v.*) ለወጠ lew-we-te / (*n.*) ለውጥ lewt
changing room መቀየሪያ ክፍል me-qey-ye-ri-ya
channel ቻናል cha-nal
chapel የጸሎት ቤት ye-tse-lot bet
chapter ምዕራፍ mi-i-raf
charge (*n.*) ዋጋ wa-ga
cheap ርካሽ rik-kash
check (*v.*) መረመረ me-rem-me-re / (*n.*) ቼክ chek
check in አልጋ ያዘ al-ga ya-ze
check out አልጋ ለቆ ወጣ al-ga leq-qo wet-ta
checkpoint ፍተሻ ኬላ fit-te-sha kel-la
cheese አይብ a-yib
chef ሼፍ shef
chemical ኬሚካል ke-mi-kal
chew አኘከ agn-gne-ke
chicken ዶሮ do-ro
chickpeas ሽምብራ shim-bi-ra

chief (*adj.*) አለቃ a-le-qa
child ልጅ lij
childcare የሕጻናት እንክብካቤ ye-hi-tsa-nat en-ki-bik-ka-be
chocolate ቸኮሌት chek-ko-let
choke አነቀ an-ne-qe
church ቤተክርስትያን be-te-ki-ris-ti-yan
cigarette ሲጋራ si-ga-ra
cinema ሲኒማ si-ni-ma
circle ክብ kibb
citizen ዜጋ ze-ga
city ከተማ ke-te-ma
civilian ሲቪል si-vil
clap አጨበጨበ a-che-bech-che-be
class ክፍል ki-fil
classic ዘመን ተሻጋሪ ze-men te-sha-ga-ri
clean ንጹህ ni-tsuh
client ደንበኛ den-begn-gna
cliff ገደል ge-del
climate አየር ንብረት ay-yer nib-ret
climb ወጣ wet-ta
clinic ክሊኒክ ki-li-nik
clock ሰዓት se-at
close (*adj.*) የቅርብ ye-qirb / (*v.*) ዘጋ zeg-ga
closed ዝግ zig
cloth ልብስ libs
clothing አልባሳት al-ba-sat
club ክለብ ki-leb
coast ጠረፍ te-ref
coat ኮት kot
cocoa ካካዎ ka-ka-wo
coconut ኮኮነት ko-ko-net
coffee ቡና bun-na
coin ፍራንክ fi-rank
cold (*adj.*) ቀዝቃዛ qez-qaz-za / (*n.*) (*illness*) ጉንፋን gun-fan
collect ሰበሰበ se-bes-se-be

color ቀለም qe-lem
comb ማበጠሪያ ma-bet-te-ri-ya
come መጣ met-ta
comedy ኮሜዲ ko-me-di
comfortable ምቹ mich-chu
commission ኮሚሽን ko-mi-shin
communication ተግባቦት teg-ba-bot
companion ጓደኛ guad-degn-gna
company ኩባንያ kub-ba-niy-ya
compare አወዳደረ aw-we-dad-de-re
compensation ካሳ ka-sa
complain አቤቱታ አቀረበ a-be-tu-ta a-qer-re-be
complicated ውስብስብ wi-sib-sib
compromise (*n.*) ስምምነት si-mim-min-net
computer ኮምፒዩተር kom-pi-yu-ter
conceal ደበቀ deb-be-qe
concert የሙዚቃ ትርኢት ye-mu-zi-qa tir-et
concrete ተጨባጭ te-cheb-bach
concussion የጭንቅላት ግጭት ye-chin-qil-lat gich-chit
condom ኮንዶም kon-dom
conductor ኮረንቲ አስተላላፊ kor-ren-ti as-te-la-la-fi
conference ጉባኤ gu-ba-e
conference room የጉባኤ አዳራሽ ye-gu-ba-ae ad-da-rash
confirm አረጋገጠ ar-re-gag-ge-te
constipated ሆድ ድርቀት ያመመው hod dir-qet yam-me-mew
constitution ህገ መንግስት hig-ge men-gist
consulate ቆንስላ qon-si-la
consult አማከረ am-mak-ke-re
contagious ተላላፊ te-lal-le-fe
contraception ወሊድ መከላከል we-lid mek-ke-la-kel
contraceptive የወሊድ መከላከያ ye-we-lid mek-ke-la-ke-ya
contract ውል wul
convenient ምቹ mich-chu
cook (*n.*) ምግብ አብሳይ mi-gib ab-say / (*v.*) አበሰለ a-bes-se-le
copy ቅጂ qij-ji

cord ሲባጎ si-ba-go
corn በቆሎ beq-qol-lo
corner ማዕዘን ma-i-zen
correct (*adj.*) ትክክለኛ ti-kik-ki-legn-gna
corrupt ብልሹ bi-lish-shu
cosmetics መዋቢያ mew-wa-bi-ya
cost ዋጋ wa-ga
cotton ጥጥ tit
cough ሳል sal
cough syrup የሳል ሽሮፕ ye-sal shi-ropp
country አገር a-ger
country code አገራዊ ኮድ a-ge-ra-wi
court ፍርድ ቤት fird bet
courtesy ትህትና ti-hi-tin-na
cover ሽፋን shi-fan
cover charge መግቢያ ክፍያ meg-bi-ya ki-fiy-ya
cream ቅባት qi-bat
credit ብድር bid-dir
credit card የብድር ካርድ ye-bid-dir kard
crime ወንጀል wen-jel
crowd ሕዝብ hizb
crutches ምርኩዝ mir-kuz
cry አለቀሰ a-leq-qe-se
culture ባህል ba-hil
cup ስኒ si-ni
cure አዳነ a-da-ne
curfew ሰዓት እላፊ se-at el-la-fi
currency ምንዛሬ mi-niz-za-re
currency exchange የውጭ ምንዛሬ ye-wuch mi-niz-za-re
customer ደንበኛ den-begn-gna
customs ጉምሩክ gum-ruk
customs declaration የጉምሩክ አዋጅ ye-gum-ruk a-waj
cut ቆረጠ qor-re-te

D

dairy የወተት ውጤቶች ye-we-tet wut-te-toch
damage (*n.*) ጉዳት gu-dat
dance እስክስታ is-kis-ta
danger አደጋ a-de-ga
dark ጨለማ chel-le-ma
date (*n.*) (*fruit*) ተምር te-mir; (*calendar*) ቀን qen, ዕለት i-let
date of birth የልደት ቀን ye-li-det qen
daughter ሴት ልጅ set lij
dawn ንጋት ni-gat
day ዕለት i-let
daytime ቀን qen
dead ሙት mut
deadline ቀነ ገደብ qe-ne ge-deb
deaf መስማት የተሳነው mes-mat yet-te-sa-new
debt እዳ i-da
decade አስርተ ዓመት as-sir-te a-met
December ታህሳስ ta-hi-sas
decide ወሰነ wes-se-ne
decision ውሳኔ wis-sa-ne
deck የመርከብ መድረክ ye-mer-keb med-rek
declare አወጀ aw-we-je
deep ጥልቅ tilq
delay መዘግየት me-zeg-yet
delicious ጥኡም ti-um
deliver አደረሰ a-der-re-se
delivery ርክክብ ri-kik-kib
demand (*n.*) ጠየቀ tey-ye-qe
democracy ዲሞ ክራሲ di-mok-ra-si
dentist የጥርስ ሐኪም ye-tirs ha-kim
deny ካደ ka-de
deodorant ዲዮድራንት di-yo-di-rant
department store ንዑስ መደብር ni-us me-deb-bir

departure መነሻ men-ne-sha
deposit ተቀማጭ te-qem-mach
depot ዴፖ dep-po
desert በረሐ be-re-ha
desk ዴስክ desk
dessert ማጣጣሚያ mat-ta-ta-mi-ya
destination መዳረሻ med-da-re-sha
detergent ማንጫ man-cha
diabetes ስኳር sik-kuar
detour ዙሮ መሄድ zu-ro me-hed
diabetic የስኳር ታማሚ ye-sik-kuar ta-ma-mi
diagnosis ምርመራ mir-me-ra
dial ማዞሪያ(የስልክ) ma-zo-ri-ya (ye-silk)
dialing code ማዞሪያ ኮድ ma-zo-ri-ya kod
diaper ዳይፐር day-per
diarrhea ተቅማጥ teq-mat
dictate አዘዘ az-ze-ze
dictionary መዝገበ ቃላት mez-ge-be qa-lat
die ሞተ mo-te
diesel ናፍታ naf-ta
different የተለየ ye-te-le-ye
difficult አስቸጋሪ as-cheg-ga-ri
dine ራት በላ rat bel-la
dining room መመገቢያ ክፍል mem-me-ge-bi-ya ki-fil
dinner ራት rat
diplomat ዲፕሎማት dip-pi-lo-mat
direction አቅጣጫ aq-tach-cha
directions መመሪያ mem-me-ri-ya
directory ማውጫ maw-cha
directory assistance የስልክ ቁጥር መረጃ አገልግሎት
ye-silk qu-tir mer-re-ja a-gel-gi-lot
dirt እድፍ i-dif
dirty ቆሻሻ qo-sha-sha
disability አካል ጉዳት a-kal gu-dat
disabled አካል ጉዳተኛ a-kal gu-da-tegn-gna
disagree አልተስማማም al-tes-mam-mam

disaster መቅሰፍት meq-seft
discount ቅናሽ qin-nash
disease በሽታ besh-shi-ta
dish ምግብ mi-gib
disposable ተወጋጅ te-weg-gaj
dispute (*v.*) አለመግባባት a-le-meg-ba-bat
district አውራጃ aw-raj-ja
disturb አወከ aw-we-ke
dive ጠለቀ tel-le-qe
dizzy ተጫጫነ te-cha-cha-ne
do አደረገ a-der-re-ge
dock የመርከብ ማራገፊያ ye-mer-keb mar-ra-ge-fi-ya
doctor ሐኪም ha-kim
document ሰነድ se-ned
dog ውሻ wush-sha
dollar ዶላር do-lar
domestic ለማዳ lem-mad-da
door በር ber
double እጥፍ e-tif
dough ሊጥ lit
down ታች tach
downtown መሐል ከተማ me-hal ke-te-ma
dozen ደርዘን der-zen
drain አደረቀ a-der-re-qe
drama ድራማ di-ra-ma
drawer መሳቢያ me-sa-bi-ya
dress (*n.*) ቀሚስ qe-mis
dress (*v.*) ለበሰ leb-be-se
drink (*n.*) መጠጥ me-tet / (*v.*) ጠጣ tet-ta
drive ነዳ ned-da
driver's license መንጃ ፈቃድ men-ja fe-qad
drown አሰመጠ a-sem-me-te
drowsy የሚያንጎላጅ yem-mi-yan-go-laj
drug መድሐኒት med-ha-nit
drugstore መድሐኒት መደብር med-ha-nit me-deb-bir
drunk ሰካራም sek-ka-ram
dry (*adj.*) ደረቅ de-req / (*v.*) ደረቀ der-re-qe

dry cleaner የንፋስ ማጽጃ ye-ni-fas mats-ja
dryer ድራየር di-ra-yer
dust (*v.*) ወለወለ we-lew-we-le
duty-free ከቀረጥ ነጻ ke-qe-ret ne-tsa
DVD ዲቪዲ di-vi-di
dye መቅለሚያ meq-le-mi-ya

E

ear ጆሮ jo-ro
earache የጆሮ ህመም ye-jo-ro hi-mem
early በጊዜ be-gi-ze
earth መሬት me-ret
earthquake መሬት መንቀጥቀጥ me-ret men-qet-qet
east ምስራቅ mis-raq
eat በላ bel-la
economy ምጣኔ ሐብት mit-ta-ne hebt
education ትምህርት ti-mi-hirt
egg እንቁላል in-qu-lal
eight ስምንት sim-mint
eighteen አስራ ስምንት as-ra sim-mint
eighty ሰማንያ se-man-ya
election ምርጫ mir-cha
electric ኮረንቲ kor-ren-ti
electricity ስነ ኮረንቲ si-ne kor-ren-ti
elevator አሳንሰር a-san-ser
eleven አስራ አንድ as-ra and
e-mail ኢሜል i-mel
embassy ኤምባሲ em-ba-si
emergency ድንገተኛ din-ge-tagn-gna
emergency room ድንገተኛ ክፍል din-ge-tegn-gna ki-fil
employee ተቀጣሪ te-qet-ta-ri
employer ቀጣሪ qe-ta-ri
empty ባዶ ba-do

end ፍጻሜ fits-tsa-me
enemy ጠላት te-lat
energy ሐይል ha-yil
engine ሞተር mo-ter
engineer መሐንዲስ me-han-dis
English language እንግሊዝኛ ቋንቋ in-gi-li-zign-gna quan-qua
engraving ቅርጽ qirts
enough በቂ be-qi
enter ገባ geb-ba
entertainment መዝናኛ mez-nagn-gna
entire በጠቅላላ be-teq-lal-la
entrance መግቢያ meg-bi-ya
entry የተመዘገበ ቃል yet-te-me-zeg-ge-be qal
entry visa መግቢያ ቪዛ meg-bi-ya vi-za
envelope ኢንቬሎፕ in-ve-lop
epileptic አውድቅ ያለበት aw-diq yal-leb-bet
equal እኩል ek-kul
equipment መሳሪያ mes-sa-ri-ya
escalator አሳንሰር a-san-ser
estimate ገመተ gem-me-te
ethnic የጎሳ ye-go-sa
Europe አውሮፓ aw-rop-pa
European አውሮፓዊ aw-rop-pa-wi
evacuate ለቆ ወጣ leq-qo wet-ta
even እኩል ik-kul
evening ምሽት mish-shit
event ሁኔታ hu-ne-ta
eventually ውሎ አድሮ wi-lo ad-ro
ever ሁልጊዜ hul-gi-ze
every እያንዳንዱ iy-yan-dan-du
exact ልክ lik
examine ፈተነ fet-te-na
example ምሳሌ mis-sa-le
except በቀር be-qer
excess የተትረፈረፈ yet-tet-re-fer-re-fe

exchange ልውውጥ li-wiw-wit
exchange rate የምንዛሬ ዋጋ ye-mi-niz-za-re wa-ga
exclude አስቀረ as-qer-re
exhaust አለፋ a-lef-fa
exhibit (*v.*) አሳየ a-say-ye / (*n.*) ኤግዚቢት aeg-zi-bit
exit መውጫ mew-cha
expense ወጪ we-chi
expensive ውድ widd
experience ልምድ limd
expiration date የአገልግሎት ጊዜ ye-a-gel-gi-lot gi-ze
explain አብራራ ab-rar-ra
export የውጭ ንግድ ye-wich nigd
express ገለጸ gel-le-tse
express train ኤክስፐረስ ባቡር e-kis-pi-res ba-bur
extra ተጨማሪ te-chem-ma-ri
eye አይን ayn
eyeglasses መነጽር me-ne-tsir

F

fabric ጨርቅ cherq
face ፊት fit
fall (*n.*) ውድቀት wid-qet; (*season*) መኸር me-kher
false ውሸት wi-shet
family ቤተሰብ be-te-seb
far ሩቅ ruq
fare መሳፈሪያ mes-sa-fe-ri-ya
farm ማሳ ma-sa
fast (*adj.*) ፈጣን fet-tan
fat ወፍራም wef-ram
father አባት ab-bat
faucet ቧምቧ መክፈቻ buam-bua mek-fe-cha
fax (*n.*) ፋክስ faks / (*v.*) ፋክስ አደረገ faks a-der-re-ge
February የካቲት ye-ka-tit

fee ክፍያ ki-fiy-ya
feel ስሜት sim-met
female እንስት i-nist
fence አጥር a-tir
ferry ማሻገሪያ mash-sha-ge-ri-ya
festival በዓል be-al
fever ትኩሳት tik-ku-sat
field መስክ mesk
fifteen አስራ አምስት as-ra sim-mint
fifty ሃምሳ ham-sa
fig በለስ be-les
fill ሞላ mol-la
film ፊልም film
find አገኘ a-gegn-ge
finger ጣት tat
fire እሳት e-sat
fire alarm የእሳት አደጋ ደወል ye-e-sat a-de-ga de-wel
firewood ማገዶ ma-ge-do
fireworks ሪችት ri-chit
first ቀዳሚ qe-da-mi
first-aid kit የመጀመሪያ ህክምና ርዳታ ቁሳቁስ ye-me-jem-me-ri-ya hik-ki-min-na ir-da-ta
first-class የማዕረግ ye-ma-i-reg
fish አሳ a-sa
fisherman አሳ አስጋሪ a-sa as-ga-ri
fishing አሳ ማስገር a-sa mas-ger
fishing license የአሳ ማስገር ፈቃድ ya-sa mas-ger fe-qad
fishing permitted አሳ ማስገር ይፈቃዳል a-sa mas-ger yif-feq-qe-dal
fishing rod አሳ ማስገሪያ ዘንግ a-sa mas-ge-ri-ya zeng
fist ቡጢ but-ti
fit ተስማሚ tes-ma-mi
fitting ልክ lik
fitting room መለኪያ ክፍል me-lek-ki-ya ki-fil
five አምስት am-mist
fix ጠገነ teg-ge-ne

flag ባንዲራ ban-di-ra
flame ነበልባል ne-bel-bal
flare ነበልባል ne-bel-bal
flash ብልጭታ bil-lich-ta
flash photography ፍላሽ ፎቶግራፊ fi-lash fo-to-gi-ra-fi
flashlight ባትሪ (የእጅ) bat-ri (ye-ijj)
flat ዝርግ zirg
flat tire የተኛ ጎማ ye-tegn-gna gom-ma
flavor ቃና qa-na
flea ቁንጫ qu-nich-cha
flea market የጎዳና ገበያ ye-go-da-na ge-be-ya
flight በረራ be-re-ra
flight number የበረራ ቁጥር ye-be-re-ra qu-tir
flood ጎርፍ gorf
floor ፎቅ foq
flour ዱቄት du-qet
flourish አበበ ab-be-be
flower አበባ a-be-ba
flu ጉንፋን gun-fan
fluent ርቱዕ ri-tu-i
fluid ፈሳሽ fe-sash
flush ውሃ ለቀቀ wu-ha leq-qe-qe
fly (*v.*) በረረ ber-re-re / (*n. / insect*) ዝንብ zinb
fog ጭጋግ chi-gag
folk የሰው ልጅ ye-sew lij
folk art ባህላዊ ኪነት ba-hi-la-wi ki-net
follow ተከተለ te-ket-te-le
food ምግብ mi-gib
food poisoning የምግብ መመረዝ ye-mi-gib mem-me-rez
foot እግር i-gir
football (soccer) እግር ኳስ i-gir kuas
footpath የእግር መንገድ ye-i-gir men-ged
forehead ግንባር gin-bar
foreign ባዕድ አገር ba-id a-ger
foreign currency የውጭ አገር ገንዘብ ye-wich a-ger gen-zeb

foreign languages የውጭ ቋንቋዎች ye-wich quan-qua-woch
forest ጫካ chak-ka
forget ረሳ res-sa
forgive ማረ ma-re
fork ሹካ shuk-ka
formal መደበኛ me-de-begn-gna
fortune እድል id-dil
fortuneteller ኮኮብ ቆጣሪ kok-kob qo-ta-ri
forty አርባ ar-ba
fountain ምንጭ minch
four አራት a-rat
fourteen አስራ አራት as-ra a-rat
fraud ማጭበርበር mach-ber-ber
free ነጻ ne-tsa
freeze አቀዘቀዘ a-qe-zeq-qe-ze
fresh ትኩስ tik-kus
Friday አርብ arb
friend ጓደኛ guad-degn-gna
front ግንባር gin-bar
front desk የፊት ለፊት ዴስክ ye-fit le-fit desk
frozen የረጋ ye-reg-ga
fruit ፍሬ fi-re
fry ጠበሰ teb-be-se
fuel ነዳጅ ne-daj
full ሙሉ mu-lu
fun ጨዋታ che-wa-ta
funeral የቀብር ስነስርዓት ye-qe-bir si-ne-sir-at
funny አስቂኝ as-si-qign
furnished ተሟልቶ የተስተካከለ te-mual-to yet-tes-te-kak-ke-le
furniture የቤት እቃ ye-bet i-qa
future የወደፊት ye-we-de-fit

G

game ግጥሚያ git-mi-ya
garden (*n.*) አትክልት ስፍራ a-ti-kilt sif-ra
gas tank ሳልቫትዮ sal-va-ti-yo
gasoline ነጭ ጋዝ nech gaz, ቤንዚን ben-zin
gear ማርሽ marsh
general (*adv.*) አጠቃላይ at-te-qa-lay
get አገኘ a-gegn-gne
gift ስጦታ si-to-ta
girl ልጃገረድ li-ja-ge-red
girlfriend የሴት ጓደኛ ye-set guad-de-gna
give ሰጠ set-te
glass ብርጭቆ bir-chiq-qo
glasses (eyeglasses) መነጽር me-ne-tsir
glue ሙጫ much-cha
go ሄደ he-de
goat ፍየል fiy-yel
gold ወርቅ werq
good ጥሩ ti-ru
goods ሸቀጥ she-qet
government መንግስት men-gist
gram ግራም gi-ram
grammar ሰዋሰው se-wa-sew
grandfather ወንድ አያት wend a-yat
grandmother ሴት አያት set a-yat
grape ወይን weyn
grass ሳር sar
great ታላቅ tal-laq
green አረንጓዴ a-ren-gua-de
greeting ሰላምታ se-lam-ta
grocery store የምግብና መጠጦች መደብር ye-mi-gi-bin-na me-tet-toch me-deb-bir
ground (*n.*) ምክንያት mi-kin-yat / (*adj.*) ምድር mi-dir
group ቡድን bu-din

guard (*n.*) ዘብ zeb / (*v.*) ጠበቀ teb-be-qe
guest እንግዳ in-gi-da
guide (*n.*) መሪ me-ri
guidebook መምሪያ mem-ri-ya
guilty ጥፋተኛ ti-fa-tegn-gna
gun ጦር መሳሪያ tor mes-sa-ri-ya
gym ጂም jim

H

hair ጸጉር tse-gur
half ግማሽ gim-mash
hall አዳራሽ ad-da-rash
halt አቆመ a-qo-me
hand እጅ ijj
handicapped አካል ጉዳተኛ a-kal gu-da-tegn-gna
happy ደስተኛ des-si-tegn-gna
harbor ወደብ we-deb
hard ጠንካራ ten-kar-ra
harm (*n.*) ጉዳት gu-dat
hat ባርኔጣ bar-net-ta
hazard አደጋ a-de-ga
he እሱ is-su
head ራስ ras
health ጤና te-na
health insurance የጤና ዋስትና ye-te-na was-tin-na
hear ሰማ sem-ma
heart ልብ libb
heart attack ልብ ድካም libb di-kam
heat ሙቀት mu-qet
heavy ከባድ keb-bad
hello ሄሎ he-lo
help ርዳታ er-da-ta
herb እጽ its
here እዚህ iz-zih

heterosexual ቅይጥ ጾታ qiy-yit tso-ta
highway አውራ ጎዳና aw-ra go-da-na
hike ሽርሽር shir-shir
hill ኮረብታ ko-reb-ta
HIV ኤች አይ ቪ ech-ay-vi
hole ጉድጓድ gud-guad
holiday በዓል be-al
holy ቅዱስ qid-dus
home መኖሪያ me-no-ri-ya
homeless ጉዳና ተዳዳሪ gu-da-na te-da-da-ri
homosexual ተመሳሳይ ጾታ te-me-sa-say tso-ta
honest ሐቀኛ haq-qegn-gna
honey ማር mar
honeymoon ጫጉላ cha-gu-la
horse ፈረስ fe-res
hospital ሆስፒታል hos-pi-tal
hospitality መስተንግዶ mes-ten-gi-do
hostage ታጋች tag-gach
hostel ሆስቴል hos-tel
hostile የጠላት ye-te-lat
hot ሙቅ muq
hotel ሆቴል ho-tel
hour ሰዓት se-at
house ቤት bet
how እንዴት in-det
hug እቅፍ አደረገ iq-qif a-der-re-ge
human ሰው sew
human rights ሰብዓዊ መብት seb-a-wi mebt
hundred መቶ me-to
hungry የተራበ yet-te-ra-be
hunt አደነ ad-de-ne
hunter አዳኝ ad-dagn
hurry ጥድፊያ tid-fi-ya
hurt ጎዳ god-da
husband ባል bal

I

I እኔ i-ne
ice በረዶ be-re-do
ID card መታወቂያ ወረቀት met-ta-we-qi-ya we-re-qet
idea አስተሳሰብ as-te-sa-seb
identification መለያ mel-le-ya
identify ለየ ley-ye
idiom ፈሊጥ fe-lit
if ከ ke
ignition ቁልፍ qulf
ignore ችላ አለ chil-la a-le
illegal ሕገ ወጥ hig-ge wet
illness ሕመም hi-mem
immigrant ስደተኛ sid-de-tegn-gna
immigration ስደት sid-det
impolite ባለጌ ba-le-ge
import አስመጣ as-met-ta
income ገቢ ge-bi
incorrect ስህተት sih-tet
individual ግለሰብ gil-le-seb
indoor የቤት ውስጥ ye-bet wist
inexpensive ውድ ያልሆነ wid yal-ho-ne
infant ጨቅላ cheq-la
infect በከለ bek-ke-le
infected የተበከለ yet-te-bek-ke-le
infection ቁስለት qus-let
influence ተጽዕኖ te-tsi-i-no
influenza ኢንፍሉዌንዛ in-fi-lu-wen-za
information መረጃ mer-re-ja
information desk የመረጃ ዴስክ ye-mer-re-ja desk
infrastructure መሰረተ ልማት me-se-re-te li-mat
inject መርፌ ወጋ mer-fe weg-ga
injury ጉዳት gu-dat
ink ብዕር bi-ir

inn ትንሽ ሆቴል tin-nish ho-tel
innocent ንጹህ ni-tsuh
inquiry ምርመራ mir-me-ra
insect ነፍሳት nef-sat
insect bite የነፍሳት ንድፊያ ye-nef-sat nid-fi-ya
insect repellant ነፍሳት ማባረሪያ nef-sat mab-ba-re-ri-ya
inside ውስጥ wist
inspect መረመረ me-rem-me-re
instant ቅጽበት qits-bet
institution ተቋም te-quam
insufficient የማይበቃ yem-may-be-qa
insulin ኢንሱሊን en-su-lin
insult ዘለፋ ze-le-fa
insurance ዋስትና was-tin-na
international አለም አቀፍ a-lem aq-qef
Internet ኢንተርኔት in-ter-net
interpret ተረጎመ te-reg-go-me
interpretation ትርጉም tir-gum
interpreter ተርጓሚ ter-gua-mi
intersection የመንገዶች መገናኛ ye-men-ge-doch meg-ge-na-gna
intimate የልብ ye-libb
introduce oneself ራስን ማስተዋወቅ ra-sin mas-te-wa-weq
intruder ሌባ le-ba
invite ጋበዘ gab-be-ze
iron (*n. / metal*) ብረት bi-ret
irritate አስቆጣ as-qot-ta
island ደሴት des-set
issue ጉዳይ gud-day
it እሱ (ለነገር) is-su (le-ne-ger)
itch እከክ i-kek
item እቃ i-qa
itinerary ጉዞ gu-zo

J

jacket ጃኬት ja-ket
jail እስር ቤት i-sir bet
jam የመኪና መጨናነቅ ye-me-ki-na mech-che-na-neq
January ጥር tirr
jar ጀሪካን je-ri-kan
jeans ጂንስ jins
Jew አይሁድ ay-hud
jewelry ጌጣጌጥ ge-ta-get
job ስራ si-ra
join ተቀላቀለ te-qe-laq-qe-le
journalist ጋዜጠኛ ga-ze-tegn-gna
judge (*n.*) ዳኛ dagn-gna
jug ጆግ jog
juice ጁስ jus
July ሐምሌ ham-le
jump ዝላይ zil-lay
jumper cables ሞተር መመንጨቂያ ሽቦ mo-ter me-men-che-qi-ya shi-bo
junction መገናኛ meg-ga-na-gna
June ሰኔ se-ne
jungle ዱር dur
just ፍትሐዊ fit-ha-wi
justice ፍትህ fi-tih

K

keep (*v.*) ያዘ ya-ze
kettle ጀበና je-be-na
key ቁልፍ qulf
kick ምት mitt
kid ታዳጊ ልጅ tad-da-gi lij

kidnap አገተ ag-ge-te
kidney ኩላሊት ku-la-lit
kill ገደለ ged-de-le
kilogram ኪሎ ግራም ki-lo gi-ram
kilometer ኪሎ ሜትር ki-lo me-tir
kind ደግ degg
kiss ሳመ sa-me
kit እቃ i-qa
kitchen ማድቤት mad-bet
knapsack ናፕሳክ nap-sak
knee ጉልበት gul-bet
knife ቢላዋ bil-la-wa
knit ሰራ ser-ra
knock አንኳኳ an-kuak-kua
knot ቋጠሮ qua-te-ro
know አወቀ aw-we-qe
kosher ኮሸር ko-sher

L

lady ወይዘሮ wey-ze-ro
lake ሐይቅ ha-yiq
lamb ጠቦት teb-bot
lamp መብራት meb-rat
land መሬት me-ret
lane ጠባብ መንገድ teb-bab men-ged
language ቋንቋ quan-qua
laptop ላፕቶፕ lap-top
large ትልቅ til-liq
last የመጨረሻ ye-me-cher-re-sha
last year አምና am-na
late ዘግይቶ zeg-yi-to
later በኋላ be-hua-la
laugh ሳቀ sa-qe

laundromat የህዝብ ላውንደሪ ye-hizb la-win-de-ri
laundry ላውንደሪ la-win-de-ri
lavatory የመጸዳጃ ክፍል ye-mets-tse-da-ja ki-fil
law ህግ higg
lawyer ጠበቃ te-be-qa
layover አዳር a-dar
leader መሪ me-ri
league ሊግ lig
learn ተማረ te-ma-re
leather ቆዳ qo-da
leave ሄደ he-de
left ግራ gi-ra
leg እግር i-gir
legal ህጋዊ hig-ga-wi
legislature ህግ አውጪ ክፍል higg aw-chi ki-fil
lemon ሎሚ lo-mi
lens ሌንስ lens
less ያነሰ yan-ne-se
letter (*written note*) ደብዳቤ deb-dab-be
lettuce ሰላጣ se-la-ta
level ደረጃ de-re-ja
library ቤተ መጻህፍት be-te me-tsa-hift
lice ቅማል qi-mal
license ፈቃድ fe-qad
lid ክዳን ki-dan
lie ውሸት wi-shet
life ሕይወት hiy-wet
lift አነሳ a-nes-sa
light (*adj.*) ቀላል qel-lal
lighting ብርሐን bir-han
like (*v.*) ወደደ wed-de-de
lime ኖራ no-ra
limit (*v.*) ወሰነ wes-se-ne / (*n.*) መጠን me-ten
lip ከንፈር ken-fer
liquid ፈሳሽ fe-sash
liquor የአልኮል መጠጥ ye-al-kol me-tet

list ዝርዝር zir-zir
listen አዳመጠ ad-dam-me-te
liter ሊትር li-tir
litter ቃሬዛ qa-re-za
little ጥቂት ti-qit
live (*v.*) ኖረ no-re / (*adj.*) ቀጥታ qet-ti-ta
liver ጉበት gub-bet
lizard እንሽላሊት in-shi-la-lit
load (*v.*) ጫነ cha-ne / (*n.*) ጫና cha-na
loaf ዳቦ dab-bo
loan (*n.*) ብድር bid-dir / (*v.*) አበደረ a-bed-de-re
lobby መተላለፊያ me-te-la-le-fi-ya
local ያገር ውስጥ ya-ger wist
location መገኛ ቦታ meg-gegn-gna bo-ta
lock ቆለፈ qol-le-fe
lock out ተዘጋበት te-zeg-gab-bet
locker ሳጥን sa-tin
long ረዥም rezh-zhim
look መልክ mel-kam
loose ልል lil
lose አጣ at-ta
lost የጠፋ ye-tef-fa
loud ጉልህ gu-lih
lounge ላውንጅ la-winj
love (*n.*) ፍቅር fi-qir / (*v.*) አፈቀረ a-feq-qe-re
low ዝቅተኛ ziq-qi-tegn-gna
lucky እድለኛ id-di-legn-gna
luggage ጓዝ guaz
lunch ምሳ mi-sa

M

machine ማሽን ma-shin
mad እብድ ibd
maid የቤት ሰራተኛ ye-bet ser-ra-tegn-gna
mail (*n.*) ፖስታ pos-ta / (*v.*) ፖስታ ላከ pos-ta la-ke
main (*adj.*) ዋና wan-na
make (*v.*) ሰራ ser-ra
man ሰው sew
mandatory የግዴታ yeigid-de-ta
manual (*n.*) መምሪያ mem-ri-ya
many ብዙ bi-zu
map ካርታ kar-ta
marketplace ገበያ ge-be-ya
marriage ጋብቻ ga-bi-cha
married ባለትዳር ba-le-ti-dar
marry አገባ a-geb-ba
massage ማሳጅ ma-saj
math ሒሳብ hi-sab
mattress ፍራሽ fi-rash
maximum የመጨረሻ ye-me-cher-re-sha
meal ምግብ mi-gib
measure ልኬት lik-ket
meat ስጋ si-ga
mechanic ሜካኒክ me-ka-nik
medication መድሐኒት med-ha-nit
medicine ሕክምና hik-ki-min-na
medium (*adj.*) መካከለኛ me-kak-ke-legn-gna
meet (*v.*) አገኘ a-gegn-gne
meeting ስብሰባ sib-se-ba
melon ሐብሐብ hab-hab
melt ቀለጠ qel-le-te
member አባል a-bal
menstruation የወር አበባ ye-wer a-be-ba
mental የአእምሮ ye-a-i-mi-ro

menu የምግብ ዝርዝር ye-mi-gib zir-zir
merchant ነጋዴ neg-ga-de
message መልዕክት me-li-ikt
messenger መልዕክተኛ me-li-ik-tegn-gna
metal ብረት bi-ret
meter ሜትር me-tir
metro station የባቡር ጣቢያ ye-ba-bur ta-bi-ya
microwave ማይክሮዌቭ may-ki-ro-wev
midday እኩለ ቀን ik-ku-le qen
middle መሃል me-hal
midnight እኩለ ሌሊት ik-ku-le le-lit
might ኃይል ha-yil
migraine ማይግሬን may-gi-ren
mild መካከለኛ me-kak-ke-legn-gna
mile ማይል ma-yil
military የጦር ሰራዊት ye-tor se-ra-wit
milk ወተት we-tet
million ሚልዮን mil-yen
mine የኔ ye-ne
minimum አነስተኛ a-nes-tegn-gna
minor (*adj.*) ቀላል qel-lal / (*n.*) ለአካለ መጠን ያልደረሰ le-ka-le me-ten yal-der-re-se
mint ሜንታ men-ta
minute ደቂቃ de-qi-qa
mirror መስታዎት mes-ta-wot
misunderstanding አለመግባባት a-le-meg-ba-bat
mix ቀላቀለ qel-lal
mobile phone ተንቀሳቃሽ ስልክ ten-qe-sa-qash silk
moment ቅጽበት qits-bet
Monday ሰኞ segn-gno
money ገንዘብ gen-zeb
monkey ዝንጀሮ zin-jo-ro
month ወር wer
monument ሐውልት ha-wilt
moon ጨረቃ che-re-qa
more (*adv.*) ይበልጥ yi-belt

morning ጧት tuat
mosque መስጊድ mes-gid
mosquito የወባ ትንኝ ye-we-ba ti-nign
mosquito net አጎበር a-go-ber
most (*adv.*) አብዛኛውን ab-zagn-gna-win
motel ሞቴል mo-tel
mother እናት in-nat
mother-in-law አማች a-mach
motion sickness ማቅለሽለሽ maq-lesh-lesh
motor ሞተር mo-ter
motorcycle ሞተርሳይክል mo-ter-say-kil
mount ጋለበ gal-le-be
mountain ተራራ te-ra-ra
mouse አይጥ a-yit
moustache ሪዝ riz
mouth አፍ af
move (*v.*) ተንቀሳቀሰ ten-qe-saq-qe-se
movie ፊልም film
movie theater ሲኒማ ቤት si-ni-ma bet
Mr. (*title*) አቶ a-to
Mrs. (*title*) ወይዘሮ wey-ze-ro
Ms. (*title*) ወይዘሪት wey-ze-rit
much ብዙ bi-zu
mud ጭቃ chi-qa
mural የግድግዳ ስዕል ye-gid-gid-da si-el
murder ግድያ gi-diy-ya
muscle ጡንቻ tun-cha
museum ሙዚየም mu-zi-yem
mushroom እንጉዳይ en-gu-day
music ሙዚቃ mu-zi-qa
musical instrument የሙዚቃ መሳሪያ ye-mu-zi-qa mes-sa-ri-ya
musician ሙዚቀኛ mu-zi-qegn-gna
Muslim ሙስሊም mus-lim
mystery እንቆቅልሽ in-qo-qil-lish

N

naked ራቁት ra-qut
name ስም sim
napkin ናፕኪን nap-kin
narrow ጠባብ teb-bab
nation አገር a-ger
native ተወላጅ te-wel-laj
nature ተፈጥሮ te-fet-ro
nausea ማቅለሽለሽ maq-lesh-lesh
navigation አሰሳ a-se-sa
navy (*n. / military*) ባህር ሐይል ba-hir ha-yil
near ቅርብ qirb
nearby በአቅራቢያ be-aq-rab-bi-ya
neck አንገት an-get
necklace ያንገት ሐብል yan-get ha-bil
need (*v.*) ፈለገ fel-le-ge
needle መርፌ mer-fe
neighbor ጎረቤት go-re-bet
neighborhood ሰፈር se-fer
nephew የወንድም (የእህት) ወንድ ልጅ ye-wen-dim (ye-i-hit) wend lij
nerve ነርቭ nerv
neutral ገለልተኛ ge-lel-tegn-gna
never (*adv.*) በፍጹም be-fits-tsum
new አዲስ ad-dis
New Year ዘመን መለወጫ ze-men me-lew-we-cha
New Year's Day የዘመን መለወጫ ዕለት (እንቁጣጣሽ) ye-ze-men me-lew-we-cha i-let (in-qu-ta-tash)
New Year's Eve የዘመን መለወጫ ዋዜማ ye-ze-men me-lew-we-cha wa-ze-ma
news ዜና ze-na
newspaper ጋዜጣ ga-ze-ta
next ቀጥሎ qet-ti-lo
next to ከ ... አጠገብ ke... a-te-geb
nice መልካም mel-kam

niece የወንድም (የእህት) ሴት ልጅ ye-wen-dim (ye-i-hit) set lij
night ሌሊት le-lit
nightlife የምሽት ሕይወት ye-mish-shit hiy-wot
nine ዘጠኝ ze-tegn
nineteen አስራ ዘጠኝ as-ra ze-tegn
ninety ዘጠና ze-te-na
no የለም yel-lem
noise ጫጫታ cha-cha-ta
non-smoking የማያጨስ yem-ma-ya-ches
noon ቀትር qe-tir
normal የተለመደ yet-te-lem-me-de
north ሰሜን se-men
northeast ሰሜን ምስራቅ se-men mis-raq
northwest ሰሜን ምዕራብ se-men mi-i-rab
nose አፍንጫ a-fin-cha
note ማስታወሻ mas-ta-we-sha
nothing ምንም mi-nim
November ህዳር hi-dar
now አሁን a-hun
nowhere የትም ቦታ ye-tim bo-ta
nuclear ኒውክሌር niw-ki-ler
nudist beach የራቁት መዝናኛ የባህር ዳርቻ ye-ra-qut mez-nagn-gna ye-ba-hir da-rich-cha
number ቁጥር qu-tir
nun መነኩሲት me-nek-ku-sit
nurse ነርስ ners
nuts ለውዝ lewz

O

occupant ነዋሪ ne-wa-ri
occupation ስራ si-ra
ocean ውቅያኖስ wiq-ya-nos
o'clock ሰዓት se-at

October ጥቅምት ti-qimt
octopus ኦክቶፐስ ok-to-pes
odor መዓዛ me-a-za
off (*adv./adj.*) የጠፋ ye-tef-fa
offend አስቀየመ as-qey-ye-me
office ቢሮ bi-ro
officer መኮንን me-kon-nin
official ባለ ስልጣን ba-le sil-tan
often (*adv.*) ባብዛኛው bab-za-gnaw
oil ዘይት ze-yit
OK/okay እሺ esh-shi
old የቆየ ye-qoy-ye
olive የወይራ ፍሬ ye-wey-ra fi-re
on ላይ lay
once አንዴ an-de
one አንድ and
one-way ባላንድ አቅጣጫ ba-land aq-tach-cha
onion ሽንኩርት shin-kurt
only ብቻ bich-cha
open ክፍት kift
opera ኦፔራ op-pe-ra
operator ኦፐሬተር op-pi-re-ter
opposite ተቃራኒ te-qa-ra-ni
option አማራጭ am-ma-rach
or ወይም we-yim
oral የቃል ye-qal
orange (*fruit*) ብርቱካን bir-tu-kan; (*color*) ብርቱካናማ bir-tu-ka-nam-ma
orchard የተክል ቦታ ye-te-kil bo-ta
orchestra የሙዚቃ ጓድ ye-mu-zi-qa guad
order ትእዛዝ ti-i-zaz
ordinary የተለመደ yet-te-lem-me-de
organ አካል a-kal
organic ተፈጥሯዊ te-fet-rua-wi
original ወጥ wett
other ሌላ le-la

ought የግድ ye-gidd
our የኛ yegn-gna
out (*adv.*) ወጣ wet-ta
outdoor (*adj.*) የውጭ ye-wich
outdoors (*n.*) ደጅ dejj
outside ውጭ wich
oven ምድጃ mi-dij-ja
over (*prep.*) ከላይ ke-lay
overdose መጠን ያለፈ me-ten yal-le-fe
overnight (*adv.*) አዳር a-dar
own (*v.*) ገዛ gez-za
owner (*n.*) ባለቤት ba-le-bet
oxygen ኦክሲጅን ok-si-jin

P

pack ጭነት chi-net
package እሽግ ish-shig
page ገጽ gets
paid ተከፍሏል te-kef-lual
pain ህመም hi-mem
painful አሳማሚ a-sam-ma-mi
painkiller ህመም ማስታገሻ hi-mem mas-ta-ge-sha
pair ጥንድ tind
pajamas ፒጃማ pi-ja-ma
pan መጥበሻ met-be-sha
pants ሱሪ sur-ri
paper ወረቀት we-re-qet
parcel ጥቅል ti-qill
pardon (*n.*) ምህረት mi-hi-ret / (*v.*) ማረ ma-re
parent ወላጅ we-laj
park (*n.*) ፓርክ park / (*v.*) አቆመ a-qo-me
parking መኪና ማቆሚያ me-ki-na ma-qo-mi-ya
parliament ፓርላማ par-la-ma

partner አጋር ag-gar
party ግብዣ gib-zha
passenger ተጓዥ te-guazh
passport ፓስፖርት pas-port
password የይለፍ ቃል ye-yi-lef qal
pasta ፓስታ pas-ta
pastry ኬክ ቤት kek bet
path የእግር መንገድ ye-i-gir men-ged
patience ትእግስት ti-i-gist
patient (*n. / medical*) ታማሚ ta-ma-mi
pavement መንገድ men-ged
pay ከፈለ kef-fe-le
payment ክፍያ ki-fiy-ya
pea አተር a-ter
peace ሰላም se-lam
peach ኮክ kok
peak ጫፍ chaf
peanuts ለውዝ lewz
pedal ፔዳል pe-dal
pedestrian እግረኛ eg-regn-gna
pen ብዕር bi-ir
penalty ቅጣት qi-tat
pencil እርሳስ ir-sas
people ሰው sew
pepper በርበሬ ber-be-re
percent መቶኛ me-togn-gna
perfect ምሉዕ mi-lu-i
period ክፍለ ጊዜ kif-le gi-ze
permanent ቋሚ qua-mi
permission ፈቃድ fe-qad
permit (*v.*) ፈቀደ fe-qe-de / (*n.*) ፈቃድ fe-qad
person ግለሰብ gil-le-seb
personal የግል ye-gill
pest ተባይ te-bay
pet ለማዳ እንስሳ lem-mad-da in-se-sa
petrol ቤንዚን ben-zin

pharmacy መድሐኒት መደብር med-ha-nit me-de-bir
phone ስልክ silk
phone booth የመንገድ ስልክ ye-men-ged silk
phone card መደወያ ካርድ me-dew-we-ya kard
phone number ስልክ ቁጥር silk qu-tir
photograph ፎቶግራፍ fo-to-gi-raf
phrase ሐረግ ha-reg
physician ሐኪም ha-kim
piano ፒያኖ pi-ya-no
pick መቆፈሪያ me-qof-fe-ri-ya
picnic ሽርሽር shir-shir
picture ምስል mi-sil
pie ፓይ pay
piece ቁራጭ qur-rach
pig አሳማ a-sa-ma
pigeon ዋኖስ wa-nos
pill ኪኒን ki-nin
pillow ትራስ ti-ras
pint መለኪያ me-lek-ki-ya
pipe ፒፓ pip-pa
place ቦታ bo-ta
plain ሜዳ me-da
plan እቅድ iq-qid
plane አውሮፕላን aw-rop-pi-lan
plant ተክል te-kil
plastic ላስቲክ las-tik
plate ሳህን sa-hin
platform መድረክ med-rek
play (*n.*) ጭውውት chi-wiw-wit / (*v.*) ተጫወተ te-chaw-we-te
pleasant አስደሳች as-des-sach
please እባክዎ i-ba-ki-wo
plug ሶኬት sok-ket
pocket ኪስ kis
poem ግጥም gi-tim
point (*n. / sports*) ነጥብ ne-tib

poison መርዝ merz
police ፖሊስ po-lis
police station ፖሊስ ጣቢያ po-lis ta-bi-ya
polite ትሁት ti-hut
politics ፖለቲካ po-le-ti-ka
pollution ብክለት bik-let
pool ገንዳ gen-da
population ሕዝብ hizb
pork የአሳማ ስጋ ye-a-sa-ma si-ga
portable ቀላል qel-lal
possibly (*adv.*) የሚቻል yem-mich-chal
post office ፖስታ ቤት pos-ta bet
postage ቴምብር tem-bir
postal code ፓስታ ሳጥን ቁጥር pos-ta sa-tin qu-tir
postbox ፖስታ ሳጥን pos-ta sa-tin
postcard ፖስትካርድ pos-ti-kard
postpone አስተላለፈ as-te-lal-le-fe
pot ማሰሮ ma-se-ro
potato ድንች din-nich
pottery ሸክላ ስራ shek-la si-ra
poultry ዶሮ do-ro
pound (*n. / monetary*) ፓውንድ pa-wind / (*v.*) ወቀጠ weq-qe-te
pour ቀዳ qed-da
poverty ድህነት di-hin-net
power ጉልበት gul-bet
pray ጸለየ tsel-le-ye
prefer መረጠ mer-re-te
pregnant ነፍሰጡር nef-se-tur
prescription የመድሐኒት ማዘዣ ye-med-ha-nit ma-ze-zha
president ፕሬዝዳንት pi-rez-dant
price ዋጋ wa-ga
priest ቄስ qes
printer ማተሚያ mat-te-mi-ya
prison ወህኒ weh-ni
prisoner እስረኛ is-regn-gna

privacy ለብቻ መሆን le-bich-cha me-hon
private የግል ye-gill
private property የግል ንብረት ye-gill nib-ret
private room የብቻ ክፍል ye-bich-cha ki-fil
prize ሽልማት shil-li-mat
probably ሊሆን የሚችል li-hon yem-mi-chil
problem ችግር chig-gir
product ውጤት wit-tet
professional ሙያዊ mu-ya-wi
professor ፕሮፌሰር pi-ro-fe-ser
profile ጎን gonn
profit ትርፍ tirf
program ፕሮግራም pi-rog-ram
prohibit ከለከለ ke-lek-ke-le
project እቅድ iq-qid
promise (*v.*) ቃል ገባ qal geb-ba / (*n.*) ቃልኪዳን qal-ki-dan
promotion የደረጃ እድገት ye-de-re-ja ed-get
pronounce አስታወቀ as-taw-we-qe
proper አግባብ ag-bab
property ንብረት nib-ret
prosecute ህግ ፊት አቀረበ higg fit a-qer-re-be
prosecution ክስ kiss
protect ተከላከለ te-ke-lak-ke-le
protest ተቃውሞ te-qaw-mo
Protestant ጴንጤ pen-te
province ጠቅላይ ግዛት teq-lay gi-zat
psychologist የስነ ልቦና ባለሙያ ye-si-ne lib-bo-na ba-le-mu-ya
public የህዝብ ye-hizb
public telephone የህዝብ ስልክ ye-hizb silk
public toilet የህዝብ መጸዳጃ ye-hizb mets-tse-da-ja
public transportation የህዝብ መጓጓዣ ye-hizb meg-gua-gua-zha
pudding ጣፋጭ (ከምግብ በኋላ) ta-fach (ke-mi-gib be-hua-la)
pull ጎተተ got-te-te

pulse ትርታ tir-ri-ta
pump ፖምፓ pom-pa
punch ቡጢ but-ti
puncture ቀዳዳ qe-da-da
punish ቀጣ qet-ta
purchase ሸመተ shem-me-te
pure ንጹህ ni-tsuh
purple ወይነጠጅ wey-ne-tejj
purpose አላማ a-la-ma
purse ቦርሳ bor-sa
push ገፋ gef-fa
puzzle እንቆቅልሽ in-qo-qil-lish
pyramid ፒራሚድ pi-ra-mid

Q

qualify አበቃ a-beq-qa
quality ጥራት ti-rat
quantity ብዛት bi-zat
quarantine ገለልታ ge-lel-ta
quarter ሩብ rub
queen ንግስት ni-gist
query (*n.*) ጥያቄ tiy-ya-qe
question (*v.*) ጠየቀ tey-ye-qe / (*n.*) ጥያቄ tiy-ya-qe
queue ረድፍ redf
quick ፈጣን fet-tan
quiet ዝምተኛ zim-mi-tegn-gna

R

radio ራዲዮ ra-di-yo
rail ሐዲድ ha-did
railroad የባቡር ሐዲድ ye-ba-bur ha-did

rain (*n.*) ዝናብ zi-nab / (*v.*) ዘነበ zen-ne-be
ramp የተጋደመ መወጣጫ yet-te-gad-de-me mew-we-ta-cha
rape (*n.*) አስገድዶ መድፈር as-ged-di-do med-fer / (*v.*) አስገድዶ ደፈረ as-ged-di-do def-fe-re
rapid ፈጣን fet-tan
rare የማይገኝ yem-ma-yig-gegn
rat አይጥ a-yit
rate (*n.*) ዋጋ wa-ga
ratio ክፍልፋይ ki-fil-fay
ration ራሽን ra-shin
raw ጥሬ ti-re
razor ምላጭ mi-lach
read አነበበ a-neb-be-be
ready ዝግጁ zi-gij-ju
rear ኋላ hua-la
reason ምክንያት mi-kin-yat
reasonable አስተዋይ as-te-way
rebel አማጺ am-ma-tsi
rebellion አመጽ a-mets
receipt ደረሰኝ der-re-segn
receive ተቀበለ te-qe-be-le
recognize ለየ ley-ye
recommend አሳሰበ a-sas-se-be
record (*n. / of events*) መዝገብ mez-geb
rectangle አራት ማዕዘን a-rat ma-i-zen
recycle ሪሳይክል ri-say-kil
red ቀይ qeyy
referee (*n.*) ዳኛ dagn-gna / (*v.*) ዳኘ dagn-gne
reference ዋቢ wa-bi
refrigerator ማቀዝቀዣ ma-qez-qe-zha
refuge መጠጊያ met-te-gi-ya
refugee ስደተኛ sid-de-tegn-gna
refund (*v.*) መለሰ mel-le-se / (*n.*) ተመላሽ ገንዘብ te-mel-lash gen-zeb
regime አገዛዝ ag-ge-zaz

region ክልል kil-lil
registration ምዝገባ miz-ge-ba
regular መደበኛ me-de-begn-gna
relationship ግንኙነት gi-nign-gnun-net
relative አንጻራዊ an-tsa-ra-wi
reliable አስተማማኝ as-ma-tegn-gna
religion ሐይማኖት hay-ma-not
remedy (*n.*) መፍትሔ mef-ti-he
remember አስታወሰ as-taw-we-se
remind አስገነዘበ as-ge-nez-ze-be
remove አስወገደ as-weg-ge-de
rent (*v.*) አከራየ ak-ke-ray-ye / (*n.*) ኪራይ ki-ray
repair ጠገነ teg-ge-ne
repair shop የጥገና መደብር ye-tig-ge-na me-deb-bir
repay መለሰ mel-le-se
repayment መልሶ ክፍያ mel-li-so ki-fiy-ya
repeat ደገመ deg-ge-me
replace ተካ tek-ka
reply መልስ mels
report ዘገባ ze-ge-ba
reporter ዘጋቢ zeg-ga-bi
republic ሪፐብሊክ ri-peb-lik
request (*v.*) ጠየቀ tey-ye-qe / (*n.*) ጥያቄ tiy-ya-qe
require ፈለገ fel-le-ge
rescue አስጣለ as-tel-la
reservation ገደብ ge-deb
reserve ተቀማጭ te-qem-mach
reservoir ቋት quat
respect (*n.*) አክብሮት ak-bi-rot / (*v.*) አከበረ a-keb-be-re
rest እረፍት e-reft
restaurant ምግብ ቤት mi-gib bet
restricted (*adj.*) የተገደበ yet-te-ged-de-be
resume (*v.*) ቀጠለ qet-te-le
retrieve አገኘ a-gegn-gne
return ተመለሰ te-mel-le-se
reverse ቀለበሰ qe-leb-be-se

revive ነፍስ ዘራ nefs zer-ra
revolution አብዮት a-bi-yot
rib ጎድን go-din
ribbon ሪባን ri-ban
rice ሩዝ ruz
ride ጋለበ gal-le-be
right (*adj.*) ትክክለኛ ti-kik-ki-legn-gna / (*n.*) መብት me-bit
ring (*n.*) (*jewelry*) ቀለበት qe-le-bet; (*sound*) የጥሪ ደወል ye-tir-ri de-wel / (*v.*) ደወለ dew-we-le
riot ረብሻ reb-sha
rip ተረተረ te-ret-te-re
risk አደጋ a-de-ga
river ወንዝ wenz
road መንገድ men-ged
road map መንገድ መምሪያ men-ged mem-ri-ya
roasted አሩስቶ ar-rus-to
rob ዘረፈ zer-re-fe
robber ዘራፊ ze-ra-fi
rock (*n.*) ድንጋይ din-gay / (*v.*) አነቃነቀ an-ne-qan-ne-qe
romance ፍቅር fi-qir
romantic የፍቅር ye-fi-qir
roof ጣሪያ ta-ri-ya
room ክፍል ki-fil
room rate የአልቤርጎ ዋጋ ye-al-ber-go wa-ga
room service የክፍል መስተንግዶ ye-ki-fil mes-ten-gi-do
rope ገመድ ge-med
rot በሰበሰ be-seb-be-se
rotten የተበላሸ yet-te-be-lash-she
rough ሸካራ she-ka-ra
round-trip ደርሶ መልስ ጉዞ der-so mels gu-zo
round-trip ticket የደርሶ መልስ ቲኬት ye-der-so mels tik-ket
route መንገድ men-ged
royalty ንጉሳዊ ቤተሰብ ni-gu-sa-wi be-te-seb
rubber ጎማ gom-ma

rude ባለጌ ba-le-ge
rug ስጋጃ si-gaj-ja
rugby ራግቢ rag-bi
ruins ፍርስራሽ fi-ris-rash
rule ደንብ denb
run ሮጠ ro-te

S

sacred ቅዱስ qid-dus
sad አሳዛኝ a-saz-zagn
saddle ኮርቻ ko-rich-cha
safe ደህና de-hi-na
safety ደህንነት deh-nin-net
sail የመርከብ ሸራ ye-mer-keb she-ra
salad ሰላጣ se-la-ta
salary ደመወዝ de-me-wez
sale ቅናሽ qin-nash
sales receipt የሽያጭ ደረሰኝ ye-shiy-yach der-re-segn
sales tax የሽያጭ ግብር ye-shiy-yach gi-bir
salon ሳሎን sa-lon
salt ጨው chew
same ተመሳሳይ te-me-sa-say
sample ናሙና na-mu-na
sanction ማዕቀብ ma-i-qeb
sanctuary መጠለያ ስፍራ met-te-le-ya sif-ra
sand አሸዋ a-she-wa
sandals ነጠላ ጫማ ne-te-la cham-ma
sandwich ሳንዱች san-duch
sanitary napkin የንጽህና ወረቀት ye-ni-tsi-hin-na we-re-qet
satellite ሳተላይት sa-te-layt
Saturday ቅዳሜ qi-da-me
sauce ስጎ si-go
sausage ቋሊማ qua-li-ma

save ቆጠበ qot-te-be
saw (*n. / tool*) መጋዝ me-gaz
say አለ a-le
scanner ስካነር is-ka-ner
scar ጠባሳ te-ba-sa
scare ፍርሃት fir-hat
scarf ያንገት ልብስ yan-get libs
scary አስፈሪ as-fer-ri
scene ስፍራ sif-ra
scenery ትዕይንት ti-ey-yint
schedule ፕሮግራም pi-rog-ram
school ትምህርት ቤት ti-mi-hirt bet
science ሳይንስ sa-yins
scissors መቀስ me-qes
score (*n.*) ነጥብ ne-tib / (*v.*) አስቆጠረ as-qot-te-re
screen ፊልም film
screw ቡሎን bu-lon
screwdriver የቡለን መፍቻ ye-bu-lon mef-cha
sculpture ቅርጻ ቅርጽ qir-tsa qirts
sea ባህር ba-hir
seafood የባህር ምግብ ye-ba-hir mi-gib
seam ስፌት si-fet
search (*n.*) ፍተሻ fit-te-sha / (*v.*) ፈተሸ fet-te-she
seasick የባህር ጉዞ ህመም ye-ba-hir gu-zo hi-mem
season ወቅት weqt
seasonal ወቅታዊ weq-ta-wi
seasoning ቅመም qi-mem
seat መቀመጫ meq-qe-me-cha
seat belt ቀበቶ qe-bet-to
seat number የወንበር ቁጥር ye-wen-ber qu-tir
second (*n. / in time*) ሰከንድ se-kend / (*adj. / ord. num.*) ሁለተኛ hu-let-tegn-gna
secondhand store ያገለገሉ እቃዎች መደብር ya-ge-leg-ge-lu e-qa-woch me-deb-bir
secret ምስጢር mis-tir
secretary ጸሐፊ tse-ha-fi

section ክፍል ki-fil
secular አለማዊ a-le-ma-wi
security ደህንነት deh-nin-net
sedative አደንዛዥ a-den-zazh
see አየ ay-ye
seed ዘር zer
seek ፈለገ fel-le-ge
seem መሰለ mes-se-le
select (*v.*) መረጠ mer-re-te
selection ምርጫ mir-cha
self-service የራስ መስተንግዶ ye-ras mes-ten-gi-do
sell ሸጠ she-te
seminar ሴሚናር se-mi-nar
senate የሕግ መወሰኛ ምክር ቤት ye-higg me-wes-se-gna mi-kir bet
senator የሕግ መወሰኛ ምክር ቤት አባል ye-higg me-wes-se-gna mi-kir bet a-bal
send ላከ la-ke
senior ከፍተኛ kef-fi-tegn-gna
sensitive ቁጡ qut-tu
sentence አረፍተ ነገር a-ref-te ne-ger
separate (*adj.*) የተለየ yet-te-ley-ye / (*v.*) ከፈለ kef-fe-le
September መስከረም mes-ke-rem
serious አደገኛ a-de-gegn-gna
servant አገልጋይ a-gel-gay
serve አገለገለ a-ge-leg-ge-le
server ሰርቨር ser-ver
service አገልግሎት a-gel-gi-lot
settlement የሰፈራ ቦታ ye-se-fe-ra bo-ta
seven ሰባት se-bat
seventeen አስራ ሰባት as-ra se-bat
seventy ሰባ se-ba
sew ልብስ ሰፋ libs se-fi
sex ጾታ tso-ta
shampoo ሻምፖ sham-po
share (*n.*) ድርሻ dir-sha

shark ሻርክ shark
sharp ስል sil
shave ላጨ lach-che
shaving cream ጺም መላጫ ሳሙና tsim me-la-cha sa-mu-na
she እሷ is-sua
sheep በግ beg
sheet አንሶላ an-so-la
shellfish ባለዛጎል ዓሳ ba-le-za-gol a-sa
shelter መጠለያ met-te-le-ya
ship (*n. / boat*) መርከብ mer-keb
shirt ሸሚዝ she-miz
shoe ጫማ cham-ma
shoot (*v.*) ተኮሰ tek-ko-se
shop ሱቅ suq
shopkeeper ባለሱቅ ba-le-suq
shoplifting ስርቆት (የሱቅ ውስጥ) sir-qot (ye-suq wist)
shopping basket ዘንቢል zen-bil
shopping center የገበያ ማዕከል ye-ge-be-ya ma-i-kel
shore ዳርቻ da-rich-cha
short አጭር ach-chir
shot ተኩስ te-kus
shoulder ትከሻ ti-kesh-sha
shout ጮኸ cho-khe
show (*v.*) አሳየ a-say-ye / (*n.*) ትርኢት tir-it
shower ገላ መታጠቢያ ge-la met-ta-te-bi-ya
shut (*v.*) ዘጋ zeg-ga
sick ህመምተኛ hi-mem-tegn-gna
side ጎን gonn
sight የአይን ብርሐን ye-ayn bir-han
sightseeing አገር ማየት a-ger ma-yet
sign ፍንጭ finch
signal ምልክት mi-lik-kit
signature ፊርማ fir-ma
silver ብር birr
sing ዘፈነ zef-fe-ne

single (*n.*) ላጤ lat-te / (*adj.*) ነጠላ ne-te-la
sink (*n.*) እቃ ማጠቢያ i-qa ma-te-bi-ya
sir ጌታዬ ge-ta-ye
siren ያደጋ ደወል ya-de-ga de-wel
sister እህት i-hit
sit ተቀመጠ te-qem-me-te
six ስድስት sid-dist
sixteen አስራ ስድስት as-ra sid-dist
sixty ስልሳ sil-sa
size መጠን me-ten
skate (*n.*) ባለጎማ ጫማ ba-le-gom-ma cham-ma / (*v.*) በባለጎማ ጫማ ተሽከረከረ be-ba-le-gom-ma cham-ma tesh-ke-rek-ke-re
ski (*v.*) ተንሸራተተ ten-she-rat-te-te
skis (*n.*) መንሸራተቻ men-she-ra-te-cha
skin ቆዳ qo-da
skirt ጉርድ ቀሚስ gurd qe-mis
skull የራስ ቅል ye-ras qil
sky ሰማይ se-may
sleep ተኛ tegn-gna
sleeping bag ባለዚፕ ብርድ ልብስ ba-le-zipp bird libs
sleeping car ባለመኝታ መኪና ba-le-megn-gni-ta me-ki-na
sleeping pills የእንቅልፍ ክኒን ye-en-qilf ki-nin
slow ዝግታ zig-gi-ta
small ትንሽ tin-nish
smell ሽታ shit-ta
smile (*n.*) ፈገግታ fe-geg-ta / (*v.*) ፈገግ አለ fe-gegg a-le
smoke ጭስ chis
smoking ማጤስ ma-tes
smooth (*adj.*) ልስልስ lis-lis
snack (*n.*) መቆያ me-qoy-ya
snake እባብ i-bab
snow (*n.*) በረዶ be-re-do / (*v.*) በረዶ ዘነበ be-re-do zen-ne-be
soap ሳሙና sa-mu-na
soccer እግር ኳስ i-gir kuas

sock ካልሲ kal-si
soft ለስላሳ les-las-sa
sold የተሸጠ yet-te-she-te
sold out ሸጦ ጨረሰ she-to cher-re-se
soldier ወታደር wet-tad-der
some የተወሰነ yet-te-wes-se-ne
someone የሆነ ሰው ye-ho-ne sew
something የሆነ ነገር ye-ho-ne ne-ger
son ወንድ ልጅ wend lij
song ዘፈን ze-fen
soon (*adv.*) ቶሎ to-lo
sore (*adj.*) ከባድ keb-bad / (*n.*) ቁስል qu-sil
sorry ይቅርታ yi-qir-ta
sound ድምጽ dimts
soup ሾርባ shor-ba
sour መራራ me-ra-ra
source ምንጭ minch
south ደቡብ de-bub
soy አኩሪ አተር a-ku-ri a-ter
spare (*adj.*) ትርፍ tirf
spare part መለዋወጫ me-le-wa-we-cha
speak ተናገረ te-nag-ge-re
special ልዩ liy-yu
speed ፍጥነት fit-net
speed limit የፍጥነት ገደብ ye-fit-net ge-deb
speedometer ፍጥነት መለኪያ fit-net me-lek-ki-ya
spell አስማት as-mat
spend አዋለ a-wa-le
spicy ቅመም የበዛበት qi-mem ye-bez-zab-bet
spider ሸረሪት she-re-rit
spine አከርካሪ a-ker-ka-ri
spoon ማንኪያ men-ki-ya
sport እስፖርት is-port
sports እስፖርቶች is-por-toch
spring (*season*) ጸደይ tse-dey; (*water*) ምንጭ minch; (*metal coil*) መንጠሪያ men-te-ri-ya

square (*town square*) አደባባይ ad-de-ba-bay; (*form*) ካሬ ka-re
stadium እስቴድየም is-te-di-yem
staff ሰራተኞች ser-ra-tegn-gnoch
stairs ፎቅ foq
stamp ማህተም mah-tem
stand መድረክ med-rek
standard ደረጃ de-re-ja
start መጀመሪያ me-jem-me-ri-ya
state ግዛት gi-zat
station ጣቢያ ta-bi-ya
statue ሐውልት ha-wult
stay ቆይታ qoy-yi-ta
steak ጥብስ tibs
steal ሰረቀ ser-re-qe
step (*v.*) ረገጠ reg-ge-te / (*n.*) መወጣጫ mew-we-ta-cha
sterile መኻን me-khan
stitch ስፋ sef-fa
stolen የተሰረቀ yet-te-ser-re-qe
stomach ሆድ hod
stone ድንጋይ din-gay
stop ማቆሚያ ma-qo-mi-ya
store መደብር me-deb-bir
storm ማዕበል ma-i-bel
stove ምድጃ mi-dij-ja
straight ቀጥታ qet-ti-ta
stranger ጸጉረ ልውጥ tse-gu-re liw-wut
street ጉዳና gu-da-na
student ተማሪ te-ma-ri
study ጥናት ti-nat
substitute ተቀያሪ te-qey-ya-ri
suburb የከተማ ዳርቻ ye-ke-te-ma da-rich-cha
subway መሿለኪያ mesh-shau-le-ki-ya
sugar ስኳር sik-kuar
suit ሙሉ ልብስ mu-lu libs
suitcase ሻንጣ shan-ta

suite ተከታዮች te-ket-ta-yoch
summer በጋ be-ga
summon ጠራ ter-ra
sun ጸሐይ tse-hay
sunblock ጸሐይ መከላከያ tse-hay mek-ke-la-ke-ya
sunburn ጸሐይ ያቃጠለው tse-hay yaq-qat-te-lew
supermarket ሱፐርማርኬት sup-per-mar-ket
supplies አስቤዛ as-be-za
surgeon ቀዶ ጠጋኝ qed-do teg-gagn
surgery ቀዶ ጥገና qed-do tig-ge-na
surname የቤተሰብ መጠሪያ ye-be-te-seb met-te-ri-ya
surprise ያልታሰበ አስደሳች ነገር yal-tas-se-be ne-ger
surrender (*v.*) እጅ ሰጠ ijj set-te
suspect (*n.*) ተጠርጣሪ te-ter-ta-ri / (*v.*) ጠረጠረ te-ret-te-re
swallow (*v.*) ዋጠ wa-te
swear መሐላ me-hal-la
sweat ላብ lab
sweet ጣፋጭ ta-fach
swelling እብጠት ib-tet
swim ዋኘ wagn-gne
symbol ትዕምርት ti-em-mirt
symptom ምልክት mi-lik-kit
synagogue ሲናጎግ si-na-gog
syringe መርፌ mer-fe
system ስርዓት sir-at

T

table ጠረጴዛ te-rep-pe-za
tag ገላጭ ወረቀት ge-lach we-re-qet
take ወሰደ wes-se-de
talk ወሬ we-re
tall ረዥም rezh-zhim
tampon ታምፑን tam-pun

tape ቴፕ tepp
taste ጣዕም ta-em
tax (*v.*) ገበረ geb-be-re / (*n.*) ግብር gi-bir
taxi ታክሲ tak-si
tea ሻይ shay
teacher አስተማሪ as-te-ma-ri
telephone ስልክ silk
television ቴሌቪዥን te-le-vi-zhin
tell ነገረ ne-ger
temperature ሙቀት mu-qet
temple ቤተ መቅደስ be-te meq-des
temporary ጊዜያዊ gi-ze-ya-wi
ten አስር as-sir
tenant ተከራይ te-ke-ray
tent ድንኳን din-kuan
territory ግዛት gi-zat
terrorist አሸባሪ ash-sheb-ba-ri
test ሙከራ muk-ke-ra
thank you አመሰግናለሁ a-me-seg-gi-nal-le-hu
that ያ ya
theater ትያትር ti-ya-tir
then (*adv.*) ያኔ yan-ne
there እዚያ ez-zi-ya
they እነሱ in-nes-su
thief ሌባ le-ba
thigh ባት bat
thin ቀጭን qech-chin
thing ነገር ne-ger
think አሰበ as-se-be
thirsty ተጠማ te-tem-ma
thirty ሰላሳ se-la-sa
this ይህ yih
thought ሐሳብ has-sab
thousand ሺ shi
threat ስጋት si-gat
threaten አሰጋ a-seg-ga

three ሶስት sost
throat ጉሮሮ gu-ro-ro
through በ be
throw ወረወረ we-rew-we-re
thumb አውራ ጣት aw-ra tat
thunder ነጎድጓድ ne-god-guad
Thursday ሐሙስ ha-mus
ticket ቲኬት tik-ket
tie (*v.*) አሰረ as-se-re / (*n.*) ከረባት ke-re-bat
time ጊዜ gi-ze
tip (*n.*) ጉርሻ gur-sha / (*v.*) አጎረሰ a-gor-re-se
tire (*v.*) ደከመ dek-ke-me / (*n.*) ጎማ gom-ma
today ዛሬ za-re
together በጋራ be-ga-ra
toilet መጸዳጃ mets-tse-ga-ja
toilet paper የመጸዳጃ ወረቀት ye-mets-tse-da-ja we-re-qet
toll (*n.*) ጉዳት gu-dat / (*v.*) ተደወለ te-dew-we-le
tomato ቲማቲም ti-ma-tim
tomorrow ነገ ne-ge
tonight ዛሬ ምሽት za-re mish-shit
tool መሳሪያ mes-sa-ri-ya
tooth ጥርስ tirs
toothache የጥርስ ህመም ye-tirs hi-mem
toothbrush የጥርስ ብሩሽ ye-tirs bi-rush
toothpaste የጥርስ ሳሙና ye-tirs sa-mu-na
top ጫፍ chaf
torture ስቃይ si-qay
total አጠቃላይ at-te-qa-lay
touch ነካ nek-ka
tourist ጎብኚ gob-gni
towel ፎጣ fo-ta
town ከተማ ke-te-ma
trade ንግድ nigd
tradition ዘልማድ zel-mad
traditional ዘልማዳዊ zel-ma-da-wi
traffic ትራፊክ ti-ra-fik

trail ዱካ duk-ka
train ባቡር ba-bur
train station ባቡር ጣቢያ ba-bur ta-bi-ya
transfer አስተላለፈ as-te-lal-le-fe
translate ተረጎመ te-reg-go-me
translator ተርጓሚ ter-gua-mi
transplant ንቅለ ተከላ niq-le te-ke-la
transport መጓጓዣ meg-gua-gua-zha
transportation መጓጓዣ meg-gua-gua-zha
trap (*v.*) አጠመደ a-tem-me-de / (*n.*) ወጥመድ wet-med
trash ቆሻሻ qo-sha-sha
travel ተጓዘ te-gua-ze
tray ትሪ ti-ri
treat አከመ ak-ke-me
trespassing ህግ መተላለፍ higg te-lal-le-fe
trial ሙከራ mik-ke-ra
triangle ሶስት ማዕዘን sost ma-e-zen
tribe ነገድ ne-ged
trick (*n.*) ተንኮል ten-kol / (*v.*) አታለለ at-tal-le-le
trip ጉዞ gu-zo
trolley የኤሌክትሪክ አውቶቡስ ye-ae-lek-ti-rik aw-to-bus
trouble ችግር chig-gir
truck የጭነት መኪና ye-chi-net me-ki-na
trunk ግንድ gind
trust (*v.*) አመነ am-me-ne / (*n.*) እምነት im-net
truth እውነት iw-net
try ሞከረ mok-ke-re
true እውነተኛ iw-ne-tegn-gna
Tuesday ማክሰኞ mak-segn-gno
tunnel ዋሻ wash-sha
turn መታጠፊያ met-ta-te-fi-ya
tutor አስጠኚ as-tegn-gni
twelve አስራ ሁለት as-ra hu-let
twenty ሃያ ha-ya
twice ሁለት ጊዜ hu-let gi-ze
twin መንታ men-ta
type (*n.*) አይነት ay-net / (*v.*) ተየበ tey-ye-be

U

umbrella ዣንጥላ zhan-ti-la
uncle አጎ ት ag-got
uncomfortable የማይመች yem-ma-yim-mech
unconscious ነፍሱን ስቶ nef-sun si-to
under ከስር ke-sir
underground በድብቅ የሚሰራ be-dib-biq
understand ተገነዘበ te-ge-nez-ze-be
underwear የውስጥ ልብስ ye-wist libs
undo ሻረ sha-re
unfamiliar እንግዳ in-gi-da
unhappy ያልተደሰተ yal-te-des-se-te
uniform አንድ አይነት and ay-net
union ህብረት hib-ret
United States አሜሪካ a-me-ri-ka
university ዩኒቨርሲቲ yu-ni-ver-si-ti
unlock ከፈተ kef-fe-te
until እስከዚያ is-kez-zi-ya
unusual ያልተለመደ yal-te-lem-me-de
up (*adv.*) ላይ lay
use (*v.*) ተጠቀመ te-tem-me-qe / (*n.*) ጠቀሜታ te-qe-me-ta
usual የተለመደ yet-te-lem-me-de

V

vacancy ክፍት የስራ ቦታ kift ye-si-ra bo-ta
vacant ባዶ ba-do
vacation የእረፍት ጊዜ ye-i-reft gi-ze
vaccinate ከተበ ket-te-be
vaccination ክትባት kit-ti-bat
vanilla ቫኒላ va-ni-la

vegetable አትክልት a-ti-kilt
vegetarian ሳር ቅጠል sar qi-tel
vehicle ተሽከርካሪ tesh-ker-ka-ri
veil አይነርግብ ay-ner-gib
vein ደም ስር dem sir
verb ግስ giss
very በጣም be-tam
video ተንቀሳቃሽ ምስል ten-qe-sa-qash mi-sil
view እይታ iy-yi-ta
village መንደር men-der
violence ብጥብጥ bi-tib-bit
virus ቫይረስ vay-res
visa ቪዛ vi-za
visit (*v.*) ጎበኘ go-begn-gne / (*n.*) ጉብኝት gu-bign-gnit
visitor ጎብኚ gob-gni
voice ድምጽ dimts
volunteer (*n.*) ፈቃደኛ fe-qa-degn-gna / (*v.*) የበጎ ፈቃድ አገልግሎት ሰጠ ye-beg-go fe-qad a-gel-gi-lot set-te
vomit ትውኪያ tiw-ki-ya
vote የምርጫ ድምጽ ye-mir-cha dimts

W

wait መጠበቅ me-teb-beq
wake ነቃ neq-qa
walk (*v.*) ተራመደ te-ram-me-de / (*n.*) ርምጃ ir-mij-ja
wall ግድግዳ gid-gid-da
wallet የገንዘብ ቦርሳ ye-gen-zeb bor-sa
want ፈለገ fel-le-ge
war ጦርነት to-rin-net
warm ሞቃት moq-qat
warn አስጠነቀቀ as-te-neq-qe-qe
warning ማስጠንቀቂያ mas-ten-qe-qi-ya
wash አጠበ at-te-be

washing machine ማጠቢያ ማሽን ma-te-bi-ya ma-shin
watch (*v.*) ተመለከተ te-me-lek-ke-te / (*n. / timepiece*) የጅ ሰዓት yejj se-at
water ውሃ wi-ha
we እኛ ign-gna
wear ለበሰ leb-be-se
weather የአየር ጠባይ ye-ay-yer te-bay
wedding ሰርግ serg
Wednesday ረቡዕ re-bu-i
week ሳምንት sam-mint
weekday የስራ ቀን ye-si-ra qen
weekend ቅዳሜና እሁድ qi-da-men-na i-hud
weigh መዘነ mez-ze-ne
welcome እንኳን ደህና መጣህ in-kuan deh-na met-tah
well (*interj.*) ደህና deh-na / (*n. / for water*) የውሃ ጉድጓድ ye-wu-ha gud-guad
west ምዕራብ mi-i-rab
what ምን min
wheat ስንዴ sin-de
wheel መሪ me-ri
wheelchair የአካል ጉዳተኛ ወንበር ye-a-kal gu-da-tegn-gna wen-ber
when መቼ me-che
where የት yet
whistle (*v.*) አፏጨ a-fua-che / (*n.*) ፉጨት fu-chet
white ነጭ nech
who ማን man
why ለምን le-min
wife ሚስት mist
wild ያልተገራ yal-te-ger-ra
win አሸነፈ ash-shen-ne-fe
wind ነፋስ nefs
window መስኮት mes-kot
wine ወይንጠጅ weyn-tejj
wing ክንፍ kinf
winter ክረምት ki-remt

wipe ጠረገ ter-re-ge
wire ሽቦ shi-bo
wireless Internet ገመድ አልባ ኢንተርኔት ge-med al-ba in-ter-net
wisdom ጥበብ ti-beb
wise ብልህ bi-lih
withdraw አገለለ a-gel-le-le
withdrawal መገለል meg-ge-lel
without ያለ yal-le
woman ሴት set
wood እንጨት in-chet
woods ጫካ chak-ka
wool ሱፍ suf
word ቃል qal
work (*n.*) ስራ si-ra / (*v.*) ሰራ ser-ra
world ዓለም a-lem
worm ትል til
worry (*v.*) አሳሰበ a-sas-se-be / (*n.*) ስጋት si-gat
wrap (*v.*) ጠቀለለ te-qel-le-le
wrist የእጅ አንጓ ye-ijj an-gua
write ጻፈ tsa-fe
wrong ስህተት sih-tet

X-Y-Z

x-ray ራጅ raj

year ዓመት a-met; **next year** ከርሞ ker-mo
yeast እርሾ ir-sho
yell ጮኸ cho-khe
yellow ቢጫ bi-cha
yes አዎ a-wo
yesterday ትናንት ti-nent
yogurt እርጎ ir-go

you አንተ an-te
young ታዳጊ tad-da-gi
youth ወጣት wet-tat

zealous ቀናኢ qe-na-i
zero ዜሮ ze-ro
zipper ቻርኔላ char-ne-la
zoo የእንስሳት ማኖሪያ ye-en-si-sat ma-no-ri-ya

ENGLISH-AMHARIC PHRASEBOOK

BASIC PHRASES

Help! እርዱኝ! ir-dugn!

Hello. ጤና ይስጥልኝ። te-na yis-til-lign / ሄሎ። he-lo
Hi! ሃይ! hay!

Goodbye. ደህና ዋል። deh-na wal / ደህና ሁን። deh-na hun

Good morning. እንዴት አደርክ? in-det ad-derk?
Good afternoon. እንዴት ዋልክ? in-det walk?
Good evening. እንዴት አመሸህ? in-det a-mesh-sheh?
Good night. ደህና እደር። deh-na i-der

Yes. አዎ። a-wo
No. አይ። ay
Okay. እሺ። ish-shi
Please. እባክህን። i-bak-ki-hin
Thank you. አመሰግናለሁ። a-me-se-gi-nal-le-hu
You're welcome. ተቀብያለሁ። te-qeb-biy-yal-le-hu
I'm Sorry. አዝናለሁ። az-nal-le-hu

It doesn't matter.
ምንም ችግር የለም።
mi-nim chig-gir yel-lem

I need . . .
. . . እፈልጋለሁ።
. . . i-fel-li-gal-le-hu

Excuse me.
(to get attention) ይቅርታ። yi-qir-ta
(to pass) ይቅርታ አድርግልኝ። yi-qir-ta a-dir-gil-lign

Where is the bathroom?
መጸዳጃ ቤቱ በየት ነው?
mets-tse-da-ja be-tu be-yet new?

Welcome!
እንኳን ደህና መጣህ!
in-kuan deh-na met-tah!

How are you?
እንዴት ነህ?
in-det neh?

I'm fine, thank you.
ደህና ነኝ፤ አመሰግናለሁ።
deh-na negn a-me-seg-gi-nal-le-hu

And you?
አንተስ?
an-tes?

What's your name?
ስምህን ማን ልበል?
sim-hin man li-bel?

My name is . . .
. . . እባላለሁ።
. . . ib-ba-lel-le-hu

Pleased to meet you.
ስለተዋወቅን ደስ ብሎኛል።
si-let-te-waw-we-qin dess bi-logn-gnal

See you . . .
. . . እንገናኛለን
. . . in-ni-ge-nagna-gnal-len

later በኋላ be-hua-la
soon በቅርብ be-qirb
tomorrow ነገ ne-ge

Take care!
ራስህን ጠብቅ!
ra-si-hin teb-biq!

Sir ጌታዬ ge-ta-ye
Madam እመቤቴ im-me-bet

Mr. አቶ a-to
Ms. ወይዘሪት wey-ze-rit
Mrs. ወይዘሮ wey-ze-ro
Dr. ዶክተር dok-ter

Who?	**What?**	**Where?**	**When?**	**Why?**
ማን?	ምን?	የት?	መቼ?	ለምን?
man?	min?	yet?	me-che?	le-min?

this ይህ yih **that** ያ ya

here እዚህ iz-zih **there** እዚያ iz-zi-ya

good ጥሩ ti-ru **bad** መጥፎ met-fo

entrance መግቢያ meg-bi-ya
exit መውጫ mew-cha

open ክፍት ነው kift new
closed ዝግ ነው zig new

LANGUAGE DIFFICULTIES

Do you speak English?
እንግሊዝኛ ትችላለህ?
in-gi-li-zign-gna ti-chi-lal-leh?

Does anyone here speak English?
እዚህ እንግሊዝኛ የሚችል ሰው አለ?
iz-zih in-gi-li-zign-gna yem-mi-chil sew al-le?

I don't speak Amharic.
አማርኛ አልችልም።
a-ma-rign-gna al-chi-lim

I speak only a little Amharic.
አማርኛ ትንሽ ትንሽ ነው የምችለው።
a-ma-rign-gna tin-nish tin-nish new yem-mi-chi-lew

I speak only English.
እንግሊዝኛ ብቻ ነው የምችለው።
in-gi-li-zign-gna bich-cha new yem-mi-chi-lew

Do you understand? ገባህ? geb-bah?

I understand.
ገብቶኛል።
geb-togn-gnal

I don't understand.
አልገባኝም።
al-geb-bagn-gnim

What does . . . mean?
. . . ምን ማለት ነው?
. . . min ma-let new?

How do you spell . . .?
. . . እንዴት ነው የሚጻፈው?
. . . in-det new yem-mits-tsa-few?

How do you say . . . in Amharic?
. . . በአማርኛ እንዴት ነው የሚባለው?
. . . be-a-ma-rign-gna in-det new yem-mib-ba-lew?

Could you please . . .?
እባክህን . . . ትችላለህ?
i-bak-ki-hin . . . ti-chi-lal-leh?

repeat that
ልትደግመው
lit-deg-mew

speak more slowly
ትንሽ በዝግታ ልትናገር
tin-nish be-zig-gi-ta lit-tin-nag-ger

speak louder
ድምጽህን ከፍ አድርገህ ልትናገር
dim-tsi-hin keff a-dir-geh lit-tin-nag-ger

point out the word for me
ቃሉን ልታመለክተኝ
qa-lun lit-ta-me-lek-ki-tegn

write that down
በጽሁፍ ልታሳየኝ
be-tsi-huf lit-ta-say-yegn

wait while I look it up
እስካየው ድረስ ልትጠብቅ
is-ka-yew di-res lit-ti-teb-biq

FAMILY

This is my . . .
ይህ/ ይህቺ . . . ነው/ ናት።
yih/yih-chi . . . new/nat

husband ባሌ ba-le
wife ሚስቴ mis-te
partner ወዳጄ we-da-je
father አባቴ ab-ba-te
mother እናቴ in-na-te
older brother ታላቅ ወንድሜ tal-laq wen-dim-me
younger brother ታናሽ ወንድሜ tan-nash wen-dim-me
older sister ታላቅ እህቴ tal-laq i-hi-te
younger sister ታናሽ እህቴ tan-nash i-hi-te
aunt አክስቴ a-kis-te
uncle አጎቴ ag-go-te
cousin ያጎቴ ልጅ yag-go-te lij
grandmother ሴት አያቴ set a-ya-te
grandfather ወንድ አያቴ wend a-ya-te
mother-in-law አማቴ a-ma-te
father-in-law አማቼ a-ma-che
brother-in-law ዋርሳዬ war-sa-ye
sister-in-law ምራቴ mi-ra-te
step-mother እንጀራ እናቴ in-je-ra in-na-te
step-father እንጀራ አባቴ in-je-ra ab-ba-te
step-sister የእንጀራ እናቴ/አባቴ ሴት ልጅ ye-en-je-ra en-na-te/ab-ba-te set lij
step-brother የእንጀራ እናቴ/አባቴ ወንድ ልጅ ye-en-je-ra en-na-te/ab-ba-te wend lij

TRAVEL & TRANSPORTATION

Arrival, Departure, and Clearing Customs

I'm here . . .
እዚህ የመጣሁት . . . ነው።
iz-zih ye-met-ta-hut . . . new

on vacation ለሽርሽር le-shir-shir
for business ለስራ le-si-ra
to visit relatives ዘመድ ለመጠየቅ ze-med le-me-tey-yeq
to study ለትምህርት le-tim-hirt

I'm just passing through.
እግረ መንገዴን እያለፍኩ ነው።
ig-re men-ge-den iy-yal-lef-ku new

I'm going to . . .
ወደ . . . ልሄድ ነው።
we-de . . . li-hed new

I'm staying at . . .
የማርፈው . . . ነው።
yem-mar-few . . . new

I'm staying for X . . .
ለ X . . . እቆያለሁ።
le X . . . i-qoy-yal-le-hu

days ቀናት qe-nat
weeks ሳምንታት sam-min-tat
months ወራት we-rat

Do I have to declare this?
ይህን ማስመዝገብ ይኖርብኝ ይሆን?
yi-hin mas-mez-geb yi-no-rib-bign yi-hon?

You Might Hear

ልታስመዘግብ የምትፈልገው ነገር አለ?
lit-tas-me-zeg-gib yem-mit-fel-li-gew ne-ger al-le?
Do you have anything to declare?

ራስህ ነህ ይህን ሻንጣ ያዘጋጀኸው?
ra-sih neh yi-hin shan-ta yaz-ze-gaj-je-khew?
Did you pack this on your own?

እባክህን ይህን ሻንጣ ክፈተው።
i-bak-ki-hin yi-hin shan-ta ki-fe-tew
Please open this bag.

ለዚህኛው ቀረጥ መክፈል ይኖርብሃል።
lez-zi-hign-gnaw qe-ret mek-fel yi-no-rib-bi-hal
You must pay duty on this.

ለምን ያህል ጊዜ ነው የምትቆየው?
le-min ya-hil gi-ze new yem-mit-qoy-yew?
How long are you staying?

የት ነው የምታርፈው?
yet new yem-mi-tar-few?
Where are you staying?

You Might See

ኢሚግሬሽን
im-mi-gi-re-shin
Immigration

ገቢዎች
ge-bi-woch
Customs

የፓስፖርት ቁጥጥር
ye-pas-port qu-tit-tir
Passport control

ኳራንታይን
kua-ran-ta-yin
Quarantine

ኢትዮጵያውያን
it-yop-ya-wi-yan
Ethiopian citizens

የውጭ ዜጎች
ye-wich ze-goch
Foreigners

ከቀረጥ ነጻ
ke-qe-ret ne-tsa
Duty-Free

የእቃ መረከቢያ
ye-i-qa mer-re-ke-bi-ya
Baggage Claim

ፖሊስ
po-lis
Police

ፍተሻ
fit-te-sha
Security Check

የመንገደኞች መግቢያ
ye-men-ge-degn-gnoch meg-bi-ya
Check-in

I have nothing to declare.
ምንም የማስመዘግበው ነገር የለም።
mi-nim yem-mas-me-zeg-gi-bew ne-ger yel-lem

I'd like to declare . . .
. . . ማስመዝገብ እፈልጋለሁ።
. . . mas-mez-geb i-fel-li-gal-le-hu

That is mine.
የኔ ነው።
ye-ne new

That is not mine.
የኔ አይደለም።
ye-ne ay-del-lem

This is for personal use.
ይሄ ለግል መገልገያ የሚውል ነው።
yi-he le-gil meg-gel-ge-ya yem-mi-wil new

This is a gift.
ይሄ ስጦታ ነው።
yi-he si-to-ta new

Here is my . . .
ይኸው . . .
yi-khew . . .

- **boarding pass** የመሳፈሪያ ቅጼ ye-mes-sa-fe-ri-ya qi-tse
- **ID** መታወቂያዬ met-ta-we-qi-ya-ye
- **passport** ፓስፖርቴ pas-por-te
- **ticket** ትኬቴ tik-ke-te
- **visa** ቪዛዬ vi-za-ye

I'm with a group.
በቡድን ነው የመጣነው።
be-bu-din new ye-met-ta-new

I'm on my own.
በግሌ ነው የመጣሁት።
be-gil-le new ye-met-ta-hut

Buying Tickets

Where can I buy a . . . ticket?
የ . . . ትኬት የት ማግኘት እችላለሁ?
ye . . . tik-ket yet ma-gign-gnet e-chi-lal-le-hu?

bus አውቶቡስ aw-to-bus
plane አውሮፕላን aw-rop-pi-lan
train ባቡር ba-bur
subway ሰብዌይ (መሿለኪያ) seb-wey (mesh-shua-le-ki-ya)

one-way አንዴ ጉዞ an-de gu-zo
round-trip ደርሶ መልስ der-so mels

first class አንደኛ ማዕረግ an-degn-gna ma-i-reg
economy class ሁለተኛ ማዕረግ hu-let-tegn-gna ma-i-reg
business class ሶስተኛ ማዕረግ sos-tegn-gna ma-i-reg

A ticket to . . . please.
እባክህን የ . . . ትኬት።
i-bak-ki-hin ye . . . tik-ket

How much?
ስንት ነው?
sint new?

One ticket, please.
እባክህን አንድ ትኬት።
i-bak-ki-hin and tik-ket

Two tickets, please.
እባክህን ሁለት ትኬት።
i-bak-ki-hin hu-let tik-ket

Is there a discount for . . .?
ለ . . . ቅናሽ አለ?
le . . . qin-nash yi-no-ral?

children ልጆች li-joch
senior citizens አዛውንት ዜጎች a-za-wint ze-goch
students ተማሪዎች te-ma-ri-woch
tourists ጎብኚዎች gob-gni-woch

You Might See

የትኬት መስኮት
ye-tik-ket mes-kot
Ticket Window

የተያዙ ቦታዎች
yet-te-ya-zu bo-ta-woch
Reservations

Can I buy a ticket on the . . .?
. . . ላይ ትኬት መግዛት እችላለሁ?
. . . lay tik-ket meg-zat i-chi-lal-le-hu?

bus አውቶቡሱ aw-to-bu-su
train ባቡሩ ba-bu-ru
subway ሰብዌዩ ውስጥ seb-we-yu wist
boat ጀልባው jel-baw

I'd like to leave . . .
. . . መውጣት እፈልጋለሁ።
. . . mew-tat i-fel-li-gal-le-hu

I'd like to arrive . . .
. . . መግባት እፈልጋለሁ።
. . . meg-bat i-fel-li-gal-le-hu

today ዛሬ za-re
tomorrow ነገ ne-ge
next week በሚቀጥለው ሳምንት bem-mi-qet-ti-lew sam-mint
in the morning ጧት ላይ tuat lay
in the afternoon ከሰዓት በኋላ ke-se-at be-hua-la
in the evening አመሻሽ ላይ a-me-shash lay
late at night ማታ አምሽቼ ma-ta am-shich-che

I have an e-ticket.
ኢትኬት ይዣለሁ።
i-tik-ket yizh-zhal-le-hu

Do I need to stamp the ticket?
ትኬቱን ማሳተም ይኖርብኝ ይሆን?
tik-ke-tun ma-sat-tem yi-no-rib-bign yi-hon?

How long is this ticket valid for?
ለምን ያህል ጊዜ ነው ይህ ትኬት የሚያገለግለው?
le-men ya-hil gi-ze new yih tik-ket yem-mi-ya-ge-leg-gi-lew?

I'd like to . . . my reservation.
ያስያዝኩትን ቦታ . . . እፈልጋለሁ።
yas-yaz-ku-tin bo-ta . . . i-fel-li-gal-le-hu

change መለወጥ me-lew-wet
cancel መሰረዝ me-ser-rez
confirm ማረጋገጥ mar-re-ga-get

Traveling by Airplane

When is the next flight to . . .?
ቀጣዩ የ . . . በረራ መቼ ነው?
qet-ta-yu ye . . . be-re-ra mech new?

Is there a bus/train to the airport?
ወደ አየር ማረፊያው የሚያደርስ የከተማ አውቶቡስ/ባቡር አለ?
we-de ay-yer ma-re-fi-yaw yem-mi-ya-ders ye-ke-te-ma aw-to-bus/ba-bur al-le?

How much is a taxi to the airport?
ወደ አየር ማረፊያው የሚያደርስ ታክሲ ምን ያህል ያስከፍላል?
we-de ay-yer ma-re-fi-yaw yem-mi-ya-ders tak-si min ya-hil yas-kef-fi-lal?

Airport, please.
እባክህን ወደ አየር ማረፊያ።
i-bak-ki-hin we-de ay-yer ma-re-fi-ya

My airline is . . .
አየር መንገዴ . . . ነው።
ay-yer men-ge-de . . . new

My flight leaves at . . .
በረራዬ የሚነሳው. . . ላይ ነው።
be-re-ra-ye yem-min-nes-saw . . . lay new

My flight number is . . .
የበረራ ቁጥሬ . . . ነው።
ye-be-re-ra qut-re . . . new

What terminal?
ተርሚናል ቁጥር ስንት?
ter-mi-nal qu-tir sint?

What gate?
መግቢያ በር ቁጥር ስንት?
meg-bi-ya ber qu-tir sint?

Where is the check-in desk?
የመንገደኞች መግቢያ ዴስኩ በየት ነው?
ye-men-ge-degn-gnoch meg-bi-ya des-ku be-yet new?

My name is . . .
. . . እባላለሁ።
. . . ib-ba-lal-le-hu

I'm going to . . .
ወደ . . . ልሄድ ነው።
we-de . . . li-hed new

Is there a connecting flight?
አገናኝ በረራ ይኖር ይሆን?
ag-ge-nagn be-re-ra yi-nor yi-hon?

How long is the layover?
የመቆሚያ ጊዜው ምን ያህል ይረዝማል?
ye-me-qo-mi-ya gi-zew min ya-hil yi-rez-mal?

You Might See

የመንገደኞች መግቢያ
ye-men-ge-degn-gnoch meg-bi-ya
Check-in

ኢትኬት የያዙ መንገደኞ መግቢያ
i-tik-ket ye-ya-zu men-ge-degn-gnoch meg-bi-ya
E-ticket check-in

የመሳፈሪያ ቅጽ **ye-mes-sa-fe-ri-ya qits** Boarding pass

መሳፈሪያ **mes-sa-fe-ri-ya** Boarding

ደህንነት **deh-nin-net** Security

እቃ መረከቢያ **i-qa mer-re-ke-bi-ya** Baggage Claim

አለም አቀፍ **a-lem aq-qef** International

አገር ውስጥ **a-ger wist** Domestic

መድረሻ **med-re-sha** Arrivals

መነሻ **men-ne-sha** Departures

አገናኝ **ag-ge-nagn** Connections

I'd like a/an . . . flight.
. . . በረራ ቢሆንልኝ እወዳለሁ።
. . . be-re-ra bi-ho-nil-lign i-wed-dal-le-hu

direct ቀጥታ qet-ti-ta
connecting አገናኝ ag-ge-nagn
overnight ሰዓት እላፊ se-at il-la-fi

I have . . .
. . . ይዣለሁ።
. . . yizh-zhal-le-hu

one suitcase አንድ ሻንጣ and shan-ta
two suitcases ሁለት ሻንጣዎች hu-let shan-ta-woch

one carry-on item
አንድ በጅ የሚንጠለጠል እቃ
and bejj yem-min-te-let-tel e-qa

two carry-on items
ሁለት በጅ የሚንጠለጠሉ እቃዎች
hu-let bejj yem-min-te-let-te-lu e-qa-woch

Do I have to check this bag?
ይህን ሻንጣ ከፍቼ ማየት ይኖርብኝ ይሆን?
yi-hin shan-ta ke-fi-che ma-yet yi-no-rib-bign yi-hon?

How much luggage is allowed?
ምን ያህል እቃ መያዝ ይፈቀዳል?
min ya-hil i-qa me-yaz yif-feq-qe-dal?

Can you seat us together?
አንድ ላይ ልታስቀምጠን ትችላለህ?
and lay lit-tas-qem-mi-ten ti-chi-lal-leh?

You Might Hear

ቀጣይ!
qet-tay!
Next!

የበረራ ቁጥር . . .
ye-be-re-ra qu-tir . . .
Flight number . . .

በር ቁጥር . . .
berr qu-tir . . .
Gate number . . .

እባክዎ ፓስፖርትዎን/ የመሳፈሪያ ቅጽዎን።
e-bak-wo pas-por-ti-won/ye-mes-sa-fe-ri-ya qits-won
Your passport/boarding pass, please.

በኪሶችዎ የያዙትን ያውጡ።
be-ki-soch-chi-wo ye-ya-zu-tin yaw-tu
Empty your pockets.

ጫማዎትን ያውልቁ።
cham-ma-wo-tin yaw-li-qu
Take off your shoes.

ማንኛውንም ብረት ነክ ቁሳቁስ ትሪው ላይ ያድርጉ።
man-nign-gna-wu-nim bi-ret nekk qu-sa-qus ti-riw lay ya-dir-gu
Place all metal items in the tray.

አሁን በመሳፈር ላይ የሚገኘው በረራ ቁጥር . . .
a-hun be-mes-sa-fer lay yem-mig-gegn-gnew be-re-ra qu-tir . . .
Now boarding flight number . . .

I'd like a/an . . . seat.
የ . . . ወንበር ባገኝ እወዳለሁ።
ye . . . wen-ber ga-gegn i-wed-dal-le-hu

window መስኮት አጠገብ mes-kot a-te-geb
aisle መተላለፊያ met-te-la-le-fi-ya
exit row መውጫ ረድፍ mew-cha redf

Is the flight . . .?
በረራው . . .?
be-re-raw . . . ?

on time ሰዓቱን የጠበቀ ነው se-a-tun ye-teb-be-qe new
delayed ዘግይቷል zeg-yi-tual
cancelled ተሰርዟል te-ser-ri-zual

Where is the baggage claim?
እቃ መረከቢያው ስፍራ በየት ነው?
i-qa mer-re-ke-bi-yaw sif-ra be-yet new?

I've lost my luggage.
እቃዬ ጠፍቶኛል።
i-qa-ye tef-togn-gnal

My luggage has been stolen.
እቃዬ ተሰርቋል።
i-qa-ye te-ser-qual

My suitcase is damaged.
ሻንጣዬ ጉዳት ደርሶበታል።
shan-ta-ye gu-dat der-sob-be-tal

Traveling by Train

Which line goes to . . . Station?
የትኛው መስመር ነው ወደ . . . ጣቢያ የሚሄደው?
ye-tign-gnaw mes-mer new we-de . . . ta-bi-ya yem-mi-he-dew?

Is it direct?
ዘላቂ ነው?
ze-la-qi new?

Is it a local train?
የከተማ ውስጥ ባቡር ነው?
ye-ke-te-ma wust ba-bur new?

Is it an express train?
አገር አቋራጭ ባቡር ነው?
a-ger aq-qua-rach ba-bur new?

I'd like to take the bullet/high-speed train.
ተወንጫፊውን/ እጅግ ፈጣኑን ባቡር ብይዝ እወዳለሁ።
te-wen-cha-fi-wun/ej-jig fet-ta-nun ba-bur bi-yiz i-wed-dal-le-hu

Do I have to change trains?
ባቡር መለወጥ ይኖርብኝ ይሆን?
ba-bur me-le-wet yi-no-rib-bign yi-hon?

Can I have a schedule?
መነሻና መድረሻውን የሚገልጽ ፕሮግራም ማግኘት እችላለሁ?
men-ne-sha-na med-re-sha-wun yem-mi-gelts pi-rog-ram ma-gign-gnet i-chi-lal-le-hu?

When is the last train back?
የመጨረሻው ባቡር የሚመለሰው መቼ ነው?
ye-me-cher-re-shaw ba-bur yem-mim-mel-le-sew me-che new?

Which track?
የትኛው መስመር?
ye-tign-gnaw mes-mer?

Where is track . . .?
መስመር . . . የት ነው?
mes-mer . . . yet new?

Where is/are the . . .?
. . . ወዴት ነው?
. . . we-det new?

dining car
መመገቢያ መኪናው
mem-me-ge-bi-ya me-ki-naw

information desk
የመረጃ ዴስኩ
ye-mer-re-ja des-ku

luggage lockers
የእቃ ማስቀመጫ ሳጥኑ
ye-i-qa mas-qem-me-cha sa-ti-nu

reservations desk
የቦታ ማስያዣ ዴስኩ
ye-bo-ta mas-ya-zha des-ku

ticket machine
የቲኬት ማሽኑ
ye-tik-ket ma-shi-nu

ticket office
የቲኬት ቢሮው
ye-tik-ket bi-row

waiting room
የእንግዳ ማረፊያው
ye-en-gi-da ma-re-fi-yaw

This is my seat.
ይህ የኔ ወንበር ነው።
yih ye-ne wen-ber new

Here is my ticket.
ይኸው ቲኬቴ።
yi-khew tik-ke-te

Can I change seats?
ወንበር መቀየር እችላለሁ?
wen-ber me-qey-yer e-chi-lal-le-hu?

What station is this?
ይህ ጣቢያ ማነው?
yih ta-bi-ya man-new?

What is the next station?
ቀጣዩ ጣቢያ ማነው?
qet-ta-yu ta-bi-ya man-new?

Does this train stop at . . .?
ይህ ባቡር . . . ላይ ይቆማል?
. . . lay yi-qo-mal?

Traveling by Bus

Where is the nearest bus stop?
በቅርብ ያለው የአውቶቡስ ማቆሚያ የት ጋር ነው?
be-qirb yal-lew ye-aw-to-bus ma-qo-mi-ya yet gar new?

Which . . .?
የትኛው . . . ?
ye-tign-gnaw . . .?

gate በር berr
line መስመር mes-mer
station ጣቢያ ta-bi-ya
stop ማቆሚያ ma-qo-mi-ya

Can I have a bus map?
የከተማ አውቶቡስ ካርታ ማግኘት እችላለሁ?
ye-ke-te-ma aw-to-bus kar-ta ma-gign-gnet e-chi-lal-le-hu?

You Might See

አውቶቡስ ማቆሚያ
aw-to-bus ma-qo-mi-ya
Bus Stop

መግቢያ
meg-bi-ya
Entrance

መውጫ
mew-cha
Exit

How far is it?
ምን ያህል ይርቃል?
min ya-hil yi-ri-qal?

Where are we?
የት ደረስን?
yet der-re-sin?

How do I get to . . .?
እንዴት ነው ወደ . . . መሄድ የምችለው?
in-det new we-de . . . me-hed yem-mi-chi-lew?

Which bus do I take for . . .?
ወደ . . . የትኛውን አውቶቡስ ልያዝ?
we-de . . . ye-tign-gna-wun aw-to-bus li-yaz?

Is this the bus to . . .?
ወደ . . . የሚያደርሰው አውቶቡስ ይህኛው ነው?
we-de . . . yem-mi-ya-der-sew aw-to-bus yi-hign-gnaw new?

When is the . . . bus to . . .?
. . . ወደ . . . የሚያደርሰው አውቶቡስ መነሻው መች ነው?
. . . we-de . . . yem-mi-ya-der-sew aw-to-bus men-ne-shaw mech new?

first የመጀመሪያው ye-me-jem-me-ri-yaw
next ቀጣዩ qet-ta-yu
last የመጨረሻው ye-me-cher-re-shaw

Do I have to change buses?
አውቶቡስ መቀየር ይኖርብኝ ይሆን?
aw-to-bus me-qey-yer yi-no-rib-bign yi-hon?

Where do I transfer?
መስመር የምቀይረው የት ነው?
mes-mer yem-mi-qey-yi-rew yet new?

Can you tell me when to get off?
መች እንደምወርድ ልትጠቁመኝ ትችላለህ?
mech in-dem-mi-werd lit-teq-qu-megn ti-chi-lal-leh?

How many stops to . . .?
. . . ድረስ ስንት ማቆሚያዎች አሉ?
. . . di-res sint ma-qo-mi-ya-woch al-lu?

Next stop, please!
እባክዎ ቀጣዩ ማቆሚያ!
i-bak-ki-wo qet-ta-yu ma-qo-mi-ya!

Stop here, please!
እባክዎ እዚህ ጋር ያቁሙልኝ!
i-bak-ki-wo iz-zih gar ya-qu-mul-lign!

Traveling by Taxi

Taxi! ታክሲ! tak-si!

Where can I get a taxi?
ታክሲ የት ጋር ማግኘት እችላለሁ?
tak-si yet gar ma-gign-gnet i-chi-lal-le-hu?

Can you call a taxi?
ታክሲ መጥራት ትችላለህ?
tak-si met-rat ti-chi-lal-leh?

I'd like a taxi now.
አሁን ታክሲ ባገኝ እወዳለሁ።
a-hun tak-si ba-gegn i-wed-dal-le-hu

I'd like a taxi in an hour.
በአንድ ሰዓት ውስጥ ታክሲ ባገኝ እወዳለሁ።
be-and se-at wust tak-si ba-gegn i-wed-dal-le-hu

Pick me up at . . .
. . . መጥተህ ውሰደኝ።
. . . met-teh wi-se-degn

Take me to . . .
ወደ . . . አድርሰኝ።
we-de . . . a-dir-segn

this address እዚህ አድራሻ iz-zih ad-rash-sha
the airport አየር ማረፊያው ay-yer ma-re-fi-yaw
the train station ባቡር ጣቢያው ba-bur ta-bi-yaw
the bus station አውቶቡስ መናኻሪያው aw-to-bus men-na-kha-ri-yaw

Can you take a different route?
ሌላ መንገድ ይዘህ ልትሔድ ትችላለህ?
le-la men-ged yi-zeh lit-hed ti-chi-lal-leh?

Can you drive faster?
ፈጠን ልትል ትችላለህ?
fe-ten lit-til ti-chi-lal-leh?

Can you drive slower?
ዝግ ልትል ትችላለህ?
zigg lit-til ti-chi-lal-leh?

Stop here.
እዚህ ጋር አቁም።
iz-zih gar a-qum

Wait here.
እዚህ ጋር ጠብቅ።
iz-zih gar teb-biq

How much will it cost?
ሒሳብ ምን ያህል ነው?
hi-sab min ya-hil new?

You said it would cost . . .
ዋጋው . . . ያህል ይሆናል አልከኝ።
wa-gaw . . . ya-hil yi-ho-nal al-kegn

Keep the change.
መልሱን ያዘው።
mel-sun ya-zew

Traveling by Car

Renting a Car

Where is the car rental?
መኪና ማከራያው ምኑ ጋር ነው?
me-ki-na mak-ke-ra-yaw mi-nu gar new?

I have an international driver's license.
አለም አቀፍ መንጃ ፈቃድ አለኝ።
a-lem aq-qef men-ja fe-qad al-legn

I don't have an international driver's license.
አለም አቀፍ መንጃ ፈቃድ የለኝም።
a-lem aq-qef men-ja fe-qad yel-legn-gnim

I'd like (a/an) . . .
. . . ባገኝ እወዳለሁ።
. . . ba-gegn i-wed-dal-le-hu

cheap car ረከስ ያለ መኪና re-kess ya-le me-ki-na
compact car እጥር ምጥን ያለ መኪና it-tir mit-tin ya-le me-ki-na
SUV ኤስ ዩ ቪ es yu vi
van ቫን van

motorcycle ሞተር ሳይክል mo-ter say-kil
scooter እስኩተር is-ku-ter

automatic transmission አውቶማቲክ ማርሽ aw-to-ma-tik marsh
manual transmission ማኑዋል ማርሽ ma-nu-wal marsh

air conditioning ኤሲ ያለው e-si yal-lew
child seat የልጅ ወንበር ያለው ye-lij wen-ber yal-lew

How much does it cost . . .?
ኪራዩ . . . ምን ያህል ነው?
ki-ra-yu . . . min ya-hil new?

per day በቀን be-qen
per week በሳምንት be-sam-mint
per kilometer በኪሎ ሜትር be-ki-lo me-tir
per mile በማይል be-ma-yil
for unlimited mileage ላልተገደበ ርቀት lal-te-ged-de-be ri-qet
with full insurance ከሙሉ ዋስትና ጋር ke-mu-lu was-tin-na gar

You Might Hear

ማስያዣ እፈልጋለሁ።
mas-ya-zha e-fel-li-gal-le-hu
I'll need a deposit.

ስም እዚህ ጋር።
sim iz-zih gar
Inital here.

ፊርማ እዚህ ጋር።
fir-ma iz-zih gar
Sign here.

What kind of fuel does it use?
ምን አይነት ነዳጅ ነው የሚጠቀመው?
min ay-net ne-daj new yem-mit-teq-qe-mew?

Are there any discounts?
የዋጋ ቅናሽ ይኖራል?
ye-wa-ga qin-nash yi-no-ral?

I don't need it until . . .
እስከ . . . አልፈልገውም።
is-ke . . . al-fel-li-ge-wum

Monday ሰኞ segn-gno
Tuesday ማክሰኞ mak-segn-gno
Wednesday ረቡዕ re-bu-i
Thursday ሐሙስ ha-mus
Friday አርብ arb
Saturday ቅዳሜ qi-da-me
Sunday እሁድ i-hud

Fuel and Repairs

Where's the gas station?
ነዳጅ ማደያው ምኑ ጋር ነው?
ne-daj mad-de-yaw mi-nu gar new?

Fill it up.
ሙሉ አድርገው።
mu-lu a-dir-gew

I need . . .
. . . እፈልጋለሁ።
. . . i-fel-li-gal-le-hu

gas ነዳጅ ne-daj
leaded የተቀላቀለ yet-te-qe-laq-qe-le
unleaded ያልተቀላቀለ yal-te-qe-laq-qe-le

regular ቤንዚን ben-zin
super ሱፐር sup-per
premium ፕሪምየም pi-rim-yem
diesel ናፍታ naf-ta

You Might See

የራስ መስተንግዶ
ye-ras mes-ten-gi-do
self-service

የተሟላ መስተንግዶ
yet-te-mual-la mes-ten-gi-do
full-service

Check the . . .
. . . ሞክር።
. . . mok-kir

battery ባትሪውን bat-ri-win
brakes ፍሬኖቹን fi-re-noch-chun
headlights የግንባር መብራቶቹን ye-gen-bar meb-ra-toch-chun
oil ዘይቱን ze-yi-tun
radiator ራዲያተሩን ra-di-ya-te-run
tail lights የኋላ መብራቶቹን ye-hua-la meb-ra-toch-chun
tires ጎማዎቹን gom-ma-woch-chun
transmission ማርሹን mar-shun

I need a . . .
. . . እፈልጋለሁ።
. . . i-fel-li-gal-le-hu

jumper cables ባትሪ ማስነሻ ሽቦ bat-ri mas-nesh-sha shi-bo
mechanic መካኒክ me-ka-nik
tow truck ጎታች መኪና got-tach me-ki-na

The car broke down.
መኪናው ተበላሸ።
me-ki-naw te-be-lash-she

The car won't start.
መኪናው አልነሳም አለ።
me-ki-naw a-lin-nes-sam a-le

I ran out of gas.
ነዳጅ አለቀብኝ።
ne-daj al-le-qeb-bign

I have a flat tire.
ጎማ ተኛብኝ።
gom-ma tegn-gnab-bign

Can you fix the car?
መኪናውን ልታስተካክለው ትችላለህ?
me-ki-na-win lit-tas-te-kak-ki-lew ti-chi-lal-leh?

When will it be ready?
መች ያልቃል?
mech yal-qal?

Driving Around

Can I park here?
እዚህ ማቆም እችላለሁ?
iz-zih ma-qom e-chi-lal-le-hu?

Where's the parking lot/garage?
መኪና ማቆሚያው/ ጋራዡ በየት ነው?
me-ki-na ma-qo-mi-yaw/ga-ra-zhu be-yet new?

How much does it cost?
ዋጋው ምን ያህል ነው?
wa-gaw min ya-hil new?

Is parking free?
ማቆሚያ በነጻ ነው?
ma-qo-mi-ya be-ne-tsa new?

What's the speed limit?
የፍጥነት ገደቡ ምን ያህል ነው?
ye-fit-net ge-de-bu min ya-hil new?

How much is the toll?
የክፍያ መንገዱ ዋጋ ምን ያህል ነው?
ye-ki-fiy-ya men-ge-du wa-ga min ya-hil new?

Can I turn here?
እዚህ ጋር ማዞር እችላለሁ?
iz-zih gar ma-zor i-chi-lal-le-hu?

There's been an accident.
አደጋ ተከስቶ ነበር።
a-de-ga te-kes-si-to neb-ber

You Might See

ቁም	አሳልፍ	አትግባ
qum	**a-sal-lif**	**at-tig-ba**
Stop	Yield	Do Not Enter

አንድ አቅጣጫ መንገድ
and aq-tach-cha men-ged
One Way

የፍጥነት ገደብ
ye-fit-net ge-deb
Speed Limit

Call the police.
ለፖሊስ ይደውሉ።
le-po-lis yid-de-wel

Call an ambulance.
አምቡላንስ ይጠራ።
am-bu-lans yit-te-ra

My car has been stolen.
መኪናዬን ተሰርቄያለሁ።
me-ki-na-yen te-se-riq-qe-yal-le-hu

My license plate number is . . .
የመኪናዬ ሰሌዳ ቁጥር . . . ነው።
ye-me-ki-na-ye se-le-da qu-tir . . . new

Can I have your insurance information?
የዋስትና መረጃህን ልትሰጠኝ ትችላለህ?
ye-was-tin-na mer-re-ja-hin lit-se-tegn ti-chi-lal-leh?

Getting Directions

Excuse me, please!
ይቅርታ፣ እባክዎ!
yi-qir-ta i-bak-ki-wo!

Can you help me?
ልትረዳኝ ትችላለህ?
lit-re-dagn ti-chi-lal-leh?

Is this the way to . . .?
ወደ . . . የሚወስደው መንገድ ይህ ነው?
we-de . . . yem-mi-wes-dew men-ged yih new?

How far is it to . . .?
. . . ድረስ ምን ያህል ይርቃል?
. . . di-res min ya-hil yi-ri-qal?

Is this the right road to . . .?
ወደ . . . ለመሄድ ትክክለኛው መንገድ ይህ ነው?
we-de . . . le-me-hed ti-kik-ki-legn-gnaw men-ged yih new?

How much longer until we get to . . .?
. . . ለመድረስ ምን ያህል ይቀራል?
le-med-res min ya-hil yi-qe-ral?

Where's . . .?
. . . በየት ነው?
. . . be-yet new?

. . . Street . . . ጎዳና . . . go-da-na
this address ይህ አድራሻ yih ad-rash-sha
the highway አውራ ጎዳናው aw-ra go-da-naw
the downtown area መሃል ከተማው አካባቢ me-hal ke-te-maw ak-ka-ba-bi

Where am I?
የት ነው ያለሁት?
yet new yal-le-hut?

I'm lost.
ጠፍቶኛል።
tef-togn-gnal

You Might Hear

. . . ያዝ . . . **yaz** Take . . .

ድልድዩን **dil-di-yun** the bridge

መውጫውን **mew-cha-win** the exit

አውራ ጎዳናውን **aw-ra go-da-na-win** the highway

ማዞሪያ ደሴቱን (አደባባይ) **ma-zo-ri-ya des-se-tun (ad-de-ba-bay)** the traffic circle

የዋሻውን መንገድ **ye-wash-sha-win men-ged** the tunnel

XX ጎዳና/አደባባይ **XX go-da-na/ad-de-ba-bay** XX Street/Avenue

ቀጥ ብለህ ሂድ።
qet bi-leh hid
Go straight ahead.

ወደ ቀኝ ታጠፍ።
we-de qegn ta-tef
Turn right.

ወደ ግራ ታጠፍ።
we-de gi-ra ta-tef
Turn left.

ከጎዳናው ባሻገር
ke-go-da-naw bash-shag-ger
across the street

እዚሁ ቅርብ
iz-zi-hu qirb
around the corner

ቀጥሎ ባለው መገናኛ
qet-ti-lo bal-lew meg-ge-na-gna
at the next intersection

ቀጥሎ ባለው ትራፊክ መብራት
qet-ti-lo bal-lew ti-ra-fik meb-rat
at the next traffic light

Can you show me on the map?
ካርታው ላይ ልታመለክተኝ ትችላለህ?
kar-taw lay lit-ta-me-lek-ki-tegn ti-chi-lal-leh?

Do you have a road map?
የመንገድ ካርታ ይዘሃል?
ye-men-ged kar-ta yi-ze-hal?

How do I get to . . .?
ወደ . . . እንዴት መድረስ እችላለሁ?
we-de . . . in-det med-res e-chi-lal-le-hu?

How long does it take . . .?
. . . ምን ያህል ጊዜ ይወስዳል?
. . . min ya-hil gi-ze yi-wes-dal?

on foot በእግር be-i-gir
by car በመኪና be-me-ki-na
using public transportation በህዝብ መጓጓዣ be-hizb meg-gua-gua-zha

You Might Hear

ወደፊት **we-de-fit** forward
ወደኋላ **we-de-hua-la** backward
ፊት ለፊት **fit le-fit** in front (of)
ከጀርባ **ke-jer-ba** behind
አጠገብ **a-te-geb** next to

በፊት **be-fit** before
በኋላ **be-hua-la** after
ቅርብ **qirb** near
ሩቅ **ruq** far

ሰሜን **se-men** north
ደቡብ **de-bub** south
ምስራቅ **mis-raq** east
ምዕራብ **mi-i-rab** west

ACCOMMODATIONS

Where is the nearest . . .?
ቅርቡ . . . የት ጋር ነው?
qir-bu . . . yet gar new?

Can you recommend a/an. . .?
ጥሩ . . . ልትጠቁመኝ ትችላለህ?
ti-ru . . . lit-teq-qu-megn ti-chi-lal-leh?

hotel ሆቴል ho-tel
inn ትንሽ ምግብ ቤት tin-nish mi-gib bet
bed-and-breakfast አልጋና ቁርስ ቤት al-gan-na qurs bet
motel ሞቴል mo-tel
guesthouse የእንግዳ ማረፊያ ye-in-gi-da ma-re-fi-ya
(youth) hostel (የወጣቶች) ክበብ (ye-wet-ta-toch) ki-beb

I'm looking for . . . accommodations.
. . . መስተንግዶ የማገኝበት ስፍራ እየፈለኩ ነው።
. . . mes-ten-gi-do yem-ma-gegn-gnib-bet sif-ra iy-ye-fel-lek-ku new

inexpensive ውድ ያልሆነ widd yal-ho-ne
luxurious የተንደላቀቀ yet-ten-de-laq-qe-qe
traditional ባህላዊ ba-hi-la-wi
clean ንጽህናው የተጠበቀ ni-tsi-hin-naw ye-teb-be-qe
conveniently located አማካይ ቦታ ላይ ያለ am-ma-kay bo-ta lay yal-le

Is there English-speaking staff?
እንግሊዝኛ የሚችል ሰራተኛ አለ እንዴ?
in-gi-li-zign-gna yem-mi-chil ser-ra-tegn-gna al-le in-de?

You Might See

ክፍት የስራ ቦታ አለ
kift ye-si-ra bo-ta al-le
Vacancy

ክፍት የስራ ቦታ የለም
kift ye-si-ra bo-ta yel-lem
No Vacancy

Booking a Room and Checking In

I have a reservation under . . .
. . . በሚል የተያዘ ክፍል ነበረኝ።
. . . bem-mil yet-te-ya-ze ki-fil neb-be-regn

I don't have a reservation.
ቀድሜ ያስያዝኩት ክፍል የለም።
qe-dim-me yas-yaz-kut ki-fil yel-lem

Do you have any rooms available?
ክፍል ይኖራችሁ ይሆን?
ki-fil yi-no-rach-chi-hu yi-hon?

I'd like a room for tonight.
ለዛሬ አዳር ክፍል ባገኝ እወዳለሁ።
le-za-re a-dar ki-fil ba-gegn i-wed-dal-le-hu

Can I make a reservation?
ቅድሚያ ቦታ ማስያዝ እችላለሁ?
qid-mi-ya bo-ta mas-yaz i-chi-lal-le-hu?

I'd like to reserve a room . . . for XX nights
. . . ክፍል ለ XX ቀናት ቅድሚያ ማስያዝ እፈልጋለሁ።
. . . ki-fil le XX qe-nat qid-mi-ya mas-yaz i-fel-li-gal-le-hu

for one person
ለአንድ ሰው የሚሆን
le-and sew yem-mi-hon

for two people
ለሁለት ሰዎች የሚሆን
le-hu-lett se-woch yem-mi-hon

with a queen-size bed
ባለትልቅ አልጋ
ba-le-til-liq al-ga

with two beds
ባለሁለት አልጋ
ba-le hu-lett al-ga

How much is it?
ዋጋው ምን ያህል ነው?
wa-gaw min ya-hil new?

How much is it per night/person?
ዋጋው በቀን/ በሰው ምን ያህል ነው?
wa-gaw be-qen/be-sew min ya-hil new?

Is breakfast included?
ቁርስን ያካትታል?
qur-sin yak-kat-ti-tal?

Does that include sales tax (VAT)?
ተእታን ጨምሮ ነው?
te-i-tan chem-mi-ro new?

Can I pay by credit card?
በክሬዲት ካርድ መክፈል እችላለሁ?
be-ki-re-dit kard mek-fel i-chi-lal-le-hu?

Do you have (a/an) . . .?
. . . አላችሁ እንዴ?
. . . al-lach-chi-hu in-de?

air conditioning ኤሲ e-si
business center የንግድ ማዕከል ye-nigd ma-i-kel
cots የሸራ አልጋዎች ye-she-ra al-ga-woch
crib የህጻናት አልጋ ye-hi-tsa-nat
elevator አሳንሰር a-san-ser
gym ጂም jim
hot water ሙቅ ውሃ muq wi-ha
kitchen ማድቤት mad-bet
laundry service የልብስ ንጽህና መስጫ ye-libs ni-tsi-hin-na mes-cha
linens የአልጋ ልብስ ye-al-ga libs
microwave ማይክሮዌቭ may-ki-ro-wev
non-smoking rooms ሲጋራ የማይጨስባቸው ክፍሎች si-ga-ra yem-ma-yich-che-sib-bach-chew kif-loch
phones ስልክ silk
pool መዋኛ ገንዳ me-wa-gna gen-da
private bathrooms የግል መታጠቢያ ክፍሎች ye-gill met-ta-te-bi-ya kif-loch
restaurant ምግብ ቤት mi-gib bet
room service የክፍል ውስጥ መስተንግዶ ye-ki-fil mes-ten-gi-do
safe ካዝና kaz-na
television ቴሌቪዥን te-le-vi-zhin
towels ፎጣዎች fo-ta-woch
wireless Internet ገመድ አልባ ኢንተርኔት ge-med al-ba in-ter-net

Is there a curfew?
ሰዓት እላፊ አለ?
se-at il-la-fi al-le?

When is check-in?
የሚገባው መቼ ነው?
yem-mig-geb-baw mech new?

May I see the room?
ክፍሉን ማየት እችላለሁ?
kif-lun ma-yet i-chi-lal-le-hu?

Do you have anything . . .?
ከዚህ . . . ያለ ቦታ ይኖራችኋል?
kez-zih . . . ya-le bo-ta yi-no-rach-chi-hual?

bigger ይበልጥ ሰፋ yi-belt se-fa
cleaner ይበልጥ ጸዳ yi-belt tse-da
quieter ይበልጥ ጸጥ yi-belt tsett
less expensive ዋጋው አነስ ያለ wa-gaw a-ness ya-le

I'll take it.
ይሁንልኝ።
yi-hu-nil-lign

Is the room ready?
ክፍሉ ተዘጋጅቷል?
kif-lu te-ze-gaj-toal?

When will the room be ready?
መች ነው ክፍሉ ዝግጁ የሚሆነው?
mech new kif-lu zi-gij-ju yem-mi-ho-new?

At the Hotel

room number ክፍል ቁጥር ki-fil qu-tir
floor ፎቅ foq
room key የክፍል ቁልፍ ye-ki-fil qulf

Where is the . . .?
. . . ምኑ ጋር ነው?
. . . mi-nu gar new?

bar ባሩ ba-ru

bathroom መታጠቢያው met-ta-te-bi-yaw

convenience store መደብሩ me-deb-bi-ru

dining room መመገቢያ አዳራሹ mem-me-ge-bi-ya ad-da-ra-shu

drugstore / pharmacy መድሐኒት ቤቱ / ፋርማሲው med-ha-nit be-tu / far-ma-siw

elevator አሳንሰሩ a-san-se-ru

information desk የመረጃ ዴስኩ ye-mer-re-ja des-ku

lobby መተላለፊያው met-te-la-le-fi-yaw

pool መዋኛ ገንዳው me-wa-gna gen-daw

restaurant ምግብ ቤቱ mi-gib be-tu

shower ገላ መታጠቢያው ge-la met-ta-te-bi-yaw

Can I have (a) . . .?
. . . ማግኘት እችላለሁ?
. . . ma-gign-gnet i-chi-lal-le-hu?

another room key ሌላ የክፍል ቁልፍ le-la ye-ki-fil qulf

blanket ብርድልብስ bir-di-libs

clean sheets ንጹህ አንሶላ ni-tsuh an-so-la

pillow ትራስ ti-ras

plug for the bath ለመታጠቢያ ቤቱ ሶኬት le-met-ta-te-bi-ya be-tu sok-ket

soap ሳሙና sa-mu-na

toilet paper የመጸዳጃ ወረቀት ye-me-tse-da-ja we-re-qet

towels ፎጣዎች fo-ta-woch

wake-up call at . . . የመንቂያ ደወል . . . ላይ ye-men-qi-ya de-wel . . . lay

I would like to place these items in the safe.
እነዚህን ቁሳቁሶች ካዝናው ውስጥ ማስቀመጥ እፈልጋለሁ።
in-nez-zi-hin qu-sa-qu-soch kaz-naw wist mas-qem-met i-fel-li-gal-le-hu

I would like to retrieve my items from the safe.
ቁሳቁሶቼን ከካዝናው ማውጣት እፈልጋለሁ።
qu-sa-qu-soch-chen ke-kaz-naw maw-tat i-fel-li-gal-le-hu

Can I stay an extra night?
ለአንድ ተጨማሪ ምሽት መቆየት እችላለሁ?
le-and te-chem-ma-ri mish-shit me-qoy-yet i-chi-lal-le-hu

There's a problem with the room.
ክፍሉ አንዳች ችግር አለበት።
kif-lu an-dach chig-gir al-leb-bet

The . . . doesn't work.
. . . አይሰራም።
. . . ay-se-ram

air conditioning ኤሲው e-siw
door lock የበሩ መቀርቀሪያ ye-ber-ru me-qer-qe-ri-ya
hot water ሙቅ ውሃው miq wi-haw
shower ሻወሩ sha-we-ru
sink መታጠቢያ ሳህኑ met-ta-te-bi-ya sa-hi-nu
toilet መጸዳጃ ቤቱ me-tse-da-ja be-tu

The lights won't turn on.
መብራቶቹ አይበሩም።
meb-ra-to-chu ay-be-rum

The room has bugs/mice.
ክፍሉ ተባይ አለበት።
kif-lu te-bay al-leb-bet

The . . . aren't clean.
. . . ንጹህ አይደሉም።
. . . ni-tsuh ay-del-lum

pillows ትራሶቹ ti-ra-soch-chu
sheets አንሶላዎቹ an-so-la-woch-chu
towels ፎጣዎቹ fo-ta-woch-chu

The room is too noisy.
ክፍሉ በሁካታ የተሞላ ነው።
kif-lu be-hu-ka-ta yet-te-mol-la new

I've lost my key.
ቁልፌ ጠፍቶብኛል።
qul-fe tef-tob-bi-gnal

I've locked myself out.
በሩ ተዘግቶብኛል።
be-ru te-zeg-tob-bi-gnal

Checking Out of a Hotel

When is check-out?
የሚለቀቀው መቸ ነው?
yem-mil-leq-qe-qew mech new?

When is the earliest I can check out?
ቀደም ብዬ ልወጣ የምችልበት ጊዜ መቸ ነው?
qe-dem biy-ye li-we-ta yem-mi-chi-lib-bet gi-ze mech new?

When is the latest I can check out?
የመጨረሻ ዘግይቼ ልወጣ የምችልበት ጊዜ መቸ ነው?
ye-me-cher-re-sha zeg-yich-che li-we-ta yem-mi-chi-lib-bet gi-ze mech new?

Can I leave my bags here until . . .?
እስከ . . . ድረስ ሻንጣዎቼን እዚህ ላስቀምጣቸው እችላለሁ?
is-ke . . . di-res shan-ta-woch-chen iz-zih las-qem-mi-tach-chew i-chi-lal-le-hu?

I would like to check out.
ለቅቄ መውጣት እፈልጋለሁ።
le-qiq-qe mew-tat i-fel-li-gal-le-hu

I would like a receipt.
ደረሰኝ እፈልጋለሁ።
der-re-segn i-fel-li-gal-le-hu

I would like an itemized bill.
በዝርዝር የተዘጋጀ የሂሳብ መክፈያ እፈልጋለሁ።
be-zir-zir yet-te-ze-gaj-je ye-hi-sab maw-we-ra-re-ja i-fel-li-gal-le-hu

There's a mistake on this bill.
ይህ ሂሳብ ስህተት አለበት።
yih hi-sab si-hi-tet al-leb-bet

Please take this off the bill.
እባክህን ይህን ከሂሳብ አውጣው።
i-bak-ki-hin yi-hin ke-hi-sab aw-taw

The total is incorrect.
ድምሩ ትክክል አይደለም።
dim-mi-ru ti-kik-kil ay-del-lem

I would like to pay . . .
. . . መክፈል እፈልጋለሁ።
. . . mek-fel i-fel-li-gal-le-hu

by credit card በክሬዲት ካርድ be-ki-re-dit kard
by traveler's check በመንገደኛ ቼክ be-men-ge-de-gna chek
in cash በጥሬ be-ti-re

Renting Accommodations

I'd like to rent (a/an) . . .
. . . መከራየት እፈልጋለሁ።
. . . mek-ke-ra-yet i-fel-li-gal-le-hu

apartment አፓርታማ ap-par-ta-ma
house ቤት bet
room ክፍል ki-fil

How much is it per week?
ዋጋው በሳምንት ምን ያህል ነው?
wa-gaw be-sam-mint min ya-hil new?

I intend to stay for XX months
XX ወራት ለመቆየት አስቤያለሁ።
XX we-rat le-me-qoy-yet as-sib-be-yal-le-hu

Is it furnished?
እቃ ተሟልቶለታል?
i-qa te-mual-tol-le-tal?

Does it have/include (a/an) . . .?
. . . አሉት/ አለው?
. . . al-lut/al-lew?

cooking utensils ብረት ድስቶች bi-ret dis-toch
dishes ሳህኖች sa-hi-noch
dryer ማድረቂያ mad-re-qi-ya
kitchen ማድቤት mad-bet
linens የአልጋ ልብሶች ye-al-ga lib-soch
towels ፎጣዎች fo-ta-woch
washing machine ማጠቢያ ማሽን ma-te-bi-ya ma-shin

Do you require a deposit?
ማስያዣ ገንዘብ ያስፈልጋል?
mas-ya-zha gen-zeb yas-fel-li-gal?

When is the rent due?
የኪራይ መክፈያው ቀን መቼ ነው?
ye-ki-ray mek-fe-yaw qen mech new?

Who is the superintendent?
ተቆጣጣሪው ማን ነው?
te-qo-ta-ta-riw man new?

Who should I contact for repairs?
ጥገና ሲያስፈልግ ማንን ነው የማነጋግረው?
tig-ge-na si-yas-fel-lig man-nin new yem-man-nag-gi-rew?

Camping and the Outdoors

Can I camp here?
እዚህ ጋር ድንኳን ልተክል እችላለሁ?
iz-zih gar din-kuan li-te-kil i-chi-lal-le-hu?

Where should I park?
መኪና የት ላቁም?
me-ki-na yet la-qum?

Do you have . . . for rent?
የሚከራይ . . . አላችሁ?
yem-mik-ke-ray . . . al-lach-chi-hu?

campsite ድንኳን መትከያ ቦታ din-kuan met-ke-ya bo-ta
cooking equipment የወጥቤት ቁሳቁስ ye-wet-bet qu-sa-qus
sleeping bags ባለዚፕ ብርድልብሶች ba-le-zip bir-di-lib-soch
tents ድንኳኖች din-kua-noch

Do you have . . .
. . . አላችሁ?
. . . al-lach-chi-hu?

electricity ኮረንቲ kor-ren-ti
laundry facilities የልብስ ንጽህና መስጫ ye-libs ni-tsi-hin-na mes-cha
showers ገላ መታጠቢያ ge-la met-ta-te-bi-ya

How much is it per . . .?
ዋጋው በ . . . ምን ያህል ነው?
wa-gaw be . . . min ya-hil new?

lot ቦታ bo-ta
person ሰው sew
night አዳር a-dar

Are there . . . that I should be careful of?
ልጠነቀቃቸው የሚገባኝ . . . አሉ?
lit-te-neq-qe-qach-chew yem-mig-geb-bagn . . . al-lu?

animals እንስሳት in-si-sat
insects ነፍሳት nef-sat
plants እጽዋት its-wat

DINING OUT

Meals

breakfast ቁርስ qurs
brunch ቁምሳ qum-sa
lunch ምሳ mi-sa
dinner ራት rat

snack መቆያ me-qoy-ya
dessert ማጣጣሚያ mat-ta-ta-mi-ya

Types of Restaurants

bar ቡና ቤት bun-na bet
bistro አነስተኛ ምግብ ቤት a-nes-tegn-gna mi-gib bet
buffet ቡፌ bu-fe
café ሻይ ቤት shay bet
fast food restaurant ፈጣን ምግቦች መሸጫ fet-tan mig-boch me-she-cha
halal restaurant የሙስሊም ምግብ ቤት ye-mus-lim mi-gib bet
kosher restaurant የአይሁድ ምግብ ቤት ye-ay-hud mi-gib bet
pizzeria ፒዛ ቤት pi-za bet
restaurant ምግብ ቤት mi-gib bet
snack bar ስናክ ባር si-nak bar
steakhouse ጥብስ ቤት tibs bet
teahouse ሻይ ቤት shay bet
vegan restaurant አትክልት ቤት a-ti-kilt bet
vegetarian restaurant የአትክልት ተመጋቢዎች ምግብ ቤት ye-a-ti-kilt te-meg-ga-bi-woch mi-gib bet

Can you recommend a/an . . .?
. . . ሊትጠቁመኝ ትችላለህ?
. . . lit-teq-qu-megn ti-chi-lal-leh?

good restaurant ጥሩ ምግብ ቤት ti-ru mi-gib bet
restaurant with local dishes ባህላዊ ምግቦች የሚገኙበት ምግብ ቤት ba-hi-la-wi mig-boch yem-mig-gegn-gnib-bet mi-gib bet
inexpensive restaurant ዋጋው ተመጣጣኝ ምግብ ቤት wa-gaw te-me-ta-tagn mi-gib bet
popular bar የታወቀ ቡና ቤት yet-taw-we-qe bun-na bet

Reservations and Getting a Table

I have a reservation for . . .
ለ . . . ቅድሚያ ቦታ አስይዣለሁ።
le . . . qid-mi-ya bo-ta as-yizh-zhal-le-hu

The reservation is under . . .
የተያዘው ቦታ . . . በሚል ነው።
yet-te-ya-zew bo-ta . . . bem-mil new

I'd like to reserve a table for . . .
ለ . . . ወንበር ቅድሚያ ማስያዝ እፈልጋለሁ?
le . . . wen-ber qid-mi-ya mas-yaz e-fel-li-gal-le-hu

Can we sit . . .?
. . . ልንቀመጥ እንችላለን?
. . . lin-niq-qem-met en-chi-lal-len?

over here እዚህ ጋ iz-zih ga
over there እዚያ ጋ iz-zi-ya ga
by a window መስኮት ጋ mes-kot ga
outside ውጪ ላይ wi-chi lay

in a non-smoking area ሲጋራ የማይጨስበት ቦታ ላይ
si-ga-ra yem-ma-yich-che-sib-bet bo-ta lay

How long is the wait?
ወረፋው ምን ያህል ነው?
we-re-faw min ya-hil new?

Ordering at a Restaurant

It's for here.
እዚሁ የምጠቀመው።
iz-zi-hu yem-mit-teq-qe-mew

It's to go.
ይዤ የምሄደው።
yizh-zhe yem-mi-he-dew

Waiter! / Waitress!
አስተናጋጅ!
as-te-na-gaj!

Excuse me!
ይቅርታ አድርግልኝ!
yi-qir-ta a-dir-gil-lign!

I'd like to order.
ማዘዝ እፈልጋለሁ።
ma-zez i-fel-li-gal-le-hu

Can I have a . . . please?
እባክህን . . . ማግኘት እችላለሁ?
i-bak-ki-hin . . . ma-gign-gnet i-chi-lal-le-hu?

menu ሜኑ me-nu
wine list የወይን ዝርዝር ye-we-yin zir-zir
drink menu የመጠጥ ሜኑ ye-me-tet me-nu
children's menu የልጆች ሜኑ ye-li-joch me-nu

Do you have a menu in English?
የእንግሊዝኛ ሜኑ ይኖራችኋል?
ye-in-gi-li-zign-gna me-nu yi-no-ra-chi-hual?

Do you have a set/fixed price menu?
ዋጋው የተገለጸበት ሜኑ ይኖራችኋል?
wa-ga yet-te-gel-le-tseb-bet me-nu yi-no-ra-chi-hual?

What are the specials?
ልዩ ምግቦቻችሁ ምን ምን ናቸው?
liy-yu mig-boch-chach-chi-hu min min nach-chew?

Do you have . . .?
. . . ይኖራችኋል?
. . . yi-no-ra-chi-hual?

Can you recommend some local dishes?
የተወሰኑ ባህላዊ ምግቦችን ልትጠቁመኝ ትችላለህ?
yet-te-wes-se-nu ba-hi-la-wi mig-boch-chin lit-teq-qu-megn ti-chi-lal-leh?

What do you recommend?
ምን ትመርጥልኛለህ?
min ti-mer-til-lign-gnal-leh?

What's this?
ይህ ምንድን ነው?
yih min-din new?

What's in this?
ይህ ምን ምን አለው?
yih min min al-lew?

Is it . . .?
. . . ነው?
. . . new?

bitter ኮምጣጣ kom-tat-ta
spicy ቅመም የበዛበት qi-mem ye-bez-zab-bet
sweet ጣፋጭ ta-fach

hot ትኩስ tik-kus
cold ቀዝቃዛ qez-qaz-za

Do you have any vegetarian dishes?
ለአትክልት ተመጋቢዎች የሚሆን ምግብ አለ?
le-a-ti-kilt te-meg-ga-bi-woch yem-mi-hon mi-gib al-le?

I'd like it with . . .
. . . ያለው ቢሆን ደስ ይለኛል።
. . . yal-lew bi-hon dess yi-legn-gnal

I'd like it without . . .
. . . የሌለው ቢሆን ደስ ይለኛል።
. . . ye-lel-lew bi-hon dess yi-legn-gnal

Are there any drink specials?
ልዩ መጠጦች አሉ?
liy-yu me-tet-toch al-lu?

I'll have . . .
. . . ይሁንልኝ።
. . . yi-hu-nil-lign

Can I have a . . .?
. . . ማግኘት እችላለሁ?
. . . ma-gign-gnet i-chi-lal-le-hu?

glass of . . . አንድ ብርጭቆ . . . and bir-chiq-qo . . .
bottle of . . . አንድ ጠርሙስ . . . and ter-mus . . .
pitcher of . . . አንድ ማንቆርቆሪያ . . . and man-qor-qo-ri-ya . . .

I'd like a bottle of . . .
አንድ ጠርሙስ . . . እፈልጋለሁ።
and ter-mus . . . i-fel-li-gal-le-hu

red wine ቀይ ወይን qey we-yin
white wine ነጭ ወይን nech we-yin
rosé wine ሮዝ ወይን roz we-yin
house wine የቤት ወይን ye-bet we-yin
dessert wine ማጣጣሚያ ወይን mat-ta-ta-mi-ya we-yin
dry wine ደረቅ ወይን de-req we-yin
champagne ሻምፓኝ sham-pagn

A light beer, please.
እባክህን ቀላል ቢራ።
i-bak-ki-hin qel-lal bi-ra

A dark beer, please.
እባክህን ጥቁር ቢራ።
i-bak-ki-hin ti-qur bi-ra

Special Dietary Needs

I'm on a special diet.
ልዩ ዳየት ላይ ነኝ።
liy-yu da-yet lay negn

Is this dish free of animal product?
ይህ ማዕድ ከእንስሳት ተዋጽኦ የጸዳ ነው?
yih ma-id ke-in-si-sat te-wa-tsi-o ye-tsed-da new?

I'm allergic to . . .
ለ . . . አለርጂክ ነኝ።
le . . . a-ler-jik negn

I can't eat . . .
. . . ልመገብ አልችልም።
. . . lim-meg-geb al-chi-lim

dairy የወተት ውጤቶች ye-we-tet wit-te-toch
eggs እንቁላል in-qu-lal
gelatin ጀላቲን je-la-tin
gluten ግሉተን gi-lu-ten
meat ስጋ si-ga
MSG ኤም ኤስ ጂ em es ji
nuts ለውዝ lewz
peanuts ኦቾሎኒ och-cho-lo-ni
seafood የባህር ምግቦች ye-ba-hir mig-boch
spicy foods ቅመም የበዛበት ምግብ qi-mem ye-bez-zab-bet mi-gib
wheat ስንዴ sin-de

I'm diabetic.
ስኳር አለብኝ።
sik-kuar al-leb-bign

Do you have any sugar-free products?
ከስኳር ነጻ የሆኑ ምርቶች አሏችሁ?
ke-sik-kuar ne-tsa ye-ho-nu mir-toch al-luach-chi-hu?

Do you have any artificial sweeteners?
ሰው ሰራሽ ማጣፈጫዎች አሏችሁ?
sew ser-rash ma-ta-fe-cha-woch al-luach-chi-hu?

I'm vegan/vegetarian.
አትክልት ተመጋቢ ነኝ።
a-ti-kilt te-meg-ga-bi negn

Complaints at a Restaurant

This isn't what I ordered.
ይህን አይደለም ያዘዝኩት።
yi-hin ay-del-lem yaz-zez-kut

I ordered . . .
ያዘዝኩት . . . ነው።
yaz-zez-kut . . . new

I cannot eat this.
ይህን ልበላ አልችልም።
yi-hin li-be-la al-chi-lim

This is . . .
ይህ . . . ።
yih . . .

cold ቀዝቅዟል qez-qi-zual
undercooked አልበሰለም al-bes-se-lem
overcooked አሯል ar-rual
spoiled ተበላሽቷል te-be-lash-tual

not fresh ትኩስ አይደለም tik-kus ay-del-lem
too spicy ቅመም በዝቶበታል qi-mem bez-tob-be-tal
too tough ገንትሯል gen-ti-rual
not vegetarian ለአትክልት ተመጋቢ የሚሆን አይደለም
le-a-ti-kilt te-meg-ga-bi yem-mi-hon ay-del-lem

Can you take it back, please?
እባክህን ልትመልሰው ትችላለህ?
i-bak-ki-hin lit-mel-li-sew ti-chi-lal-leh?

How much longer until we get our food?
ምግባችን እስኪደርስ ምን ያህል ይቆያል?
mig-bach-chin is-ki-ders min ya-hil yi-qoy-yal?

We cannot wait any longer.
ከዚህ በላይ ልንጠብቅ አንችልም።
kez-zih be-lay lin-teb-biq an-chi-limm

We're leaving.
መውጣታችን ነው።
mew-ta-tach-chin new

Paying at a Restaurant

Check, please!
እባክህን ደረሰኝ!
i-bk-ki-hin der-re-segn!

We'd like to pay separately.
ለየብቻ መክፈል እንፈልጋለን።
ley-ye-bich-cha mek-fel in-fel-li-gal-len

Can we have separate checks?
ደረሰኝ ለየብቻ ልናገኝ እንችላለን?
der-re-segn ley-ye-bich-cha lin-na-gegn in-chi-lal-len?

We're paying together.
በጋራ ነው የምንከፍለው።
be-ga-ra new yem-min-kef-lew

Is service included?
አገልግሎትም ተካቷል?
a-gel-gi-lo-timm te-kat-toal?

What is this charge for?
ይህኛው ክፍያ ለምንድን ነው?
yi-hign-gnaw ki-fiy-ya le-min-din new?

There is a mistake in this bill.
ይህ ቢል ስህተት አለበት።
yih bil sih-tet al-leb-bet

I didn't order that.
ይህን አላዘዝኩም።
yi-hin a-laz-zez-kum

I ordered . . .
. . . አዝዣለሁ።
. . . a-zizh-zhal-le-hu

Can I have a receipt, please?
እባክህን ደረሰኝ ማግኘት እችላለሁ?
i-bak-ki-hin der-re-segn ma-gign-gnet i-chi-lal-le-hu?

Can I have an itemized bill, please?
ዝርዝር የያዘ ቢል ማግኘት እችላለሁ?
zir-zir ye-ya-ze bil ma-gign-gnet i-chi-lal-le-hu?

It was delicious!
ጣፋጭ ነበር!
ta-fach neb-ber!

FOOD & DRINK

Cooking Methods

baked የተጠበሰ yet-te-teb-be-se
boiled የተቀቀለ yet-te-qeq-qe-le
braised በመጠኑ የተጠበሰ be-me-te-nu yet-te-teb-be-se
breaded የተጋገረ yet-te-gag-ge-re
creamed ክሬም የተቀባ ki-rem yet-te-qeb-ba
diced በማዕዘን የተቆረጠ be-ma-e-zen yet-te-qor-re-te
filleted አጥንቱ የወጣለት a-tin-tu ye-wet-tal-let
grilled ግሪል ላይ የተጠበሰ gi-ril lay yet-te-teb-be-se
microwaved በማይክሮዌቭ የሞቀ be-may-ki-ro-wev ye-mo-qe
poached የተቋጠረ yet-te-quat-te-re
re-heated መልሶ የተሞቀ mel-li-so yet-te-mo-qe
roasted አሩስቶ ar-rus-to
sautéed በዘይት የተጠበሰ be-ze-yit yet-te-teb-be-se
smoked በጭስ የበሰለ be-chis ye-bes-se-le
steamed በእንፋሎት የተጋገረ be-en-fa-lot yet-te-gag-ge-re
stewed ወጥ የተሰራ wet yet-te-ser-ra
stir-fried ተገላብጦ የተጠበሰ te-ge-lab-to yet-te-bes-se-le
stuffed ውስጥ የተሞላ wust yet-te-mol-la
toasted የተጠበሰ yet-te-teb-be-se

rare ለብለብ leb-bi-lebb
medium rare ገባ ያለ ge-ba ya-le
well-done የበሰለ ye-bes-se-le

on the side በጎን የሚቀርብ be-gon yem-mi-qerb

Tastes

bitter ኮምጣጣ kom-tat-ta
bland ቅመም የሌለው qi-mem ye-lel-lew
salty ጨዋማ che-wam-ma
sour መራራ me-ra-ra
spicy ቅመም የበዛበት qi-mem ye-bez-zab-bet
sweet ጣፋጭ ta-fach

Dietary Terms

decaffeinated ካፊን አልባ ka-fin al-ba
free-range በተፈጥሮ የተጣለ (እንቁላል) be-te-fet-ro yet-te-ta-le (en-qu-lal)
genetically modified በዘረመል የተቀነባበረ be-ze-re-mel yet-te-qe-ne-bab-be-re
gluten-free ከግሉቲን ነጻ ke-gi-lo-tin ne-tsa
kosher የአይሁድ ye-ay-hud
low-fat ስብ ያልበዛበት sib yal-bez-zab-bet
low in cholesterol ዝቅተኛ ኮሌስትሮል ziq-qi-tegn-gna ko-les-ti-rol
low in sugar ዝቅተኛ ስኳር ziq-qi-tegn-gna sik-kuar
organic የተፈጥሮ ye-te-fet-ro
salt-free ከጨው ነጻ ke-chew ne-tsa
vegan ለአትክልት ተመጋቢ le-a-ti-kilt te-meg-ga-bi
vegetarian ለአትክልት ተመጋቢ le-a-ti-kilt te-meg-ga-bi

Breakfast Foods

bacon በጨው የታሸ ያሳማ ስጋ be-chew yet-tash-she ya-sa-ma si-ga
bread ዳቦ dab-bo
butter ቅቤ qi-be
cereal ጥራጥሬ ti-ra-ti-re
cheese አይብ a-yib
eggs እንቁላል in-qu-lal
granola ግራኖላ gi-ra-no-la
honey ማር mar
jam ጃም jam
jelly ቅባት qi-bat
omelet ኦምሌት om-let
sausage ቋሊማ qua-li-ma
yogurt እርጎ ir-go

Vegetables አትክልት a-ti-kilt

asparagus አስፓራገስ as-pa-ra-ges
avocado አቩካዶ a-vu-ka-do
beans ባቄላ ba-qe-la
broccoli ጥቅል ጎመን ti-qill gom-men
cabbage ጎመን gom-men
carrot ካሮት ka-rot
cauliflower ጥቅል ጎመን ti-qill gom-men
celery ሴለሪ se-le-ri
chickpeas ሽምብራ shim-bi-ra
corn በቆሎ beq-qol-lo
cucumber ከከምበር ke-kem-ber
eggplant ብሪንጃል bi-rin-jal

garlic ነጭ ሽንኩርት nech shin-kurt
lentils ምስር mis-sir
lettuce ሰላጣ se-la-ta
mushrooms እንጉዳይ en-gu-day
okra ኦክራ ok-ra
olives የወይራ ፍሬ ye-wey-ra fi-re
onion ሽንኩርት shin-kurt
peas አተር a-ter
pepper ቃሪያ qa-ri-ya
potato ድንች din-nich
radish ራዲሽ ra-dish
spinach ቆስጣ qos-ta
sweet potato ስኳር ድንች sik-kuar din-nich
tomato ቲማቲም ti-ma-tim

Fruits and Nuts ፍራፍሬና ጥራጥሬ fi-ra-fi-ren-na ti-ra-ti-re

apricot አፕሪኮት ap-ri-kot
apple ፖም pom
banana ሙዝ muz
blueberry ኢጋም a-gam
cashew አደንጓሬ a-den-guar-re
cherry በለስ be-les
clementine ፍሬ የሌለው መንደሪን fi-re ye-lel-lew men-de-rin
coconut ኮኮናት ko-ko-nat
date ቴምር te-mir
fig በለስ be-les
grape ወይን we-yin
grapefruit የወይን ፍሬ ye-we-yin fi-re

lemon ሎሚ lo-mi
lime ኮምጣጤ kom-tat-te
mandarin መንደሪን men-de-rin
melon ሃብሃብ hab-hab
orange ብርቱካን bir-tu-kan
peanut ኦቾሎኒ och-cho-lo-ni
peach ኮክ kok
pear ፕሪም pi-rim
pineapple አናናስ a-na-nas
plum ኮክ kok
pomegranate ፖም pom
raspberry እንኮይ in-koy
strawberry እንጆሪ in-jor-ri
tangerine መንደሪን men-de-rin
walnut ትሪንጎ ti-rin-go
watermelon ሃብሃብ hab-hab

Meats የስጋ አይነት ye-si-ga ay-net

beef የበሬ ስጋ ye-be-re si-ga
burger በርገር ber-ger
chicken ዶሮ do-ro
duck ዳክዬ dak-kiy-ye
goat ፍየል fiy-yel
ham የአሳማ ስጋ ye-a-sa-ma si-ga
lamb የበግ ስጋ ye-beg si-ga
pork የአሳማ ስጋ ye-a-sa-ma si-ga
rabbit ጥንቸል tin-chel
steak ጥብስ tibs
turkey ተርኪ ter-ki
veal የጥጃ ስጋ ye-tij-ja si-ga

Seafood የባህር ምግብ ye-ba-hil mi-gib

calamari ካላማሪ ka-la-ma-ri
clams ሞለስክ mo-lesk
crab ክራብ ki-rab
fish ዓሳ a-sa
lobster ሎብስተር lo-bis-ter
mussels ሙሰል mu-sel
octopus ኦክቶፐስ ok-to-pus
salmon ሳልመን sal-men
shrimp ሽሪምፕ shi-rimp

Desserts ማጣጣሚያ mat-ta-ta-mi-ya

cake ኬክ kek
cookie ኩኪስ ku-kis
ice cream አይስ ክሬም ays ki-rem
pastries ኬኮች ke-koch
pie ፓይ pay
pudding ፐዲንግ pe-ding
whipped cream የተመታ ክሬም yet-te-met-ta ki-rem

Drinks መጠጦች me-tet-toch

Non-alcoholic drinks

apple juice የፖም ጭማቂ ye-pom chim-ma-qi
coffee (black) ቡና (ጥቁር) bun-na (ti-qur)
coffee with milk ቡና በወተት bun-na be-we-tet
hot chocolate ትኩስ ቼኮሌት tik-kus chek-ko-let
lemonade ሎሚ lo-mi
milk ወተት we-tet

mineral water የማዕድን ውሃ ye-ma-id-din wi-ha
orange juice የብርቱካን ጭማቂ ye-bir-tu-kan chim-ma-qi
sparkling water አምቦ ውሃ am-bo wi-ha
soda / soft drink ለስላሳ les-las-sa
soymilk ሶይ ወተት soy we-tet
tea ሻይ shay
water ውሃ wi-ha

Alcoholic drinks

beer ቢራ bi-ra
  bottled beer የጠርሙስ ቢራ ye-ter-mus bi-ra
  canned beer የቆርቆሮ ቢራ ye-qor-qo-ro bi-ra
  draft beer ድራፍት di-raft
brandy ብራንዲ bi-ran-di
champagne ሻምፓኝ sham-pagn
cocktail ኮክቴል kok-tel
gin ጂን jin
liqueur አልኮል al-kol
margarita ማርጋሪታ mar-ga-ri-ta
martini ማርቲኒ mar-ti-ni
rum ሪም rem
scotch ስካች es-kach
tequila ቲኪላ ti-ki-la
vermouth ቨርሙዝ ver-muz
vodka ቮድካ vod-ka
whiskey ዊስኪ wis-ki
wine ወይን we-yin
  dessert wine ማጣጣሚያ ወይን mat-ta-ta-mi-ya we-yin
  dry wine ደረቅ ወይን de-req we-yin
  red wine ቀይ ወይን qeyy we-yin
  rosé wine ሮዝ ወይን roz we-yin
  white wine ነጭ ወይን nech we-yin

Grocery Shopping

Where is the nearest market/supermarket?
በቅርብ ያለው ገበያ/ ሱፐርማርኬት ወዴት ነው?
be-qirb yal-lew ge-be-ya/sup-per-mar-ket we-det new?

Where are the baskets/carts?
ዘንቢሎቹ/ ጋሪዎቹ የት አሉ?
zen-bi-lo-chu/gar-ri-wo-chu yet al-lu?

I'd like some of this/that.
ከእነዚህ/ ከእነዚያ የተወሰኑትን እፈልጋለሁ።
ke-in-nez-zih/ke-in-nez-zi-ya yet-te-wes-se-nu-tin
i-fel-li-gal-le-hu

Can I have (a) . . .?
. . . ማግኘት እችላለሁ?
. . . ma-gign-gnet i-chi-lal-le-hu?

(half) kilo of . . . ግማሽ ኪሎ . . . gim-mash ki-lo . . .
liter of . . . አንድ ሊትር . . . and li-tir . . .
piece of . . . አንድ ፍሬ . . . and fi-re . . .
two pieces of . . . ሁለት ፍሬ . . . hu-let fi-re . . .
little more ትንሽ ጨመር tin-nish chem-mer
little less ትንሽ ቀነስ tin-nish qen-nes

Can I have a little of . . . please?
እባክህ ትንሽ . . . ማግኘት እችላለሁ?
i-bak-ki-hin tin-nish . . . ma-gign-gnet i-chi-lal-le-hu?

Can I have a lot of . . . please?
እባክህን በርከት ያለ . . . ማግኘት እችላለሁ?
i-bak-ki-hin ber-kett ya-le . . . ma-gign-gnet i-chi-lal-le-hu?

That's enough, thanks.
ይበቃኛል፣ አመሰግናለሁ።
yi-be-qagn-gnal a-me-seg-gi-nal-le-hu

Where can I find . . .?
. . . የት ማግኘት እችላለሁ?
. . . yet ma-gign-gnet i-chi-lal-le-hu?

cleaning products የጽዳት ምርቶች ye-tsi-dat mir-toch
dairy products የወተት ውጤቶች ye-we-tet wit-te-toch
deli section የአይብና የስጋ ሱቅ ye-ayb-na ye-si-ga suq
fresh produce ትኩስ ምርት tik-kus mirt
fresh fish ትኩስ አሳ tik-kus a-sa
frozen foods የቀዘቀዙ ምግቦች ye-qe-zeq-qe-zu mig-boch
household goods የቤት ቁሳቁስ ye-bet qu-sa-qus
meats ስጋ si-ga
poultry ዶሮ do-ro

I need to go to the . . .
ወደ . . . መሄድ ይኖርብኛል።
we-de . . . me-hed yi-no-rib-bign-gnal

bakery ዳቦ ቤት dab-bo bet
butcher shop ልኳንዳ li-kuan-da
convenience store መደብር me-deb-bir
fish market ዓሳ መሸጫ a-sa me-she-cha
produce market እህል ተራ i-hil te-ra
supermarket ሱፐርማርኬት sup-per-mar-ket

You Might See

በ . . . ይሸጥ።
be . . . yish-shet
Sell by . . .

ማቀዝቀዣ ውስጥ ይቀመጥ
ma-qez-qe-zha wist yiq-qe-met
Keep refrigerated

ከተከፈተ በኋላ በ . . . ውስጥ ይበላ።
ket-te-kef-fe-te be-hua-la be . . . qe-nat wist yib-be-la
Eat within . . . days of opening.

ከመጠቀምህ በፊት መልሰህ አሙቀው።
ke-met-te-qe-mih be-fit mel-li-she a-mu-qew
Reheat before consuming.

ለአትክልት ተመጋቢዎች ተስማሚ
le-a-ti-kilt te-meg-ga-bi-woch tes-ma-mi
Suitable for vegetarians

በማይክሮዌቭ ሊሞቅ የሚችል
be-may-ki-ro-wev lim-moq yem-mi-chil
microwaveable

የአይሁድ **ye-ay-hud** kosher

የተፈጥሮ **ye-te-fet-ro** organic

Paying for Groceries

Where is the checkout?
መውጫው በየት በኩል ነው?
mew-chaw be-yet bek-kul new?

Do I pay here?
እዚህ ጋር እከፍላለሁ?
iz-zih gar i-kef-lal-le-hu?

Do you accept credit cards?
ክሬዲት ካርድ ትቀበላላችሁ?
ki-re-dit kard tiq-qeb-be-lal-lach-chi-hu?

I'll pay in cash.
በጥሬው እከፍላለሁ።
be-ti-rew i-kef-lal-le-hu

I'll pay by credit card.
በክሬዲት ካርድ እከፍላለሁ።
be-ki-re-dit kard i-kef-lal-le-hu

Paper, please.
እባክህን፣ ካኪ።
i-bak-ki-hin ka-ki

Plastic, please.
እባክህን፣ ፌስታል።
i-bak-ki-hin fes-tal

I don't need a bag.
መያዣ አያስፈልገኝም።
me-ya-zha a-yas-fel-li-gegn-gnim

I have my own bag.
የራሴ መያዣ አለኝ።
ye-ra-se me-ya-zha al-legn

MONEY & BANKING

Where can I exchange money?
ገንዘብ መመንዘር የምችለው የት ነው?
gen-zeb me-men-zer yem-mi-chi-lew yet new?

Is there a currency exchange office nearby?
የውጭ ምንዛሬ ቢሮ በአቅራቢያ ይገኛል?
ye-wi-chi mi-niz-za-re bi-ro be-aq-rab-bi-ya yig-gegn-gnal?

I'd like to exchange . . . for . . .
. . . ወደ . . . መመንዘር እፈልጋለሁ።
we-de . . . me-men-zer i-fel-li-gal-le-hu

US dollars የአሜሪካ ዶላር ye-a-me-ri-ka do-lar
pounds ፓውንድ pa-wind
Canadian dollars የካናዳ ዶላር ye-ka-na-da do-lar
euros ዩሮ yu-ro
traveler's checks የመንገደኛ ቼክ ye-men-ge-de-gna chek
birr ብር birr *(Ethiopian currency)*

What is the exchange rate?
ምንዛሬው ምን ያህል ነው?
mi-niz-za-rew min ya-hil new?

What is the commission change?
የኮሚሽን ክፍያው ምን ያህል ነው?
ye-ko-mi-shin ki-fiy-yaw min ya-hil new?

Can you write that down for me?
ያልከውን ልትጽፍልኝ ትችላለህ?
yal-ke-win lit-tsi-fil-lign ti-chi-lal-leh?

Banking

Is there a bank near here?
እዚህ ቅርብ ባንክ ይገኛል?
iz-zih qirb bank yig-gegn-gnal?

Where is the nearest ATM?
ቅርቡ ኤቲኤም ምኑ ጋር ነው?
qir-bu e-ti-em mi-nu gar new?

What time does the bank open?
ባንኩ የሚከፈተው ስንት ሰዓት ነው?
ban-ku yem-mik-kef-fe-tew sint se-at new?

What time does the bank close?
ባንኩ የሚዘጋው ስንት ሰዓት ነው?
ban-ku yem-miz-zeg-gaw sint se-at new?

Can I cash this check here?
ይህን ቼክ እዚህ መመንዘር እችላለሁ?
yi-hin chek iz-zih me-men-zer i-chi-lal-le-hu?

I would like to get a cash advance.
ቅድሚያ ክፍያ በጥሬው ማግኘት እፈልጋለሁ።
qid-mi-ya ki-fiy-ya be-ti-rew ma-gign-gnet i-fel-li-gal-le-hu

I would like to cash some traveler's checks.
የተወሰኑ የመንገደኛ ቼኮችን መመንዘር እፈልጋለሁ።
yet-te-wes-se-nu ye-men-ge-de-gna che-koch-chin me-men-zer i-fel-li-gal-le-hu

I've lost my traveler's checks.
የመንገደኛ ቼኮቼ ጠፍተውብኛል።
ye-men-ge-de-gna che-koch-che tef-te-wib-bign-gnal

The ATM ate my card.
ኤቲኤሙ ካርዴን ውጦ ዝም አለ።
e-ti-em-mu kar-den wi-to zimm a-le

You Might See at an ATM

ካርድ ያስገቡ **kard yas-geb-bu** insert card
መለያ ቁጥር **mel-le-ya qu-tir** PIN number
ያስገቡ **yas-geb-bu** enter
ያውጡ **yaw-tu** clear
ይሰርዙ **yi-ser-ri-zu** cancel
ተቀማጭ **te-qem-mach** checking
ቁጠባ **qut-te-ba** savings
ወጪ **we-chi** withdrawal
ገቢ **ge-bi** deposit
መቀበያ **meq-qe-be-ya** receipt

SHOPPING

Where's the . . .?
. . . የት ጋር ነው?
. . . yet gar new?

antiques store የጥንት ቁሳቁሶች መደብሩ ye-tint qu-sa-qu-soch me-deb-bi-ru
bakery ዳቦ ቤቱ dab-bo be-tu
bookstore የመጻህፍት መደብሩ ye-me-tsa-hift me-deb-bi-ru
camera store የካሜራ መሸጫው ye-ka-me-ra me-she-chaw
clothing store አልባሳት መደብሩ al-ba-sat me-deb-bi-ru
convenience store መደብሩ me-deb-bi-ru
delicatessen የውጭ አገር ምግቦች መሸጫ መደብሩ ye-wu-chi a-ger mig-boch me-she-cha me-deb-bi-ru
department store ንኡስ መደብር ni-us me-deb-bi-ru
electronics store የኮረንቲ ቁሳቁስ መደብሩ ye-kor-ren-ti qu-sa-qus me-deb-bi-ru
gift shop የስጦታ እቃዎች መሸጫው ye-si-to-ta i-qa-woch me-she-chaw
grocery store የምግብ ሸቀጣ ሸቀጥ ገበያ ye-mi-gib she-qe-ta she-qet ge-be-ya
health food store የጤና አጠባበቅ ምግቦች መሸጫ መደብሩ ye-te-na at-te-ba-beq mig-boch me-she-cha me-deb-bi-ru
jeweler ጌጣጌጥ መሸጫው ge-ta-get me-she-chaw
liquor store የመጠጥ መደብሩ ye-me-tett me-deb-bi-ru
mall ሞሉ mo-lu
market ገበያው ge-be-yaw
music store የሙዚቃ መደብሩ ye-mu-zi-qa me-deb-bi-ru
pastry shop ኬክ ቤቱ kek be-tu
pharmacy መድሐኒት መደብሩ med-ha-nit me-deb-bi-ru

shoe store ጫማ ቤቱ cham-ma be-tu
souvenir store የባህላዊ ቁሳቁስ መደብሩ ye-ba-hi-la-wi qu-sa-qus me-deb-bi-ru
supermarket ሱፐርማርኬቱ sup-per-mar-ke-tu
toy store የአሻንጉሊት መደብሩ ye-a-shan-gul-lit me-deb-bi-ru

Getting Help at a Store

Where's the . . .?
. . . የት አለ?
. . . yet al-le?

cashier ገንዘብ ተቀባዩ gen-zeb te-qeb-ba-yu
escalator ተንቀሳቃሽ ደረጃው ten-qe-sa-qash de-re-jaw
elevator አሳንሰሩ a-san-se-ru
fitting room መሞከሪያ ክፍሉ me-mok-ke-ri-ya kif-lu
store map የመደብሩ ካርታ ye-me-deb-bi-ru kar-ta

Can you help me?
ልትረዳኝ ትችላለህ?
lit-re-dagn ti-chi-lal-leh?

I'm looking for . . .
. . . ፈልጌ ነበር።
. . . fel-lig-ge neb-ber

I would like . . .
. . . እፈልጋለሁ።
. . . i-fel-li-gal-le-hu

Where can I find . . .?
. . . ላገኝ የምችለው የት ነው?
. . . la-gegn yem-mi-chi-lew yet new?

I'm just looking.
ዝም ብዬ እያየሁ ነው።
zim biy-ye iy-yay-ye-hu new

I want something . . .
የሆነ . . . ነገር እፈልጋለሁ።
ye-ho-ne . . . ne-ger i-fel-li-gal-le-hu

big ተለቅ te-leqq **small** አነስ a-ness
cheap ረከስ re-kess **expensive** ወደድ we-dedd
local አገር በቀል a-ger beq-qel
nice ደስ የሚል dess yem-mil

Can you show me that?
ያንን ልታሳየኝ ትችላለህ?
yan-nin lit-ta-say-yegn ti-chi-lal-leh?

Can I see it?
ላየው እችላለሁ?
la-yew i-chi-lal-le-hu?

Is it authentic?
እውነተኛ ነው?
iw-ne-tegn-gna new?

Do you have any others?
ሌሎች አይነቶች አሉህ?
le-loch ay-ne-toch al-luh?

Do you have this in . . .?
ይህኛው በ . . . አለህ?
yi-hign-gnaw be . . . al-leh?

black ጥቁር ti-qur
blue ሰማያዊ se-ma-ya-wi
brown ቡኒ bun-ni
gray ግራጫ gi-rach-cha
green አረንጓዴ a-ren-gua-de
orange ብርቱካናማ bir-tu-ka-nam-ma
pink ሐምራዊ ham-ra-wi
purple ወይነጠጅ wey-ne-tejj
red ቀይ qeyy
white ነጭ nech
yellow ቢጫ bi-cha

Do you have anything lighter?
ነጣ ያለ ነገር ይኖርሃል?
ne-ta ya-le ne-ger yi-no-ri-hal?

Do you have anything darker?
ጠቆር ያለ ነገር ይኖርሃል?
te-qorr ya-le ne-ger yi-no-ri-hal?

That's too expensive.
ይህማ በጣም ውድ ነው።
yi-him-ma be-tam widd new

Do you have anything cheaper?
ረከስ ያለ ነገር ይኖርሃል?
re-kess ya-le ne-ger yi-no-ri-hal?

I can only pay . . .
. . . ብቻ ነው ልከፍል የምችለው።
. . . bich-cha new li-kefl yem-mi-chi-lew

I'll give you . . .
. . . እሰጥሃለሁ።
. . . i-se-ti-hal-le-hu

Is that your best price?
እሱ ነው የመጨረሻ ዋጋህ?
is-su new ye-me-cher-re-sha wa-gah?

Can you give me a discount?
ቅናሽ ልታደርግልኝ ትችላለህ?
qin-nash lit-ta-der-gil-lign ti-chi-lal-leh?

I'll have to think about it.
ላስብበት ይገባል።
las-si-bib-bet yig-geb-bal

That's not quite what I want.
በርግጥ እሱ የፈለግኩት አይነት አይደለም።
ber-git is-su ye-fel-leg-kut ay-net ay-del-lem

I don't like it.
አልወደድኩትም።
al-wed-ded-ku-tim

It's too expensive.
በጣም ውድ ነው።
be-tam widd new

I'll take it.
እወስደዋለሁ።
i-wes-de-wal-le-hu

Can you ship this?
ይህን ልትልክልኝ ትችላለህ?
yi-hin lit-li-kil-lign ti-chi-lal-leh?

Can you wrap this?
ይህን ልትጠቀልልልኝ ትችላለህ?
yi-hin lit-te-qel-li-lil-lign ti-chi-lal-leh?

Paying at a Store

Where can I pay?
የት ጋር ነው ልከፍል የምችለው?
yet gar new li-ke-fil yem-mi-chi-lew?

How much?
ስንት?
sint?

Does the price include tax?
ዋጋው ታክስን ይጨምራል?
wa-gaw tak-sin yi-chem-mi-ral?

I'll pay in cash.
በጥሬው እከፍላለሁ።
be-ti-rew i-kef-lal-le-hu

I'll pay by credit card.
በክሬዲት ካርድ እከፍላለሁ።
be-ki-re-dit kard i-kef-lal-le-hu

Do you accept traveler's checks?
የመንገደኛ ቼኮች ትቀበላላችሁ?
ye-men-ge-de-gna che-koch tiq-qeb-be-lal-lach-chi-hu?

I have a/an . . .
. . . አለኝ።
. . . al-legn

ATM card የኤቲኤም ካርድ ye-e-ti-eam kard
credit card ክሬዲት ካርድ ki-re-dit kard
debit card የብድር ካርድ ye-bid-dir kard
gift card የስጦታ ካርድ ye-si-to-ta kard

Can I have a receipt?
ደረሰኝ ማግኘት እችላለሁ?
der-re-segn ma-gign-gnet i-chi-lal-le-hu?

Complaining at a Store

This is broken.
ይህ ተበላሽቷል።
yih te-be-lash-toal

It doesn't work.
አይሰራም።
ay-se-ram

I'd like . . .
. . . እፈልጋለሁ።
. . . i-fel-li-gal-le-hu

to exchange this ይህን በሌላ መለወጥ yi-hin be-le-la me-lew-wet
to return this ይህን መመለስ yi-hin me-mel-les

a refund ገንዘቤ እንዲመለስልኝ gen-ze-be en-dim-mel-le-sil-lign

to speak to the manager ማናጀሩን ማናገር ma-na-je-run man-na-ger

Grocery Shopping. *See page 210*

Pharmacy. *See page 266*

SERVICES

bank ባንክ bank
barber ጸጉር አስተካካይ tse-gur as-te-ka-kay
dry cleaner የንፋስ ማጸጃ ye-ni-fas mats-ja
hair salon የጸጉር ሳሎን ye-tse-gur sa-lon
laundromat ላውንድሮማት la-win-di-ro-mat
nail salon የጥፍር ሳሎን ye-ti-fir sa-lon
spa እስፓ is-pa
travel agency የጉዞ ወኪል ye-gu-zo we-kil

At the Hair Salon / Barber

I'd like a . . .
. . . እፈልጋለሁ።
. . . i-fel-li-gal-le-hu

color ቀለም መቀባት qe-lem meq-qe-bat
cut መስተካከል mes-te-ka-kel
perm ፐርም መቀባት perm meq-qe-bat
shave መላጨት mel-la-chet
trim መከርከም mek-ker-kem

Cut about this much off.
ይህን ያህል ቆርጠህ አስተካክለው።
yi-hin ya-hil qor-teh as-te-ka-ki-lew

Can I have a shampoo?
በሻምፑ መታጠብ እችላለሁ?
be-sham-pu met-ta-teb e-chi-lal-le-hu

Cut it shorter here.
እዚህ ጋር አጠር አርገህ ቁረጠው።
iz-zih gar a-terr ar-geh qu-re-tew

Leave it longer here.
እዚህ ጋር ረዘም አርገህ ተወው።
iz-zih gar re-zemm ar-geh te-wew

At a Spa / Nail Salon

I'd like (a) . . .
. . . እፈልጋለሁ።
. . . i-fel-li-gal-le-hu

aromatherapy ጠረን ማስተካከል te-ren mas-te-ka-kel
acupuncture አኩፐንክቸር ak-ku-pen-ki-cher
facial ፊት መሰራት fit mes-se-rat
manicure እጅ መሰራት ijj mes-se-rat
massage ማሳጅ ma-saj
pedicure እግር መሰራት i-gir mes-se-rat
sauna ሳውና saw-na
wax ዋክስ waks

At a Laundromat

Is there . . .?
. . . ይኖራል?
. . . yi-no-ral?

full-service የተሟላ አገልግሎት yet-te-mual-la a-gel-gi-lot
self-service ራስን ማስተናገድ ra-sin mas-te-na-ged
same-day service በአንድ ቀን የሚያልቅ አገልግሎት
be-and qen yem-mi-yalq a-gel-gi-lot

How does this work?
ይህ እንዴት ነው የሚሰራው?
yih en-det new yem-mi-se-raw?

Do you have . . .?
. . . ይኖርሃል?
. . . yi-nor-hal?

bleach ማንጫ man-cha
change ዝርዝር ሳንቲም zir-zir san-tim
detergent ፈሳሽ ሳሙና fe-sash sa-mu-na
dryer sheets ጨርቅ ማለዘቢያ አንሶላ cherq ma-lez-ze-bi-ya an-so-la
fabric softener ጨርቅ ማለዘቢያ cherq ma-lez-ze-bi-ya

This machine is broken.
ይህ ማሽን ተበላሽቷል።
yih ma-shin te-be-lash-toal

When will my clothes be ready?
መቼ ነው ልብሶቼ ዝግጁ የሚሆኑት?
mech new lib-soch-che zi-gij-ju yem-mi-ho-nut?

whites ነጫጭ ne-chach
colors ባለቀለም ba-le-qe-lem
delicates ከፋይ ke-fay
hand wash በእጅ የሚታጠብ be-ijj yem-mi-ta-teb
permanent press የማይጨማደድ ልብስ ye-may-che-ma-ded libs
dry clean only በደረቁ ብቻ የሚታጠብ be-de-re-qu bich-cha yem-mit-tat-teb

cold water ቀዝቃዛ ውሃ qez-qaz-za wi-ha
warm water ሙቅ ውሃ muq wi-ha
hot water የፈላ ውሃ ye-fel-la wi-ha

Banking. *See page 215*

NATIONALITIES & COUNTRIES

I'm . . .
. . . ነኝ።
. . . negn

American አሜሪካዊ a-me-ri-ka-wi
Australian አውስትራሊያዊ a-wis-ti-ra-li-ya-wi
Canadian ካናዳዊ ka-na-da-wi
English እንግሊዛዊ in-gi-li-za-wi
Irish አየርላንዳዊ a-yer-lan-da-wi
a New Zealander ኒውዚላንዳዊ niw-zi-lan-da-wi
Scottish ስኮትላንዳዊ is-kot-lan-da-wi
Welsh ዌልሳዊ wel-sa-wi

Where are you from?
ከወዴት ነህ?
ke-we-det neh?

Where were you born?
የት ነው የተወለድከው?
yet new yet-te-wel-led-kew?

I'm from . . .
ከወደ . . .
ke-we-de . . .

I was born in . . .
የተወለድኩት . . . ነው።
yet-te-wel-led-kut . . . new

Australia አውስትራሊያ a-wis-ti-ra-li-ya
Canada ካናዳ ka-na-da
England እንግሊዝ in-gi-liz
Ethiopia ኢትዮጵያ **it-yo-p'i-ya**
Ireland አየርላንድ a-yer-land
New Zealand ኒውዚላንድ niw-zi-land
the United States አሜሪካ a-me-ri-ka
the United Kingdom ዩናይትድ ኪንግደም yu-nay-tid king-dem
Wales ዌልስ wels

RELIGIONS

What religion are you?
ሐይማኖትህ ምንድን ነው?
hay-ma-no-tih min-din new?

I am . . .
እኔ . . . ነኝ
i-ne . . . negn

agnostic አግኖስቲክ ag-nos-tik
atheist በፈጣሪ ከማያምኑት be-fe-ta-ri kem-ma-yam-nut
Buddhist ቡድሂስት bud-hist
Catholic ካቶሊክ ka-to-lik
Christian ክርስትያን ki-ris-ti-yan
Hindu ሂንዱ hin-du
Jewish አይሁድ ay-hud
Muslim ሙስሊም mus-lim

INTERESTS & LEISURE

Arts

Do you like . . .?
. . . ትወዳለህ?
. . . ti-wed-dal-leh?

art ኪነጥበብ ki-ne-ti-beb
cinema ሲኒማ si-ni-ma
music ሙዚቃ mu-zi-qa
sports እስፖርት is-port
theater ትያትር ti-ya-tir

Yes, very much.
አዎ፤ በጣም።
a-wo be-tam

Not really.
እምብዛም አይደል።
em-bi-zam ay-del

A little.
በጥቂቱ።
be-ti-qi-tu

I like . . .
. . . እወዳለሁ።
. . . i-wed-dal-le-hu

I don't like . . .
. . . አልወድም።
. . . al-wed-dim

Can you recommend a good . . .?
ጥሩ . . . ልትጠቁመኝ ትችላለህ?
ti-ru . . . lit-teq-qu-mugn ti-chi-lal-leh?

book መጽሐፍ mets-haf
exhibit ኤግዚቢሽን eg-zi-bi-shin
museum ሙዝየም muz-yem
film ፊልም film
play ትያትር ti-ya-tir

What's playing tonight?
ዛሬ ማታ ምንድን ነው የሚታየው?
za-re ma-ta min-din new yem-mit-tay-yew?

I like . . . films/movies.
. . . ፊልሞች ደስ ይሉኛል።
. . . fil-moch dess yi-lugn-gnal

action የድርጊት ye-dir-git
art ስዕላዊ si-i-la-wi
comedy አስቂኝ as-si-qign
drama ድራማ di-ra-ma
foreign የውጭ አገር ye-wuch a-ger
horror አስፈሪ as-fe-ri
indie ኢንዲ in-di
musical ሙዚቃዊ mu-zi-qa-wi
mystery እንቆቅልሽ in-qo-qil-lish
romance የፍቅር ye-fi-qir
suspense ልብ አንጠልጣይ libb an-tel-tay

What are the movie times?
የፊልም መታያ ጊዜያት የትኞቹ ናቸው?
ye-film met-ta-ya gi-ze-yat ye-tign-gnoch-chu nach-chew?

Sports

When's the game?
ግጥሚያው መች ነው?
git-mi-yaw mech new?

Would you like to go to the game with me?
ወደ ግጥሚያው አብረኸኝ ልትሄድ ትችላለህ?
we-de git-mi-yaw ab-re-khegn lit-hed ti-chi-lal-leh?

What's the score?
ስንት ለስንት ናቸው?
sint le-sint nach-chew?

Who's winning?
ማን ነው የሚያሸንፈው?
man new yem-mi-yash-shen-ni-few?

Do you want to play?
መጫወት ትፈልጋለህ?
mech-cha-wet ti-fel-li-gal-leh?

Can I join in?
አብሬያችሁ ልጫዎት እችላለሁ?
a-bir-re-yach-chi-hu lich-cha-wet i-chi-lal-le-hu?

I like . . .
. . . እወዳለሁ።
. . . i-wed-dal-le-hu

baseball ቤዝቦል bez-bol
basketball ቅርጫት ኳስ qir-chat kuas
bicycling የብስክሌት ውድድር ye-bis-ki-let wi-did-dir
boxing ቦክስ boks
diving ውሃ ጠለቃ wi-ha te-le-qa
football (American) የአሜሪካ እግር ኳስ ye-a-me-ri-ka i-gir kuas
golf ጎልፍ golf
hiking ጀልባ ቀዘፋ jel-ba qe-ze-fa
martial arts ማርሻል አርት mar-shal art
skiing የበረዶ መንሸራተት ye-be-re-do men-she-ra-tet
soccer እግር ኳስ i-gir kuas
surfing ሰርፊንግ ser-fing
swimming ውሃ ዋና wi-ha wa-na
tennis ሜዳ ቴንስ me-da te-nis
volleyball መረብ ኳስ me-reb kuas

FRIENDS & ROMANCE

What are your plans for . . .?
. . . እቅድህ ምንድን ነው?
. . . iq-qi-dih min-din new?

tonight የዛሬ ye-za-re
tomorrow የነገ ye-ne-ge
the weekend የቅዳሜና እሁድ ye-qi-da-men-na e-hud

Would you like to get a drink?
መጠጥ ማግኘት ትፈልጋለህ?
me-tett ma-gign-gnet ti-fel-li-gal-leh?

Where would you like to go?
የት ነው መሄድ የምትፈልገው?
yet new me-hed yem-mit-fel-li-gew?

Would you like to go dancing?
ወደ ጭፈራ ቤት መሄድ ትፈልጋለህ?
we-de chif-fe-ra bet me-hed ti-fel-li-gal-leh?

I'd like that.
ደስ ይለኛል።
dess yi-legn-gnal

That sounds great!
አሪፍ ነው!
a-rif new!

I'm busy.
ስራ በዝቶብኛል።
si-ra bez-tob-bign-gnal

No, thank you.
አይ፤ አመሰግናለሁ።
ay a-me-seg-gi-nal-le-hu

Go away!
ሂድልኝ!
hi-dil-lign!

Stop it!
ተው!
tew!

I'm here with my . . .
እዚህ ከ . . . ጋር ነኝ።
iz-zih ke . . . gar negn

boyfriend ወንድ ጓደኛዬ wend guad-degn-gna-ye
girlfriend ሴት ጓደኛዬ set guad-degn-gna-ye
husband ባሌ ba-le
wife ሚስቴ mis-te
partner ወዳጄ we-da-je
friend(s) ጓደኛዬ / ኞቼ guad-degn-gna-ye / gno-che

I'm . . .
. . . ነኝ።
. . . negn

single ላጤ lat-te
married ባለትዳር ba-le-ti-dar
separated የተለያየሁ yet-te-ley-ye-hu
divorced የተፋታሁ yet-te-fat-ta-hu
seeing someone የከንፈር ወዳጅ ይዣለሁ ye-ken-fer we-daj yizh-zhal-le-hu

Do you like men or women?
የምትፈልገው ወንዶችን ነው ሴቶችን?
yem-mit-fel-li-gew wen-doch-chin new se-toch-chin?

I'm . . .
. . . ነኝ።
. . . negn

bisexual ባይሴክሹዋል bay-sek-shual
heterosexual ሄትሮሴክሹዋል het-ro-sek-shual
homosexual ሆሞሴክሹዋል ho-mo-sek-shual

Can I kiss you?
ልስምሽ እችላለሁ?
li-si-mish i-chi-lal-le-hu?

I like you.
እወድሃለሁ።
i-wed-di-hal-le-hu

I love you.
አፈቅርሃለሁ።
a-feq-ri-hal-le-hu

COMMUNICATIONS

Mail

Where is the post office?
ፖስታ ቤቱ የት ጋ ነው?
pos-ta be-tu yet ga new?

Is there a mailbox nearby?
የፖስታ ማስገቢያ ሳጥን በቅርብ አለ እንዴ?
ye-pos-ta mas-geb-bi-ya sa-tin be-qirb al-le en-de?

Can I buy stamps?
ቴምብር መግዛት እችላለሁ?
tem-bir meg-zat i-chi-lal-le-hu?

I would like to send a . . .
. . . መላክ እፈልጋለሁ።
. . . me-lak i-fel-li-gal-le-hu

letter ደብዳቤ deb-dab-be
postcard ፖስት ካርድ post kard
package ጥቅል ti-qill **parcel** እሽግ ish-shig

It contains . . .
በውስጡ . . . ይዟል።
be-wus-tu . . . yi-zual

Please send this via . . .
እባክህን ይህን በ . . . ላክልኝ።
i-bak-ki-hin yi-hin be . . . la-kil-lign

air mail ኤንቬሎፕ en-ve-lop
registered mail ሪኮማንዴ ፖስታ ri-ko-man-de pos-ta
priority mail አስቸኳይ ፖስታ as-chek-kuay pos-ta
regular mail መደበኛ ፖስታ me-de-begn-gna pos-ta

It's going to . . .
ወደ . . . የሚሄድ ነው።
we-de . . . yem-mi-hed new

Australia አውስትራሊያ a-wis-ti-ra-li-ya
Canada ካናዳ ka-na-da
Ireland አየርላንድ a-yer-land
New Zealand ኒውዚላንድ niw-zi-land
Scotland ስኮትላንድ is-kot-land
the United Kingdom ዩናይትድ ኪንግደም yu-nay-tid king-dem
the United States አሜሪካ a-me-ri-ka

How much does it cost?
ምን ያህል ያስከፍላል?
min ya-hil yas-kef-fi-lal

When will it arrive?
መች ይደርሳል?
mech yi-der-sal?

What is . . .?
. . . ምንድን ነው?
. . . min-din new?

your address
አድራሻህ
ad-rash-shah

the address for the hotel
የሆቴሉ አድራሻ
ye-ho-te-lu ad-rash-sha

the address I should have my mail sent to
ፖስታዬን መላክ የሚኖርብኝ አድራሻ
pos-ta-yen me-lak yem-mi-no-rib-bign ad-rash-sha

Can you write down the address for me?
አድራሻውን በጽሁፍ ሊታሰፍርልኝ ትችላለህ?
ad-rash-sha-win be-tsi-huf lit-ta-sef-ril-lign ti-chi-lal-leh?

Is there any mail for me?
የመጣልኝ ፖስታ አለ እንዴ?
ye-met-tal-lign pos-ta al-le en-de?

international አለም አቀፍ a-lem aq-qef
domestic አገር ውስጥ a-ger wist
postage ቴምብር tem-bir
stamp ማህተም mah-tem
envelope ኤንቬሎፕ ean-ve-lop
postal code ፖስታ ሳጥን ቁጥር pos-ta sa-tin qu-tir
postal insurance የፖስታ ዋስትና ye-pos-ta was-tin-na
customs ቀረጥ qe-ret

Telephones

Where is a pay phone?
የግድግዳ ስልክ የት ይገኛል?
ye-gid-gid-da silk yet yig-gegn-gnal?

Can I use your phone?
ስልክ ልታስደውለኝ ትችላለህ?
silk lit-tas-dew-wu-legn ti-chi-lal-leh?

I would like to . . .
. . . እፈልጋለሁ።
. . . i-fel-li-gal-le-hu

make an overseas phone call
የውጭ አገር የስልክ ጥሪ ማድረግ
ye-wich a-ger ye-silk tir-ri mad-reg

make a local call
የአገር ውስጥ ጥሪ ማድረግ
ye-a-ger wist tir-ri mad-reg

send a fax
ፋክስ መላክ
faks me-lak

What number do I dial for . . .?
. . . ስንት ቁጥር ላይ ነው የምደውለው።
. . . sint qu-tir lay new yem-mi-dew-wu-lew?

information መረጃ ለማግኘት mer-re-ja le-ma-gign-gnet
an outside line ለውጭ መስመር le-wich mes-mer
an operator የጥሪ ማዕከል ሰራተኛ ለማግኘት ye-tir-ri ma-i-kel ser-ra-tegn-gna le-ma-gign-gnet

What is the phone number for the . . .?
የ. . . ስልክ ቁጥር ስንት ነው?
ye . . . silk qu-tir sint new?

hotel ሆቴሉ ho-te-lu
office ቢሮው bi-row
restaurant ምግብ ቤቱ mi-gib be-tu
embassy ኤምባሲው em-ba-siw

What is your . . .?
. . . ስንት ነው?
. . . sint new?

phone number ስልክ ቁጥርህ silk qut-rih
cell phone number ሞባይል ስልክ ቁጥርህ mo-ba-yil silk qut-rih
home phone number የመኖሪያ ቤትህ ስልክ ቁጥር ye-me-no-ri-ya be-tih silk qu-tir
work phone number የመስሪያ ቤትህ ስልክ ቁጥር ye-mes-ri-ya be-tih silk qu-tir
extention (number) ኤክስቴንሽን ቁጥርህ e-kis-ten-shin qut-rih
fax number ፋክስ ቁጥርህ faks qut-rih

My number is . . .
ቁጥሬ . . . ነው።
qut-re . . . new

Can you write down your number for me?
ቁጥርህን በጽሁፍ ልታስፍርልኝ ትችላለህ?
qut-ri-hin be-tsi-huf-ril-lign ti-chi-lal-leh?

What is the country code for . . .? *(see page 229)*
የ. . . አገራዊ ኮዷ ስንት ነው?
ye . . . a-ge-ra-wi ko-dua sint new?

I would like to buy a/an . . .
. . . መግዛት እፈልጋለሁ።
. . . meg-zat i-fel-li-gal-le-hu

domestic phone card
አገር ውስጥ መደወያ ካርድ
a-ger wist me-dew-we-ya kard

international phone card
አለም አቀፍ መደወያ ካርድ
a-lem aq-qef me-dew-we-ya kard

disposible cell phone
ተጠቅሞ የሚጣል ተንቀሳቃሽ ስልክ
te-teq-mo yem-mit-tal ten-qe-sa-qash silk

SIM card
ሲም ካርድ
sim kard

cell phone recharge card
የሞባይል ሂሳብ መሙሊያ ካርድ
ye-mo-ba-yil hi-sab me-mu-li-ya kard

pre-payed cell phone
የቅድሚያ ክፍያ ተንቀሳቃሽ ስልክ
ye-qid-mi-ya ki-fiy-ya ten-qe-sa-qash silk

What is the cost per minute?
ክፍያው በደቂቃ ስንት ነው?
ki-fiy-yaw be-de-qi-qa sint new?

I need a phone with XX minutes.
XX ደቂቃ ያለው ስልክ እፈልጋለሁ።
XX de-qi-qa yal-lew silk i-fel-li-gal-le-hu

How do I make calls?
ጥሪዎችን እንዴት ነው የማደርገው?
tir-ri-woch-chin n-det new yem-ma-der-gew?

collect call
የተደወለለት ሰው የሚከፍልበት የስልክ ጥሪ
ye-te-dew-we-le-let sew ye-mik-flibet tiri

toll-free ከክፍያ ነጻ ke-ki-fiy-ya ne-tsa
phonebook የስልክ ማውጫ ye-silk maw-cha
voicemail የድምጽ መልዕክት ye-dimts me-li-ikt

On the Phone

Hello.	**This is . . .**
ሄሎ።	. . . ነኝ።
he-lo	. . . negn

May I speak to . . .?
. . . ን ማግኘት እችላለሁ?
. . . n ma-gign-gnet i-chi-lal-le-hu?

. . . isn't here; may I take a message?
. . . የለም፤ መልዕክት ካለህ?
. . . yel-lem mel-ikt kal-leh?

I would like to leave a message for . . .
ለ . . . መልዕክት መተው እፈልጋለሁ።
le . . . mel-ikt me-tew i-fel-li-gal-le-hu

Sorry, wrong number.
ይቅርታ፤ ተሳስተሃል።
yi-qir-ta te-sa-si-te-hal

Please call back later.
እባክህን ወደ በኋላ መልሰህ ደውል።
i-bak-ki-hin we-de be-hua-la mel-li-she dew-wil

I'll call back later.
በኋላ መልሼ እደውላለሁ።
be-hua-la mel-lish-she i-dew-wi-lal-le-hu

Goodbye. ደህና ዋል። deh-na wal

Computers and the Internet

computer ኮምፒዩተር kom-pi-yu-ter
laptop ላፕቶፕ lap-top
USB port የዩኤስቢ መሰኪያ ye-yu-es-bi me-sek-ki-ya
ethernet cable ኔትወርክ ገመድ net-werk ge-med
CD ሲዲ si-di
DVD ዲቪዲ di-vi-di
e-mail ኢሜይል i-me-yil

Windows ዊንዶውስ win-dows
Macintosh ማኪንቶሽ ma-kin-tosh
Linux ሊነክስ li-neks

Where is the nearest . . .?
በቅርብ የሚገኘው . . . የት ጋር ነው?
be-qirb yem-mig-gegn-gnew . . . yet gar new?

Internet café ኢንተርኔት ካፌ in-ter-net ka-fe
computer repair shop የኮምፒዩተር ጥገና መደብር
ye-kom-pi-yu-ter tig-ge-na me-deb-bir

Do you have . . .?
. . . አላችሁ?
. . . al-lach-chi-hu?

available computers ያልተያዙ ኮምፒዩተሮች
yal-te-ya-zu kom-pi-yu-te-roch
(wireless) Internet (ገመድ አልባ) ኢንተርኔት
(ge-med al-ba) in-ter-net
a printer ፐሪንተር pi-rin-ter
a scanner ስካነር is-ka-ner

How do you . . .?
. . . እንዴት ነው?
. . . in-det new?

turn on this computer ይህን ኮምፒዩተር የምትከፍተው
yi-hin kom-pi-yu-ter yem-mit-kef-tew
log in የምትገባው yem-mit-ge-baw
connect to the wi-fi ከዋይፋይ ጋር የምታገናኘው
ke-way-fay gar yem-mit-tag-ge-nagn-gnew
type in English በእንግሊዝኛ የምትጽፈው be-in-gi-li-zign-gna yem-mit-tsi-few

What is the password?
የይለፍ ቃሉ ምንድን ነው?
ye-yi-lef qa-lu min-din new?

How much does it cost for . . .?
ለ . . . ምን ያህል ያስከፍላል?
le . . . min ya-hil yas-kef-fi-lal?

15 minutes 15 ደቂቃ as-ra am-mist de-qi-qa
30 minutes 30 ደቂቃ se-la-sa de-qi-qa
one hour አንድ ሰዓት and se-at

My computer . . .
ኮምፒዩተሬ . . .
kom-pi-yu-te-re . . .

doesn't work አይሰራም ay-se-ram
is frozen ድርቅ ብሎ ቀረ dir-riqq bi-lo qer-re
won't turn on አልከፈት አለ a-lik-ke-fet a-le
crashed ተደመሰሰ te-de-mes-se-se
doesn't have an Internet connection ኢንተርኔት የለውም in-ter-net yel-le-wim

PROFESSIONS

What do you do?	**I'm a/an . . .**
ስራህ ምንድን ነው?	. . . ነኝ።
si-rah min-din new?	. . . negn

accountant ሒሳብ ሰራተኛ hi-sab ser-ra-tegn-gna
admisistrative assistant ተላላኪ te-la-la-ki
aid worker የርዳታ ሰራተኛ yer-da-ta ser-ra-tegn-gna
architect አርኪቴክት ar-ki-tekt
artist አርቲስት ar-tist
assistant ረዳት red-dat
banker የባንክ ሰራተኛ ye-bank ser-ra-tegn-gna
businessman/businesswoman ነጋዴ neg-ga-de
carpenter አናጺ a-na-tsi
CEO ዋና ስራ አስኪያጅ wan-na si-ra as-ki-yaj
clerk የሽያጭ ሰራተኛ shach
computer engineer የኮምፒዩተር መሃንዲስ ye-kom-pi-yu-ter me-han-dis
computer programmer የኮምፒዩተር ፕሮግራመር ye-kom-pi-yu-ter pi-rog-ra-mer
consultant አማካሪ am-ma-ka-ri
construction worker የግንባታ ሰራተኛ ye-gin-ba-ta ser-ra-tegn-gna
contractor ተቋራጭ te-qua-rach
coordinator አስተባባሪ as-te-ba-ba-ri
dentist የጥርስ ሐኪም ye-tirs ha-kim
director ዳይሬክተር day-rek-ter
doctor ዶክተር dok-ter
editor አርታኢ ar-ta-i
electrician የኮረንቲ ባለሙያ ye-kor-ren-ti ba-le-mu-ya
engineer መሐንዲስ me-han-dis

intern ኢንተርን in-tern
journalist ጋዜጠኛ ga-ze-te-gna
lawyer ጠበቃ te-be-qa
librarian የቤተ መጻህፍት ባለሙያ ye-be-te mets-haft ba-le-mu-ya
manager ማናጀር ma-na-jer
nurse ነርስ ners
politician ፖለቲከኛ po-le-ti-kegn-gna
secretary ጸሐፊ tse-ha-fi
student ተማሪ te-ma-ri
supervisor ዋና ተቆጣጣሪ wan-na te-qo-ta-ta-ri
teacher መምህር mem-mi-hir
writer ደራሲ de-ra-si

I work in . . .
. . . ላይ ተሰማርቻለሁ።
. . . lay te-se-ma-rich-chal-le-hu

academia አካደሚያ ak-ka-de-mi-ya
accounting የሒሳብ መዝገብ አያያዝ ye-hi-sab mez-geb ay-ya-yaz
advertising የማስታወቂያ ስራ ye-mas-ta-we-qi-ya si-ra
the arts ኪነጥበብ ki-ne-ti-beb
banking ባንክ bank
business ንግድ nigd
computers ኮምፒዩተር kom-pi-yu-ter
education ትምህርት tim-hirt
engineering ምህንድስና mi-hin-di-din-na
finance ፋይናንስ fay-nans
government የመንግስት ስራ ye-men-gist si-ra
journalism ጋዜጠኝነት ga-ze-tegn-gnan-net
law ህግ higg

manufacturing ማኑፋክቸሪንግ ma-nu-fak-che-ring
marketing ማርኬቲንግ mar-ke-ting
the medical field ሕክምና hik-ki-min-na
politics ፖለቲካ po-le-ti-ka
public relations የህዝብ ግንኙነት ye-hizb gi-nign-gnun-net
publishing ህትመት ስራ hit-met si-ra
a restaurant የምግብ ቤት ስራ ye-mi-gib bet si-ra
sales ሽያጭ shiy-yach
a store ሽቀጣ ሽቀጥ she-qe-ta she-qet
social services ማህበራዊ አገልግሎት ma-hi-be-ra-wi a-gel-gi-lot
the travel industry የጉዞ ውክልና ስራ ye-gu-zo wik-ki-lin-na si-ra

BUSINESS INTERACTIONS

I have a meeting/appointment with . . .
ከ . . . ጋር ስብሰባ/ቀጠሮ ነበረኝ።
ke . . . gar sib-se-ba/qe-te-ro neb-be-regn

Where's the . . .?
. . . የት ጋር ነው?
. . . yet gar new?

business center የንግድ ማዕከሉ ye-nigd ma-i-ke-lu
convention hall የጉባኤ አዳራሹ ye-gu-ba-e ad-da-ra-shu
meeting room የመሰብሰቢያው ክፍል ye-mes-seb-se-bi-yaw ki-fil

Can I have your business card?
ቢዝነስ ካርድህን ማግኘት እችላለሁ?
biz-nes kar-di-hin ma-gign-gnet i-chi-lal-le-hu?

Here's my name card.
ይኸው በስሜ የተዘጋጀ ካርድ።
yi-khew be-si-me yet-te-ze-gaj-je kard

I'm here for a . . .
እዚህ የመጣሁት ለ . . . ነው።
iz-zih ye-met-ta-hut le . . . new

conference ጉባኤ gu-ba-ea
meeting ስብሰባ sib-se-ba
seminar ሴሚናር se-mi-nar

My name is . . .
. . . እባላለሁ።
. . . ib-ba-lal-le-hu

You Might Hear

በመምጣትህ እናመሰግናለን።
be-mem-ta-tih in-na-me-seg-gi-nal-len
Thank you for coming.

ቀጠሮ ይዘሃል?
qe-te-ro yi-ze-hal?
Do you have an appointment?

ከማን ጋር?
ke-man gar?
With whom?

እባክህን አንድ ጊዜ።
i-bak-ki-hin and gi-ze
One moment, please.

እባክህን ተቀመጥ።
i-bak-ki-hin te-qe-met
Please have a seat.

እሱ/እሷ . . .
is-su/is-sua . . .
He/She . . .

ስብሰባ ላይ ነው/ናት **sib-se-ba lay new/nat** is in a meeting

ለስራ ጉዳይ ጉዞ ላይ ነው/ናት **le-si-ra gud-day gu-zo lay new/nat** is on a business trip

እረፍት ላይ ነው/ናት **e-reft lay new/nat** is away on vacation

አሁን ወጣ/ወጣች **a-hun wet-ta/wet-tach** just stepped out

አንተን አሁን ያገኝሃል/ታገኝሃለች **an-ten a-hun ya-gegn-gni-hal/ta-gegn-gni-hal-lech** will be right with you

አሁን ያስተናግድሃል/ ታስተናግድሃለች **a-hun yas-te-nag-gi-di-hal/tas-te-nag-gi-di-hal-lech** will see you now

May I introduce my colleague . . .
የስራ ባልደረባዬን . . . ተዋወቀው።
ye-si-ra bal-de-re-ba-yen . . . te-wa-we-qew

Pleased to meet you.
ስለተዋወቅን ደስ ብሎኛል።
si-let-te-waw-we-qin dess bi-logn-gnal

I'm sorry I'm late.
ይቅርታ ስለዘገየሁ።
yi-qir-ta si-le-ze-gey-ye-hu

You can reach me at . . .
በ . . . ልታገኘኝ ትችላለህ።
be . . . lit-ta-gegn-gnegn ti-chi-lal-leh

I'm here until . . .
እስከ . . . ድረስ እዚህ እኖራለሁ።
is-ke . . . di-res iz-zih i-no-ral-le-hu

I need to . . .
. . . ይኖርብኛል።
. . . yi-no-rib-bign-gnal

make a photocopy ፎቶኮፒ ማድረግ fo-to kop-pi mad-reg

make a telephone call ስልክ መደወል silk-me-dew-wel

send a fax ፋክስ ማድረግ faks mad-reg

send a package (overnight)(አዳሬን) እቃ መላክ (a-da-ren) i-qa me-lak

use the Internet ኢንተርኔት መጠቀም in-ter-net met-te-qem

It was a pleasure meeting you.
ከአንተ ጋር በመገናኘቴ የላቀ ደስታ ተሰምቶኛል።
ke-an-te gar be-meg-ge-na-gne-te ye-la-qe des-ta te-sem-togn-gnal

I look forward to meeting with you again.
ከአንተ ጋር በድጋሜ ለመገናኘት በጉጉት እጠብቃለሁ።
ke-an-te gar be-dig-ga-me le-meg-ge-na-gnet be-gug-gut i-teb-bi-qal-le-hu

Business Vocabulary

advertisment ማስታወቂያ mas-ta-we-qi-ya
advertising የማስታወቂያ ስራ ye-mas-ta-we-qi-ya si-ra
bonus ጉርሻ gur-sha
boss አለቃ a-le-qa
briefcase ቦርሳ bor-sa
business ስራ ጉዳይ si-ra gud-day
business card ቢዝነስ ካርድ biz-nes kard
business casual *(dress)* የስራ የክት (አለባበስ) ye-si-ra ye-kitt (al-le-ba-bes)
business plan የስራ እቅድ ye-si-ra eq-qid
casual *(dress)* የክት (አለባበስ) ye-kitt (al-le-ba-bes)
cell phone number የሞባይል ስልክ ቁጥር ye-mo-ba-yil silk qu-tir
certification የምስክር ወረቀት አሰጣጥ ye-mi-sik-kir we-re-qet as-se-tat
certified የተመሰከረለት yet-te-me-sek-ke-rel-let
colleague ባልደረባ bal-de-re-ba
company ኩባንያ kub-ba-niy-ya
competition ውድድር wi-did-dir
competitor ተወዳዳሪ te-we-da-da-ri

computer ኮምፒዩተር kom-pi-yu-ter
conference ጉባኤ gu-ba-ea
contract ውል wil
course ዘዴ ze-de
cubicle አነስተኛ ክፍል a-nes-tegn-gna ki-fil
CV ሲቪ si-vi
deduction ቅናሽ qin-nash
degree ዲግሪ dig-ri
desk ዴስክ desk
dress አለባበስ al-le-ba-bes
  business casual የስራ የክት ye-si-ra ye-kitt
  casual የክት ye-kitt
  formal መደበኛ me-de-begn-gna
e-mail address የኢሜይል አድራሻ ye-i-me-yil ad-rash-sha
employee ተቀጣሪ te-qet-ta-ri
employer ቀጣሪ qe-ta-ri
equal opportunity እኩል ተሳትፎ ik-kul te-sat-fo
expenses ወጪዎች we-chi-woch
experience የስራ ልምድ ye-si-ra limd
fax number የፋክስ ቁጥር ye-faks qu-tir
field መስክ mesk
formal *(dress)* መደበኛ (አለባበስ) me-de-begn-gna (al-le-ba-bes)
full-time የሙሉ ጊዜ ye-mu-lu gi-ze
global አለም አቀፍ a-lem aq-qef
income ገቢ ge-bi
income tax የገቢ ግብር ye-ge-bi gi-bir
insurance ዋስትና was-tin-na
job ስራ si-ra
joint venture የሽርክና ስራ ye-shir-kin-na si-ra
license ፈቃድ fe-qad

mailing ፖስታ pos-ta
marketing ግብይት gi-biy-yit
meeting ስብሰባ sib-se-ba
minimum wage ዝቅተኛ የደመወዝ ጣሪያ ziq-qi-tegn-gna ye-de-me-wez ta-ri-ya
multinational በተለያዩ አገራት ላይ የሚሰራ bet-te-le-yay-yu a-ge-rat lay yem-mi-se-ra
office ቢሮ bi-ro
office phone number የቢሮ ስልክ ቁጥር ye-bi-ro silk qu-tir
paperwork የወረቀት ስራ ye-we-re-qet si-ra
part-time የትርፍ ጊዜ ye-tirf gi-ze si-ra
phone number ስልክ ቁጥር silk qu-tir
  cell phone number የሞባይል ስልክ ቁጥር ye-mo-ba-yil silk qu-tir
  office phone number የቢሮ ስልክ ቁጥር ye-bi-ro silk qu-tir
printer ፕሪንተር pi-rin-ter
profession ሙያ mu-ya
professional ሙያዊ mu-ya-wi
project ፕሮጀክት pi-ro-jekt
promotion የደረጃ እድገት ye-de-re-ja id-get
raise ጭማሪ chim-ma-ri
reimbursement ለወጣ ወጪ የሚተካ ክፍያ le-wet-ta we-chi yem-mit-tek-ka ki-fiy-ya
resumé ቀጠለ qet-te-le
salary ደመወዝ de-me-wez
scanner ስካነር is-ka-ner
seminar ሴሚናር se-mi-nar
suit ሙሉ ልብስ mu-lu libs
supervisor ዋና ተቆጣጣሪ wan-na te-qo-ta-ta-ri
tax ID የግብር መለያ ye-gi-bir mel-le-ya
tie ከረባት ke-re-bat

trade fair የንግድ አውደርዕይ ye-nigd aw-de-ri-iyy
uniform መለያ ልብስ ye-denb libs
union ማህበር mah-ber
visa ቪዛ vi-za
wages ደመወዝ de-me-wez
work number የስራ ቁጥር ye-si-ra qu-tir
work permit የስራ ፈቃድ ye-si-ra fe-qad

MEDICAL

Can you recommend a good doctor?
ጥሩ ዶክተር ልትጠቁመኝ ትችላለህ?
ti-ru dok-ter lit-teq-qu-megn ti-chi-lal-leh?

At the Doctor

I'd to make an appiontment for . . .
ለ . . . ቀጠሮ መያዝ እፈልጋለሁ።
le . . . qe-te-ro me-yaz e-fel-li-gal-le-hu

today ዛሬ za-re
tomorrow ነገ ne-ge
next week ቀጣዩ ሳምንት qet-ta-yu sam-mint
as soon as possible በተቻለ ፍጥነት bet-te-cha-le fit-net

Can the doctor come here?
ዶክተሩ እዚህ ሊመጣ ይችላል?
dok-te-ru iz-zih li-me-ta yi-chi-lal?

What are the office hours?
የቢሮው ሰዓት መቼ መቼ ነው?
ye-bi-row se-at mech mech new?

It's urgent.
አስቸኳይ ነው።
as-chek-kuay new

How long is the wait?
ወረፋው ምን ያህል ነው?
we-re-faw min ya-hil new?

I need a doctor who speaks English.
እንግሊዝኛ የሚችል ዶክተር እፈልጋለሁ።
in-gi-li-zign-gna yem-mi-chil dok-ter i-fel-li-gal-le-hu

I've been sick for . . . days.
ለ . . . ቀናት ታምሜ ነበር።
le . . . qe-nat ta-mim-me neb-ber

You Might Hear

አለርጂ አለብህ?
a-ler-ji al-leb-bih?
Do you have any allergies?

እየወሰድክ ያለኸው መድሐኒት አለ?
iy-ye-wes-sedk yal-le-khew med-ha-nit al-le?
Are you on any medications?

እዚህ ጋር ፈርም።
iz-zih gar fer-rim
Sign here.

I have . . .
. . . አለብኝ
. . . al-leb-bign

I need medication for . . .
ለ . . . መድሐኒት እፈልጋለሁ።
le . . . med-ha-nit i-fel-li-gal-le-hu

allergies አለርጂ a-ler-ji
an allergic reaction የአለርጂ መቀስቀስ ye-a-ler-ji meq-qes-qes
arthritis አርቲራይቲስ ar-ti-ray-tis
asthma አስም asm
a backache የጀርባ ህመም ye-jer-ba hi-mem
bug bites የተባይ ንድፊያ ye-te-bay nid-fi-ya
chest pain የደረት ህመም ye-de-ret hi-mem
a cold ጉንፋን gun-fan
cramps ቁርጠት qur-tet
diabetes ስኳር sik-kuar
diarrhea ተቅማጥ teq-mat
an earache የጆሮ ህመም ye-jo-ro hi-mem

You Might Hear

በጥልቀት ተንፍስ።
be-til-qet ten-fis
Breathe deeply.

እባክህን አስል።
i-bak-ki-hin as-sil
Cough please.

እባክህን ልብስህን አወላልቅ።
i-bak-ki-hin lib-si-hin a-we-laiq
Undress, please.

እዚህ ጋር ያማል?
iz-zih gar yam-mal?
Does it hurt here?

አፍህን ክፈት።
af-hin ki-fet
Open your mouth.

ስፔሻሊስት ሐኪም ማየት አለብህ።
is-pe-sha-list ha-kim ma-yet al-leb-bih
You should see a specialist.

ወደ ሆስፒታል መሄድ አለብህ።
we-de hos-pi-tal me-hed al-leb-bih
You must go to the hospital.

ከሁለት ሳምንት በኋላ ተመልሰህ ና።
ke-hu-lett sam-mint be-hua-la te-mel-li-she na
Come back in two weeks.

ክትትል ማድረግ ይኖርብሃል።
ki-tit-til mad-reg yi-no-rib-bi-hal
You need a follow-up.

ተሰብሯል **te-seb-roal** broken
ተላላፊ **te-la-la-fi** contagious
ተበክሏል **te-bek-ki-loal** infected
ወለም ብሎታል **we-lem bi-lo-tal** sprained

a fever ትኩሳት tik-ku-sat

the flu ጉንፋን gun-fan

a fracture ስብራት sib-bi-rat

a heart condition የልብ ችግር ye-libb chig-gir

high blood pressure ከፍተኛ የደም ግፊት kef-fi-tegn-gna ye-dem gif-fit

an infection ቁስለት qus-let

indigestion የምግብ አለመፈጨት ye-mi-gib a-le-mef-fe-chet

low blood pressure ዝቅተኛ የደም ግፊት ziq-qi-tegn-gna ye-dem gif-fit

pain ስቃይ si-qay

a rash የሰውነት መቅላት ye-se-win-net meq-lat

swelling እብጠት eb-tet

a sprain ወለምታ we-lem-ta

a stomchache የሆድ ህመም ye-hod hi-mem

sunburn የጸሃይ መለብለብ ye-tse-hay mel-leb-leb

sunstroke ሰንስትሮክ se-nis-ti-rok

a toothache የጥርስ ህመም ye-tirs hi-mem

a urinary tract infection የሽንት ቱቦ ቁስለት ye-shint tub-bo qus-let

a venereal disease የአባለዘር በሽታ ye-a-ba-le-zer besh-shi-ta

I'm . . .
እኔ . . .
ine . . .

anemic ደም ማነስ አለብኝ dem ma-nes al-leb-bign

bleeding የደም መፍሰስ ችግር አለብኝ ye-dem mef-ses chig-gir al-leb-bign

consitpated የሆድ ድርቀት አለብኝ ye-hod dir-qet al-leb-bign

dizzy ያዞረኛል ya-zo-regn-gnal

You Might Hear

. . . አዝልሃለሁ።
. . . az-zil-li-hal-le-hu
I'm prescribing you . . .

አንቲባዮቲክስ **an-ti-ba-yo-tiks** antibiotics
ጸረ ቫይረስ **tse-re vay-res** anti-virals
የሚቀባ ነገር **yem-miq-qeb-ba** an ointment
የህመም ማስታገሻ **ye-hi-mem mas-ta-ge-sha** painkillers

. . . ያስፈልግሃል።
. . . yas-fel-li-gi-hal
You need a/an . . .

የደም ምርመራ **ye-dem mir-me-ra** blood test
መርፌ **mer-fe** injection
ግሉኮስ **gi-luk-kos** IV
የአክታ ምርመራ **ye-ak-ki-ta mir-me-ra** strep test
የሽንት ምርመራ **ye-shint mir-me-ra** urine test

having trouble breathing መተንፈስ እየተቸገርኩ ነው me-ten-fes ey-ye-te-cheg-ger-ku new
late for my period የወር አበባዬ ዘግይቷል ye-wer a-be-ba-ye zeg-yi-toal
nauseous ያጥወለውለኛል yat-we-lew-wi-legn-gnal
pregnant ነፍሰጡር ነኝ nef-se-tur negn
vomiting ያስመልሰኛል yas-mel-li-segn-gnal

It hurts here.
እዚህ ጋር ያማል።
iz-zih gar yam-mal

It's gotten worse/better.
ተባብሷል/ ተሻሽሏል
te-ba-bi-soal/te-sha-shi-loal

Do I need a prescription medicine?
በሐኪም የታዘዘ መድሐኒት ያስፈልገኝ ይሆን?
be-ha-kim yet-taz-ze-ze med-ha-nit yas-fel-li-gegn yi-hon?

Can you prescribe a generic drug?
ሁሉን አቀፍ መድሐኒት ሊታዝልኝ ትችላለህ?
hul-lun aq-qef med-ha-nit lit-taz-zil-lign ti-chi-lal-leh?

Is this over the counter?
ሼልፍ ላይ ነው?
shelf lay new?

How much do I take?
ምን ያህል ነው የምወስደው?
min ya-hil new yem-mi-wes-dew?

How often do I take this?
ለምን ያህል ጊዜ ነው ይህን የምወስደው?
le-min ya-hil gi-ze new yi-hin yem-mi-wes-dew?

Are there side effects?
ተጓዳኝ ችግሮች አሉት?
te-gua-dagn chig-gi-roch al-lut?

Is this safe for children?
ለልጆች ምንም ችግር አያመጣም?
le-li-joch mi-nim chig-gir a-ya-me-tam?

I'm allergic to . . .
ለ . . . አለርጅክ ነኝ።
le . . . a-ler-jik negn

antibiotics አንቲባዮቲክስ an-ti-ba-yo-tiks
anti-inflammatories ጸረ ቁስለት መድሐኒት tse-re qus-let med-ha-nit
aspirin አስፕሪን as-pi-rin
codeine ኮዴይን ko-de-yin
penicillin ፔንሲሊን pen-si-lin

I have insurance.
ዋስትና አለኝ።
was-tin-na al-legn

Do you accept . . .?
. . . ትቀበላላችሁ?
. . . tiq-qeb-be-lal-la-chi-hu?

How much does it cost?
ክፍያው ምን ያህል ነው?
ki-fiy-yaw min ya-hil new?

Can I have an itemized receipt for my insurance please?
ለዋስትናዬ እንዲሆነኝ እባክህን በዝርዝር የተዘጋጀ ደረሰኝ ማግኘት እችላለሁ?
le-was-tin-na-ye in-di-ho-negn i-bak-ki-hin be-zir-zir yet-te-ze-gaj-je der-re-segn ma-gign-gnet i-chi-lal-le-hu?

Can I pay by credit card?
በክሬዲት ካርድ መክፈል እችላለሁ?
be-ki-re-dit kard mek-fel i-chi-lal-le-hu?

Will my insurance cover this?
ዋስትናዬ ይህን ይሸፍንልኛል?
was-tin-na-ye yi-hin yi-shef-fi-nil-lign-gnal?

At the Optometrist

I need an eye exam.
አይኔን መታየት እፈልጋለሁ።
ay-nen met-ta-yet i-fel-li-gal-le-hu

I've lost . . .
. . . ጠፍቶብኛል።
. . . tef-tob-bign-gnal

a lens ሌንስ lens
my contacts ኮንታክት ሌንሴ kon-takt len-se
my glasses መነጽሬ me-ne-tsi-re

Should I continue to wear these?
እነሁኑ ማድረጌን ልቀጥል?
in-ni-hu-nu mad-re-gen li-qet-til?

Can I select new frames?
አዲስ ፍሬም መምረጥ እችላለሁ?
ad-dis fi-rem mem-ret i-chi-lal-le-hu?

How long will it take?
በምን ያህል ጊዜ ይደርሳል?
be-min ya-hil gi-ze yi-der-sal?

I'm nearsighted.
የሩቁን ማየት አልችልም።
ye-ru-qun ma-yet al-chi-lim

I'm farsighted.
የቅርቡን ማየት አልችልም።
ye-qir-bun ma-yet al-chi-lim

At the Dentist

I have a toothache.
ጥርሴን አምሞኛል።
tir-sen am-mogn-gnal

This tooth hurts.
ይህኛው ጥርስ ያመኛል።
yi-hign-gnaw tirs yam-megn-gnal

My tooth is broken.
ጥርሴ ተሸርፏል።
tir-se te-sher-foal

My teeth are sensitive.
ጥርሴን ቶሎ ይሰማኛል።
tir-sen to-lo yis-sem-magn-gnal

I've lost a filling.
የተሞላ ጥርሴ ተበላሽቷል።
yet-te-mol-la tir-se te-be-lash-toal

I have a cavity.
ጥርሴ ተቦርቡሯል።
tir-se te-bor-bu-roal

Can you fix these dentures?
እነዚህን ሰው ሰራሽ ጥርሶች ሊታስተካክሉልኝ ትችላለህ?
en-nez-zi-hin sew ser-rash tir-soch lit-tas-te-kak-ki-lil-lign ti-chi-lal-leh?

You Might Hear

ማስሞላት ይኖርብሃል።
mas-mol-lat yi-no-rib-bi-hal
You need a filling.

መርፌ/ባህላዊ ማደንዘዣ ልሰጥህ ነው።
mer-fe/ba-hi-la-wi ma-den-ze-zhi-ya li-se-tih new
I'm giving you an injection/a local anesthetic.

ይህን ጥርስ ነቅዬ ማውጣት አለብኝ።
yi-hin tirs ne-qiy-ye maw-tat al-leb-bign
I have to extract this tooth.

ለ . . . ሰዓታት ምንም ነገር አትብላ።
le . . . se-a-tat mi-nim ne-ger at-tib-la
Don't eat anything for . . . hours.

At the Gynecologist

I have cramps.
ቁርጠት ይዞኛል።
qur-tet yi-zogn-gnal

I have an infection.
ቁስለት አጋጥሞኛል።
qus-let ag-gat-mogn-gnal

My period is late.
የወር አበባዬ ዘግይቶብኛል።
ye-wer a-be-ba-ye zeg-yi-tob-bign-gnal

My last period was . . .
የመጨረሻው የወር አበባዬ . . . ላይ ነበር።
ye-me-cher-re-shaw ye-wer a-be-ba-ye . . . lay neb-ber

I'm on the Pill.
የወሊድ መቆጣጠሪያ ክኒን እየወሰድኩ ነው።
ye-we-lid meq-qo-ta-te-ri-ya ki-nin iy-ye-wes-sed-ku new

I'm not pregnant.
ነፍሰጡር አይደለሁም።
nef-se-tur ay-del-le-hum

I'm . . . months pregnant.
የ . . . ወራት ነፍሰጡር ነኝ።
ye . . . we-rat nef-se-tur negn

I need . . .
. . . እፈልጋለሁ።
. . . i-fel-li-gal-le-hu

a contraceptive የወሊድ መቆጣጠሪያ ye-we-lid meq-qo-ta-te-ri-ya

the morning-after pill የወሊድ መቆጣጠሪያ ክኒን ye-we-lid meq-qo-ta-te-ri-ya ki-nin

a pregnancy test የእርግዝና ምርመራ ye-ir-gi-zin-na mir-me-ra

an STD test የአባላዘር በሽታ ምርመራ ye-a-ba-la-zer besh-shi-ta mir-me-ra

At the Pharmacy

Where's the nearest (24-hour) pharmacy?
በቅርብ ያለው (24 ሰዓት የሚሰራ) የመድሐኒት መደብር ምኑ ጋር ነው?
be-qirb yal-lew (24 se-at yem-mi-se-ra) ye-med-ha-nit me-deb-bir mi-nu gar new?

What time does the pharmacy open?
የመድሐኒት መደብሩ የሚከፈተው ስንት ሰዓት ላይ ነው?
ye-med-ha-nit me-deb-bi-ru yem-mik-kef-fe-tew sint se-at lay new?

What time does the pharmacy close?
የመድሐኒት መደብሩ የሚዘጋው ስንት ሰዓት ላይ ነው?
ye-med-ha-nit me-deb-bi-ru yem-miz-zeg-gaw sint se-at lay new?

Can you fill this prescription?
ይህን ማዘዣ መሙላት ትችላለህ?
yi-hin ma-ze-zha me-mu-lat ti-chi-lal-leh?

How long is the wait?
ወረፋው ምን ያህል ነው?
we-re-faw min ya-hil new?

I'll come back for it.
ልወስደው ተመልሼ እመጣለሁ
li-wes-dew te-mel-lish-she i-me-tal-le-hu

What do you recommend for (a/an) . . .?
ለ . . . ምን ትመክረኛለህ?
le . . . min ti-mek-regn-gnal-leh?

allergies አለርጂ a-ler-ji
cold ጉንፋን gun-fan
cough ሳል sal
diarrhea ተቅማጥ teq-mat
hangover ሃንጎቨር han-go-ver
motion sickness ጉዞ ላይ ማጥወልወል gu-zo lay mat-wel-wel
post-nasal drip ንፍጥ መዝረብረብ nift mez-reb-reb
sore throat ጉሮሮ መቁሰል gu-ro-ro me-qu-sel
upset stomach ጨጓራ ማቃጠል cheg-gua-ra maq-qa-tel

Do I need a prescription?
የሐኪም ማዘዣ ያስፈልገኝ ይሆን?
ye-ha-kim ma-ze-zha yas-fel-li-gegn yi-hon?

I'm looking for . . .
. . . ፈልጌ ነበር።
. . . fel-lig-ge neb-ber

Do you have . . .?
. . . ይኖራችኋል?
. . . yi-no-rach-chi-hual?

aftershave አፍተርሼቭ af-ter-shev
anti-diarrheal ጸረ ተቅማጥ tse-re teq-mat
antiseptic rinse ጸረ ተህዋስያን ማለቅለቂያ tse-re the-wa-si-yan ma-leq-le-qi-ya
aspirin አስፕሪን as-pi-rin
baby wipes የህጻናት ማበሻ ye-hi-tsa-nat mab-be-sha
bandages ባንዴጅ ban-dej
cold medicine የጉንፋን መድሐኒት ye-gun-fan med-ha-nit
a comb ማበጠሪያ ma-be-te-ri-ya
conditioner ኮንዲሽነር kon-di-shi-ner
condoms ኮንዶም kon-dom

You Might See/Hear

. . . ይወሰድ።
. . . yiw-we-sed
Take . . .

ከምግብ በኋላ **ke-mi-gib be-hua-la** after eating
ከመኝታ በፊት **ke-megn-gni-ta be-fit** before bed
ከምግብ በፊት **ke-mi-gib be-fit** before meals
ጧት **tuat** in the morning
በባዶ ሆድ **be-ba-do hod** on an empty stomach
በአፍ **be-af** orally
በቀን ሁለቴ **be-qen hu-let-te** twice daily
በብዙ ውሃ **be-bi-zu wi-ha** with plenty of water

ለውጫዊ አካል አገልግሎት ብቻ
le-wuch-cha-wi a-kal a-gel-gi-lot bich-cha
for external use only

እንዳለ ይዋጥ
in-dal-le yiw-wat
swallow whole

የመጫጫን ስሜት ሊያስከትል ይችላል
ye-mech-cha-chan sim-met li-yas-ket-til yi-chi-lal
may cause drowsiness

ከአልኮል ጋር አይወሰድ
ke-al-kol gar a-yiw-we-sed
do not mix with alcohol

cotton balls ፋሻ fa-sha

dental floss ለጥርስ ማፅጃ የሚውል ክር le tirs mats-ja ye-mi-wil kirr

deodorant ዲዮድራንት di-yo-di-rant

diapers ዳይፐር day-per

gauze ሻሽ shash

a hairbrush የጸጉር መላጊያ ye-tse-gur me-la-gi-ya

hairspray የጸጉር መርጫ ye-tse-gur mer-chi-ya

hand lotion የእጅ ቅባት ye-ejj qi-bat

ibuprofen አይብዩፕሮፊን ay-bi-yu-pi-ro-fin

insect repellant የነፍሳት ማባረሪያ ye-nef-sat mab-ba-re-ri-ya

moisturizer ሞይስቸራይዘር mo-yis-che-ray-zer

mousse (hair) የጸጉር ውበት መጠበቂያ ye-tse-gur wu-bet me-teb-be-qi-ya

mouthwash የአፍ ማጠቢያ ye-af ma-te-bi-ya

razor blades ጺም መላጫ tsim me-la-cha

rubbing alcohol ቁስል መጥረጊያ አልኮል qu-sil met-re-gi-ya al-kol

shampoo ሻምፖ sham-po

shaving cream የጺም መላጫ ክሬም ye-tsim me-la-cha ki-rem

soap ሳሙና sa-mu-na

sunblock የጸሐይ ጨረር መከላከያ ቅባት ye-tse-hay che-rer mek-ke-la-ke-ya qi-bat

tampons ታምፑን tam-pun

a thermometer የሙቀት መጠን መለኪያ ye-mu-qet me-ten me-lek-ki-ya

throat lozenges የጉሮሮ ኪኒን ye-gu-ro-ro ki-nin

tissues ሶፍት soft

toilet paper የመጸዳጃ ቤት ወረቀት ye-mets-tse-da-ja bet we-re-qet

a toothbrush የጥርስ ብሩሽ ye-tirs bi-rush

toothpaste የጥርስ ሳሙና ye-tirs sa-mu-na
vitamins ቪታሚን vi-ta-min

PARTS OF THE BODY

abdomen ሆድ hod
anus ፊንጢጣ fin-ti-ta
appendix ትርፍ አንጀት tirf an-jet
arm ክንድ kind
back ጀርባ jer-ba
belly button እምብርት em-birt
bladder የሽንት ፊኛ ye-shint fign-gna
bone አጥንት a-tint
buttocks ቂጥ qit
breast ጡት tut
chest ደረት de-ret
ear ጆሮ jo-ro
elbow ክርን kirn
eye አይን ayn
face ፊት fit
finger የእጅ ጣት ye-ijj tat
foot እግር i-gir
gland እጢ i-ti
hair ጸጉር tse-gur
hand እጅ ijj
heart ልብ libb
hip ዳሌ dal-le
intestines አንጀት an-jet
jaw መንጋጭላ men-ga-chil-la
joint መገጣጠሚያ meg-ge-ta-te-mi-ya
kidney ኩላሊት ku-la-lit
knee ጉልበት gul-bet
knuckles አጽቅ atsq
leg እግር e-gir
lip ከንፈር ken-fer
liver ጉበት gub-bet
lung ሳንባ san-ba
mouth አፍ af
muscle ጡንቻ tun-cha
neck አንገት an-get
nose አፍንጫ a-fin-cha
penis ጀላ jel-la
rectum ቂጥ qit
rib ጎድን go-din
shoulder ትከሻ ti-kesh-sha
skin ቆዳ qo-da
stomach ጨጓራ cheg-gua-ra
testicles ቆለጥ qo-let
thigh ባት bat
throat ጉሮሮ go-ro-ro
thumb አውራ ጣት aw-ra tat
toe የእግር ጣት ye-i-gir tat
tooth/teeth ጥርስ tirs
tongue ምላስ mi-las
tonsils እንጥል en-til
urethra የሽንት ቱቦ ye-shint tub-bo
uterus ማህጸን ma-hi-tsen
vagina እምስ ems
vein ደም ስር dem sir
waist ወገብ we-geb
wrist የእጅ አንጓ ye-ijj an-gua

GENERAL EMERGENCIES

Help! እርዱኝ! er-dugn!
Fire! እሳት! e-sat!
Thief! ሌባ! le-ba!
Police! ፖሊስ! po-lis!
Stop! ቁም! qum!
Quickly! በፍጥነት! be-fit-net!
Be careful! ተጠንቀቅ! te-ten-qeq!
Go away! ሂድልኝ! hi-dil-lign
Leave me alone! በቃ ተወኝ! beq-qa te-wegn

It's an emergency!
ድንገተኛ ነው!
din-ge-tegn-gna new!

There's been an attack!
ጥቃት ተፈጽሟል!
ti-qat te-fets-tsi-mual

There's been an accident!
ድንገተኛ አደጋ ተከስቷል!
din-ge-tegn-gna a-de-ga te-kes-si-tual!

Call . . .!
. . . ጥራ!
. . . ti-ra!

an ambulance አምቡላንስ am-bu-lans
a doctor ዶክተር dok-ter
the fire department እሳት አደጋ e-sat a-de-ga
the police ፖሊስ po-lis

You Might See/Hear

ድንገተኛ **din-ge-tegn-gna** Emergency
ሆስፒታል **hos-pi-tal** Hospital
ፖሊስ **po-lis** Police
ፖሊስ ጣቢያ **po-lis ta-bi-ya** Police Station

Is anyone here . . .?
እዚህ ውስጥ . . . አለ?
iz-zih wust . . . al-le?

a doctor ዶክተር dok-ter
trained in CPR በሲ ፒ አር የሰለጠነ be-si pi ar ye-se-let-te-ne

Where is the . . .?
. . . ምኑ ጋር ነው?
. . . mi-nu gar new?

American embassy የአሜሪካ ኢምባሲ ye-a-me-ri-ka em-ba-si
bathroom መጸዳጃ ቤቱ mets-tse-da-ja be-tu
hospital ሆስፒታሉ hos-pi-ta-lu
police station ፖሊስ ጣቢያው po-lis ta-bi-yaw

Can you help me?
ልትረዳኝ ትችላለህ?
lit-re-dagn ti-chi-lal-leh?

I'm lost.
ጠፍቻለሁ።
te-fich-che-yal-le-hu

Can I use your phone?
ስልክህን ልታስጠቅመኝ ትችላለህ?
sil-ki-hin lit-tas-teq-qi-megn ti-chi-lal-leh?

Talking to Police

I've been . . .
[*meaning included in phrases given in Amharic*]

assaulted ተደብድቤያለሁ te-deb-dib-be-yal-le-hu
mugged ተመናጭቄያለሁ te-me-na-chiq-qe-yal-le-hu
raped ተደፍሬያለሁ te-de-fir-re-yal-le-hu
robbed ተዘርፌያለሁ te-ze-rif-fe-yal-le-hu
swindled ተጭበርብሬያለሁ tech-ber-bir-re-yal-le-hu

That person tried to . . . me.
ያ ግለሰብ . . . ሞከረ።
ya gil-le-seb . . . mok-ke-re

assault ሊደበድበኝ li-de-bed-di-begn
mug ሊያመናጭቀኝ li-yam-me-nach-chi-qegn
rape ሊደፍረኝ li-def-regn
rob ሊዘርፈኝ li-zer-fegn

I've lost my . . .
. . . ጠፍቷል።
. . . tef-tual

My . . . was stolen.
. . . ተሰርቋል
. . . te-ser-qual

bag(s) ሻንጣዬ shan-ta-ye
credit card ክሬዲት ካርዴ ki-re-dit kar-de
driver's license መንጃ ፈቃዴ men-ja fe-qa-de
identification መታወቂያዬ met-ta-we-qi-ya-ye
keys ቁልፌ qul-fe
laptop (computer) ላፕቶፔ (ኮምፒዩተር) lap-top-pe (kom-pi-yu-ter)
money ገንዘቤ gen-ze-be
passport ፓስፖርቴ pas-por-te

purse ቦርሳዬ bor-sa-ye

traveler's checks የመንገደኛ ቼኬ ye-men-ge-degn-gna che-ke

visa ቪዛዬ vi-za-ye

wallet የኪስ ቦርሳዬ ye-kis bor-sa-ye

Please show me your badge.
እባክህን ባጅህን አሳየኝ።
i-bak-ki-hin ba-ji-hin a-say-yegn

Please take me to your superior/the police station.
እባክህን ወደ አለቃህ/ ፖሊስ ጣቢያው አድርሰኝ።
i-bak-ki-hin we-de a-le-qah/po-lis ta-bi-yaw lit-ta-der-segn ti-chi-lal-leh

I have insurance.
ዋስትና አለኝ።
was-tin-na al-legn

I need a police report.
የፖሊስ ሪፖርት እፈልጋለሁ።
ye-po-lis ri-port i-fel-li-gal-le-hu

This person won't leave me alone.
ይህ ሰው አልተዎኝ ብሏል።
yih sew al-te-wegn bi-loal

My son/daughter is missing.
ልጄ ጠፍቷል/ ጠፍታለች።
li-je tef-toal/tef-tal-lech

He/She is XX years old.
XX አመቱ/ አመቷ ነው።
XX a-me-tu/a-me-tua new

I last saw the culprit XX minutes/hours ago.
ወንጀለኛውን ለመጨረሻ ጊዜ ያየሁት ከXX ደቂቃ/ሰዓት በፊት ነው።
wen-je-legn-gna-win le-me-cher-re-sha gi-ze yay-ye-hut keXX de-qi-qa/se-at be-fit new

You Might Hear

ይህ የተከሰተው የት ነው?
yih yet-te-kes-se-tew yet new?
Where did this happen?

የተከሰተው ስንት ሰዓት ላይ ነው?
yet-te-kes-se-tew sint se-at lay new?
What time did it occur?

ሰውየው/ሴትዮዋ ምን ይመስላል/ትመስላለች?
se-wiy-yew/se-tiy-yo-wa min yi-mes-lal/ti-mes-lal-lech?
What does he/she look like?

What is the problem?
ምንድን ነው ችግሩ?
min-din new chig-gi-ru?

What am I accused of?
በምን ጉዳይ ነው የተከሰስኩት?
be-min gud-day new yet-te-kes-ses-kut?

I didn't realize that it wasn't allowed.
የማይፈቀድ መሆኑን አላስተዋልኩም።
yem-ma-yif-feq-qed me-ho-nun a-las-te-wal-kum

I apologize.
ይቅርታ እለምናለሁ።
yi-qir-ta i-lem-mi-nal-le-hu

You Might Hear

ሰላም ማደፍረስ se-lam ma-def-res
disturbing the peace

የትራፊክ ደምብ መተላለፍ
ye-ti-ra-fik demb met-te-la-lef
traffic violation

መኪና አላገባብ የማቆም መቀጫ
me-ki-na a-lag-bab ye-ma-qom meq-qe-cha
parking fine

ከፍጥነት በላይ የማሽከርከር መቀጫ
ke-fit-net be-lay ye-mash-ker-ker meq-qe-cha
speeding ticket

የቪዛ ቀነ ገደብ አሳልፎ መቆየት
ye-vi-za qe-ne ge-deb a-sal-li-fo me-qoy-yet
overstaying your visa

ስርቆት sir-qot
theft

I didn't do anything.
ምንም አላጠፋሁም።
mi-nim a-la-tef-fa-hum

I'm innocent.
እኔ ንጹህ ነኝ።
i-ne ni-tsuh negn

I need to make a phone call.
ስልክ መደወል ይኖርብኛል።
silk me-dew-wel yi-no-rib-bign-gnal

I want to contact my embassy/consulate.
ኢምባሲዬን/ቆንሲላዬን ማግኘት እፈልጋለሁ።
im-ba-si-yen/qon-si-la-yen ma-gign-gnet i-fel-li-gal-le-hu

I want to speak to a lawyer.
ጠበቃ ማናገር እፈልጋለሁ።
te-be-qa man-na-ger i-fel-li-gal-le-hu

I speak English.
እንግሊዝኛ እናገራለሁ።
in-gi-li-zign-gna in-nag-ge-ral-le-hu

I need an interpreter.
አስተርጓሚ ያስፈልገኛል።
as-ter-gua-mi yas-fel-li-gegn-gnal

NUMBERS

Cardinal Numbers

1 ፩ አንድ and
2 ፪ ሁለት hu-let
3 ፫ ሶስት sost
4 ፬ አራት a-rat
5 ፭ አምስት am-mist
6 ፮ ስድስት sid-dist
7 ፯ ሰባት se-bat
8 ፰ ስምንት sim-mint
9 ፱ ዘጠኝ ze-tegn
10 ፲ አስር as-sir
11 ፲፩ አስራ አንድ as-ra and
12 ፲፪ አስራ ሁለት as-ra hu-let
13 ፲፫ አስራ ሶስት as-ra sost
14 ፲፬ አስራ አራት as-ra a-rat
15 ፲፭ አስራ አምስት as-ra am-mist
16 ፲፮ አስራ ስድስት as-ra sid-dist
17 ፲፯ አስራ ሰባት as-ra se-bat
18 ፲፰ አስራ ስምንት as-ra sim-mint
19 ፲፱ አስራ ዘጠኝ as-ra ze-tegn
20 ፳ ሃያ ha-ya
21 ፳፩ ሃያ አንድ ha-ya and

22 ፳፪ ሃያ ሁለት ha-ya hu-let

30 ፴ ሰላሳ se-la-sa

31 ፴፩ ሰላሳ አንድ se-la-sa and

32 ፴፪ ሰላሳ ሁለት se-la-sa hu-let

40 ፵ አርባ ar-ba

50 ፶ ሃምሳ ham-sa

60 ፷ ስልሳ sil-sa

70 ፸ ሰባ se-ba

80 ፹ ሰማንያ se-man-ya

90 ፺ ዘጠና ze-te-na

100 ፻ አንድ መቶ and me-to

101 ፻፩ አንድ መቶ አንድ and me-to and

200 ፪፻ ሁለት መቶ hu-let me-to

500 ፭፻ አምስት መቶ am-mist me-to

1,000 ፲፻ አንድ ሺ and shi

10,000 ፼ አስር ሺ as-sir shi

100,000 ፲፼ አንድ መቶ ሺ and me-to shi

1,000,000 ፻፼ አንድ ሚሊዮን and mi-li-yon

Ordinal Numbers

first አንደኛ an-degn-gna

second ሁለተኛ hu-let-tegn-gna

third ሶስተኛ sos-tegn-gna

fourth አራተኛ a-rat-tegn-gna

fifth አምስተኛ am-mis-tegn-gna

sixth ስድስተኛ si-dis-tegn-gna
seventh ሰባተኛ se-bat-tegn-gna
eighth ስምንተኛ sim-min-tegn-gna
ninth ዘጠንኛ ze-te-nign-gna
tenth አስረኛ as-si-regn-gna

Fractions ክፍልፋዮች ki-fil-fa-yoch

one-quarter ሩብ rub
one-half ግማሽ gim-mash
three-quarters ሶስት አራተኛ sost a-rat-tegn-gna
one-third ሲሶ si-so
two-thirds ሁለት ሶስተኛ hu-let sos-tegn-gna

all ሁሉም hul-lumm
none ምንም mi-nimm

QUANTITY & SIZE

one dozen አንድ ደርዘን and der-zen
half a dozen ግማሽ ደርዘን gim-mash der-zen

a pair of . . . አንድ ጥንድ . . . and tind . . .
a couple of . . . የተወሰነ . . . yet-te-wes-se-ne . . .
some (of) . . . ጥቂት . . . ti-qit . . .

a half ግማሽ gim-mash

a little ትንሽ tin-nish **a lot** ብዙ bi-zu

more የሚበልጥ yem-mi-belt **less** የሚያንስ yem-mi-yans

enough በቂ be-qi **not enough** የማይበቃ yem-may-be-qa

too many/much በጣም ብዙ be-tam bi-zu

extra small (XS) የትንሽ ትንሽ ye-tin-nish tin-nish
small (S) ትንሽ tin-nish
medium (M) መካከለኛ me-kak-ke-legn-gna
large (L) ትልቅ til-liq
extra-large (XL) የትልቅ ትልቅ ye-til-liq til-liq

big ትልቅ til-liq
bigger ተለቅ ያለ te-leqq ya-le
biggest በጣም ትልቅ be-tam til-liq

small ትንሽ tin-nish
smaller አነስ ያለ a-ness ya-le
smallest በጣም ትንሽ be-tam tin-nish

fat ወፍራም wef-ram **skinny** ቀጫጫ qe-cha-cha

wide ሰፊ sef-fi **narrow** ጠባብ teb-bab

tall ረዥም rezh-zhim **short** አጭር ach-chir
long ረዥም rezh-zhim

WEIGHTS & MEASUREMENTS

inch ኢንች inch
foot ጫማ cham-ma
mile ማይል ma-yil

meter ሜትር me-tir
millimeter ሚሊ ሜትር mi-li me-tir
centimeter ሴንቲ ሜትር sen-ti me-tir
kilometer ኪሎ ሜትር ki-lo me-tir

squared ካሬ ka-re **cubed** ኩብ kubb

milliliter ሚሊ ሊትር mi-li li-tir
liter ሊትር li-tir

kilogram ኪሎ ግራም ki-lo gi-ram

ounce ወቄት we-qet
cup ኩባያ kub-bay-ya
pint ቡትሌ but-til-le
quart ሁለት ቡትሌ hu-let but-til-le
gallon ጋሎን ga-lon

TIMES & DATES

Telling Time

What time is it?
ስንት ሰዓት ነው?
sint se-at new?

It's 5 A.M./P.M.
ከቀኑ/ ከምሽቱ 5 ሰዓት።
ke-qe-nu/ke-mish-shi-tu am-mist se-at ho-noual

It's 6 o'clock.
6 ሰዓት ሆኗል።
sid-dist se-at ho-noual

It's 6:30.
6:30 ሆኗል።
sid-dist tek-kul ho-noual

Five past three
ሶስት ከአምስት
sost ke-am-mist

Half past two
ሁለት ተኩል
hu-let tek-kul

Quarter to eight
ሩብ ጉዳይ ለስምንት
rub gud-day le-sim-mint

Twenty to four
ሃያ ጉዳይ ለአራት
ha-ya gud-day le-a-ratt

noon ቀትር qe-tir
midnight እኩለ ሌሊት ek-ku-le le-lit

at night ምሽት be-mish-shit

early በጊዜ be-gi-ze **late** ዘግይቶ zeg-yi-to

In the . . .
. . . ላይ
. . . lay

morning ጧት tuat
afternoon ከሰዓት በኋላ ke-se-at be-hual
evening አመሻሽ a-me-shash

At 1 P.M.
ከቀኑ 1 ሰዓት ላይ
ke-qe-nu and se-at lay

A.M. ከጧት ke-tuat **P.M.** ከሰዓት በላይ ke-se-at be-lay

Duration

for . . . ለ . . . le . . .

one month አንድ ወር and wer
two months ሁለት ወራት hu-let we-rat

one week አንድ ሳምንት and sam-mint
three weeks ሶስት ሳምንታት sost sam-min-tat

one day አንድ ቀን and qen
four days አራት ቀናት a-rat qe-nat

one hour አንድ ሰዓት and se-at
a half hour ግማሽ ሰዓት gim-mash se-at

one minute አንድ ደቂቃ and de-qi-qa
five minutes አምስት ደቂቃ am-mist de-qi-qa

one second አንድ ሰከንድ and se-kend
five seconds አምስት ሰከንድ am-mist se-kend

since ከ ጀምሮ ke . . . jem-mi-ro
during በ ጊዜ be . . . gi-ze

before በፊት be-fit
after በኋላ be-hua-la

one year ago ከአንድ ዓመት በፊት ke-and a-met be-fit
five years ago ከአምስት አመታት በፊት ke-am-mist a-me-tat be-fit
six months ago ከመንፈቅ በፊት ke-men-feq be-fit

in two years በሁለት ዓመት ውስጥ be-hu-let a-met wust
in five months በአምስት ወር ውስጥ be-am-mist wer wust
in two weeks በሁለት ሳምንት ውስጥ be-hu-lett sam-min-tat wust
in twelve days በአስራ ሁለት ቀናት ውስጥ be-as-ra hu-let qe-nat wust
in three hours በሶስት ሰዓታት ውስጥ bo-sost se-a-tat wust
in five minutes በአምስት ደቂቃ ውስጥ be-am-mist de-qi-qa wust
in ten seconds በአስር ሰከንድ ውስጥ be-as-sir se-kend wust

yesterday ትናንት ti-nant
today ዛሬ za-re
tomorrow ነገ ne-ge

week ሳምንት sam-mint
this week ይህ ሳምንት yih sam-mint
next week ቀጣዩ ሳምንት qet-ta-yu sam-mint
last week ያለፈው ሳምንት yal-le-few sam-mint

month ወር wer
this month ይህ ወር yih wer
next month ቀጣዩ ወር qet-ta-yu wer
last month ያለፈው ወር yal-le-few wer

year ዓመት a-met
this year ይህ ዓመት yih a-met
next year ከርሞ ker-mo
last year አምና am-na

Days of the Week

Monday ሰኞ segn-gno
Tuesday ማክሰኞ mak-segn-gno
Wednesday ረቡዕ re-bu-i
Thursday ሐሙስ ha-mus
Friday አርብ arb
Saturday ቅዳሜ qi-da-me
Sunday እሁድ i-hud

Months of the Year

January ጥር tirr
February የካቲት ye-ka-tit
March መጋቢት meg-ga-bit
April ሚያዝያ mi-ya-zi-ya
May ግንቦት gin-bot
June ሰኔ se-ne
July ሐምሌ ham-le
August ነሐሴ ne-ha-se
September መስከረም **mes-ke-rem**
October ጥቅምት ti-kimt
November ህዳር hi-dar
December ታህሳስ tah-sas

Seasons of the Year

Winter ክረምት ki-remt
Spring ጸደይ tse-dey
Summer በጋ be-ga
Fall/Autumn መኸር me-kher

www.ingramcontent.com/pod-product-compliance
Lightning Source LLC
Jackson TN
JSHW050807140125
77033JS00040B/699

* 9 7 8 0 7 8 1 8 1 3 8 2 2 *